THE LADIES
OF SENECA FALLS

THE LADIES OF SENECA FALLS *The Birth of the Woman's Rights Movement*

MIRIAM GURKO

SCHOCKEN BOOKS • NEW YORK

All rights reserved under International and Pan-American
Copyright Conventions. Published in the United States
by Schocken Books Inc., New York. Distributed by
Pantheon Books, a division of Random House, Inc., New York.

Published by arrangement with Macmillan Publishing Co., Inc.

Library of Congress Cataloging in Publication Data

Gurko, Miriam.
    The ladies of Seneca Falls.

    (Studies in the life of women)
    Reprint of the ed. published by Macmillan, New York.
    Bibliography: p. 316
    Includes index.
    1. Women—United States—Biography.   2. Women
    —Suffrage—United States.   3. Women's rights—
    United States.   I. Title.

[HQ1412.G85   1976]   301.41′ 2′ 0973   76-9144

ISBN 0-8052-0545-4

Picture credits: Illustrations are from the collection of
the Library of Congress with the exception of plates 2
and 32 from the New York Public Library Picture
Collection; plates 6, 20, 22, 26, and 27 from New-
York Historical Society, New York City; plate 13 from
Eighty Years and More by Elizabeth Cady Stanton
(Unwin, 1898); and plate 15 from *James and Lucretia
Mott* by Anna Davis Hallowell (Houghton Mifflin,
1884).

Manufactured in the United States of America

B9876543

First SCHOCKEN edition published in 1976

Author's Note

Most histories contain, if anything, only the briefest allusion to the woman's rights movement in the nineteenth century—perhaps no more than a sentence to include it in the general upsurge of reform. Here and there the name of a woman's rights leader might be mentioned, generally that of Susan B. Anthony, sometimes Elizabeth Cady Stanton. The rest might never have existed so far as the general run of historical sources is concerned. Women and their doings are practically invisible in these volumes and even in the biographies of men who were involved in the feminist movement. It has often been asked why, if women are presumably as capable as men, they haven't appeared more on the pages of history. One answer might be that female accomplishments were usually not recorded by male historians.

But outside the standard sources, in books, pamphlets, and speeches by women themselves, and in biographies of nineteenth-century female figures, the women of this period become strikingly visible and as active as many male performers on the historical scene. I hope this book will help to increase that visibility in the present day. I first thought of writing it after a conversation I had one evening with some young women who spoke of the current liberation movement as though it had no antecedents and had sprung up the day before yesterday. The women of all generations before their own, they remarked accusingly, had been either completely unaware of their inferior position, or at least passively resigned to it. These young women may have heard something of the suffrage movement and of Susan B. Anthony, but they knew little or nothing of the agonizing struggles for rights far more fundamental than that of voting, or of the origin of ideas which they themselves had unwittingly taken over from such women as Mary Wollstonecraft, Margaret Fuller, or Elizabeth Cady Stanton. This book was written, therefore, to bring to a new generation the story of the remarkable ladies of Seneca Falls, their forerunners and associates, and the extraordinary movement which they inaugurated.

Many of the volumes used in the preparation of this book have long been out of print. For assistance in locating them, and for their generosity in making them available to me, my warm thanks go to the Hofstra University Library, to my good friends at the Hart Memorial Library of Shrub Oak, New York, and to Robert Littauer of the Tower House, Greenwich, Connecticut.

MIRIAM GURKO

New York, 1974

Contents

Contents

Illustrations

Between pages 92 and 93:

1

The Ladies
of Seneca Falls

I suffered with mental hunger, which, like an empty stomach, is very depressing. I had . . . no stimulating companionship. . . . I now fully understood the practical difficulties most women had to contend with in the isolated household, and the impossibility of woman's best development if in contact, the chief part of her life, with servants and children.

—Elizabeth Cady Stanton, *Eighty Years and More*, 1898

Behind the veneer of modern emancipation is a woman isolated in an apartment or suburban home, exclusively responsible for the care of young children, dependent on her husband for an income.

—Alice S. Rossi, 1969

While man enjoys all the rights, he preaches all the duties to a woman.

—Elizabeth Cady Stanton

Who were the ladies of Seneca Falls? Originally there were five: five ladies sitting around a tea table in 1848 in the small town of Waterloo in upstate New York. Four of them, the Quaker preacher Lucretia Mott of Philadelphia, her sister Martha Wright, Jane Hunt, and Mary Ann McClintock, listened while the fifth, Elizabeth Cady Stanton of nearby Seneca Falls, suddenly began to pour out her "discontent . . . with woman's portion as wife, mother, housekeeper."

Until the previous year, Mrs. Stanton had led a highly stimulating life. As the wife of Henry Stanton, the abolitionist orator, she had attended the turbulent World Anti-Slavery Convention in London—where she first met Lucretia Mott—visited Paris, then settled in Boston in one of the richest periods of that city's history.

It was a time of great reform movements—the abolition of slavery, temperance, religious agitation, campaigns to eliminate war—in which the Stantons took a leading part. They had three sons, but with a comfortable house and good servants, domestic life ran smoothly and she was free to enjoy the exhilarations of Boston.

It wasn't until they had to leave the city because of Henry Stanton's health and move to Seneca Falls in 1847 that Elizabeth Stanton began to live more like the average housewife. Their house was older, less convenient, and harder to run than their Boston home; she found it impossible to get good servants. Above all, she missed the intellectual activity and companionship she had enjoyed in Boston. Henry Stanton was often away on business, and she was left alone with just the children. The dimensions of her life quickly shrank to painfully narrow limits.

By the time she went to Waterloo for a reunion with Lucretia Mott, her dissatisfactions had become so acute that, over the teacups, she found herself releasing "the torrent of my long-accumulating discontent, with such vehemence and indignation that I stirred myself, as well as the rest of the party, to do and dare anything."

What they dared—and in those days it took monumental daring—was to call a woman's rights convention. The possibility of such a convention had occurred to Mrs. Mott and Mrs. Stanton at their first meeting eight years before, but nothing had come of it. Now, however, they and the other ladies took action. That evening they wrote an announcement which appeared the next day, July 14, 1848, in the *Seneca County Courier*. It invited women to attend "A Convention to discuss the social, civil, and religious condition and rights of woman" in the Wesleyan Chapel at Seneca Falls on the 19th and 20th of July.

They had no idea of how to organize such a meeting, or what the outcome would be. It was the first time in history that women had ever done anything remotely like it. Yet from this almost offhand, accidental beginning would arise the dynamic woman's rights and suffrage movements in the United States, and these would in turn inspire similar movements in other parts of the world.

In a sense the convention could be said to have arisen spontaneously from Elizabeth Stanton's discontent, but even with Mrs. Stanton it wasn't quite that spontaneous. Her early life, her experience at the London Anti-Slavery Convention, her observations and awareness of "the wearied, anxious look of the majority of women," topped by her own personal frustrations, had all led to this moment. "It seemed as if all the elements had conspired to impel me to some onward step."

But individuals, even as fiercely independent and forceful as Elizabeth Stanton, do not act in a historical vacuum. A long series of earlier events and stirrings helped establish a foundation for such a convention. The year itself, 1848, known as the "year of revolutions," contributed its impetus. And though Mrs. Stanton's complaints seemed relatively simple—too much domestic drudgery and too little mental activity, too much isolation and too little adult companionship—the problem was far more complex. Mrs. Stanton herself would explore not only the legal and social bases of her discontent, but the subtle psychological fogs through which women had to grope before understanding themselves and their relationship to the world.

Indeed, defining the problem was in some ways as difficult as solving it. What, after all, was wrong with the way women lived, as distinguished from all the things that might be wrong with the world as a whole? What, after all, did women really want?

2

"What Does a Woman Want?"

The souls of women are so small
That some believe they've none at all.
—Samuel Butler, *Hudibras*, 1663

A woman, especially, if she have the misfortune of knowing anything, should conceal it as well as she can.
—Jane Austen, *Northanger Abbey*, 1798

"It is a very poor thing to be a woman," [Emily] said to her sister.

"It is perhaps better than being a dog," said Nora; "but, of course, we can't compare ourselves to men."
—Anthony Trollope, *He Knew He Was Right*, 1868–9

People sometimes wonder what is the secret of the extra-ordinary knowledge of women which I shew in my plays. . . . I have always assumed that a woman is a person exactly like myself, and that is how the trick is done.
—George Bernard Shaw, 1927

W hat does a woman want?" asked Sigmund Freud. It is a question, said the father of psychoanalysis, "that has never been answered, and which I have not yet been able to answer despite my thirty years of research into the feminine soul."

Freud, and the hordes of other men who have been baffled by female discontent, might have gotten a clue if the word "woman" were changed to "person." What does any person want? What did Freud himself, as an adult, rational human being, want?

More than half a century earlier, the ladies of Seneca Falls had an answer for him. In 1849 the journalist Richard Henry Dana ridiculed the demands of the Seneca Falls movement for civil and political rights; he offered instead a model for self-effacing feminine behavior of which Freud would have approved. Lucretia Mott, replying to him, said: "The question is often asked, 'What does woman want, more than she enjoys? What is she seeking to obtain? Of what rights is she deprived? What privileges are withheld from her?' I answer . . . she wants to be acknowledged a moral, responsible being. She is seeking not to be governed by laws in the making of which she has no voice. . . . Her exclusion . . . her duties marked out for her by her equal brother man, subject to creeds, rules, and disciplines made for her by him, is unworthy [of] her true dignity. . . .

"She has so long been subject to the disabilities and restrictions with which her progress has been embarrassed, that she has become enervated, her mind to some extent paralyzed. . . . I would, therefore, urge that woman be placed in such a situation in society, by the recognition of her rights, and have such opportunities for growth and development, as shall raise her from this low, enervated, and paralyzed condition. . . . Let woman then go on, not asking favors, but claiming as right, the removal of all hindrances to her elevation in the scale of being;

6

let her receive encouragement for the proper cultivation of all her powers, so that she may enter profitably into the active business of life."

Long before and after Lucretia Mott, women have thought and written about this "low, enervated, and paralyzed condition." Thousands of women could have told Freud that what they wanted was to be regarded as human beings, not just as females. They wanted no barriers placed in their way because of their sex. They did not want to be cherished and protected as helpless children, or adored as angels. They did not want to function simply as appendages to men. They wanted to be accepted and allowed to live as responsible adults, capable of thinking for themselves and of making their own decisions as to how to spend their lives.

In the good—or bad—old days, women's lives were supposed to follow a clearly defined pattern; "role conflicts" hadn't appeared yet. A baby girl was dressed in soft pink pastels, given dolls and toy dishes, and taught that when she grew up she would become a mommy and have a dear little house of her own to take care of. She took it for granted that she would receive less education than her brother (as a housewife, she wouldn't need any more), wouldn't engage in strenuous sports (girls were delicate), or concern herself with politics, science, and abstract thought in general (too complicated for her pretty little head).

As she grew up, her future was planned exclusively in terms of marriage. Unless misfortune struck, she would spend her life as the dependent of a man. Papa would take care of her before marriage; her husband would support her afterward. Both would guide her thinking and conduct. In return, she would take care of the house and children, prepare tasty meals, keep herself attractive and amiable. Security for her, home comforts for him. A satisfactory arrangement all around. Or at least a pretty picture of it.

7

But there have always been women who felt, or at the very least suspected, that there was something wrong with this picture. They realized that their lives were bottled up by all kinds of social and legal restrictions. They were aware, too, of the internal barriers—the fears and self-doubts—which women themselves placed in the way of their own possible growth. Feminine consciousness did not begin with today's young women.

Everyone knows how women fought for and won the right to vote, but that was just one dramatically publicized highpoint in a long, slogging, bitterly contested effort to be treated like rational beings. Women fought for the right to control their own property, to work and keep their own earnings from that work, to have a voice in decisions affecting their own children. They insisted on a real education and demanded entrance into professions closed to them. They battled against hampering laws, religious beliefs, and social customs. They broke down the major obstacles to woman's progress, and cleared away the underbrush of a thousand petty taboos.

They did all this against an avalanche of hostility and ridicule that today's young militants can scarcely imagine. Every institution—government, church, press, school—was angrily or scornfully against them. Women had few rights and little respect if they weren't married, and a grudging acceptance but even fewer rights as married women.

Once a woman married, she forfeited her legal existence. She couldn't sign a contract, make a will, or sue in a court of law. If she received property from her father or other source, her husband could sell it and keep the money for himself. If she worked, her husband was entitled to her earnings. He could apprentice her children against her wishes, or assign them to a guardian of his own choosing. In the eyes of the law, explained the great legal authority Blackstone, "the husband and the wife are one person," and that person was the husband. If women were considered apart from their husbands, it was to be classed, in the language of many statutes, with infants and idiots. Any effort by women to retain even a fragment of legal identity or independence while married was firmly squashed.

Legally and economically, an unmarried woman might be better off than if she married. She could at least control her own property, if she was lucky enough to inherit any, or keep her own earnings, though there were few ways in which she could get any earnings to keep. Depending on her social position, she could become a servant, a factory worker, a schoolteacher, or a paid companion; or she could do needlework, open a small shop, run a boardinghouse. Not much else was possible, no matter how much talent and ambition a woman might have. Or she could live as a dependent in the home of a more or less reluctant relative, helping with the children or housework, melting unobtrusively into the background, and silently enduring the anguish of humiliation and helplessness.

Socially, she was far worse off. She would be pitied as being too unattractive to snare a husband, mocked as an "old maid," doomed to eccentricity and angularity, uninvited to social affairs where couples were the basic unit. The only path to any kind of acceptance by society was through marriage. She must live through her husband and children. This was the pattern laid down for her, and very little deviation was permitted without penalty.

The church, too, was determined to keep her in her place. A woman must remain in "her proper sphere," which is the home. The Congregationalist ministers of Massachusetts declared she must be "unobtrusive, mild, dependent," conscious of "that weakness which God has given her for her protection." When she tries to act or even think independently, she becomes unnatural or worse. "We do not believe women . . . are fit to have their own head," wrote the Catholic spokesman Orestes Brownson. ". . . Without masculine direction or control, she is out of her element, and a social anomaly, sometimes a hideous monster."

Eve caused the fall of man, thundered the preachers, "and brought sin and all our woe into the world." Therefore all women, daughters of Eve, must suffer and obey St. Peter's admonition to "be in subjection to your husbands." A girl was made to feel that "she should be ashamed at the very thought that she is a woman," and "should live in continuous penance, on account of the curses she has brought upon the world."

Outside the church, things were not much better. Girls received a minimum of formal education. An American college president found the very thought of a woman aspiring to higher learning "too ridiculous to appear credible." A woman speaking in public was considered either shocking or preposterous. When Samuel Johnson heard of a woman preaching at a Quaker meeting, he said: "Sir, a woman's preaching is like a dog's walking on its hind legs. It is not done well; but you are surprised to find it done at all."

And finally, there was the opposition of the press. Newspaper editors led the public in jeering at or denouncing any effort by women to change or improve their lives. A typical comment on a woman's rights convention was that of the Syracuse *Daily Star*, which labeled the proceedings as a "mass of corruption, heresies, ridiculous nonsense, and reeking vulgarities which these bad women have vomited forth for the past three days."

All these deeply encrusted beliefs had to be scraped away before a positive step could be taken to raise women to full human status. It was especially difficult because women generally agreed with these images of themselves. After a lifetime of hearing how weak and inferior they were, it took a formidable degree of independence and courage, first to recognize the image as false, and then to go about changing it.

In doing so, the early feminists touched upon practically

everything that women of today are saying. Update the language and style of something said by Mary Wollstonecraft in the eighteenth century, or by Margaret Fuller, Elizabeth Cady Stanton, and a hundred others in the nineteenth, and it could pass for a statement issued today.

The earliest solution proposed for woman's "low, enervated, and paralyzed condition" was to improve her education. It was grossly unfair, argued the writers of the seventeenth and eighteenth centuries, to criticize women for being frivolous, ignorant, or capricious. How could they be anything else when they were treated like simpleminded children and denied the training that would help them become mature adults?

In England, Mary Astell expressed what was then a novel idea: that girls had as much capacity for learning as boys. In her *Serious Proposal to the Ladies*, written in 1694, she urged the establishment of what might have been the first school to provide girls with an education equal to that of their brothers. When Queen Anne came to the throne in 1702, Mary Astell hoped she would encourage such a school for her own sex, but the idea was ridiculed and rejected.

For the next hundred years, the question was endlessly argued: Should women be educated? How much and what kind of training should they—and were they able to—receive? Many people believed that women's mental capacities were inferior to men's; others felt that though they might not be inferior, they were very different, so that boys and girls should be given different subjects and different methods of instruction.

The same arguments were used to oppose coeducation above the earliest grades. Aside from the moral objections to putting genteel and gentle young women into the same classrooms with young men—an almost certain road to improper behavior—it would be virtually impossible to teach them on the same level. The feebler female brain, it was said, would be seriously overburdened if it had to compete with the stronger male intellect.

It was taken for granted that female standards would have to be much lower.

Above all other considerations, would higher learning interfere with a woman's performance as wife, mother, and housekeeper? There were people who warned that advanced study was too taxing for the delicate female, that neither her mind nor her body could absorb the strain; she would be unable to have healthy babies as a result. Even those who denied this, and who believed strongly in female education, always kept a woman's primary roles firmly in mind. The chief aim of education, they said, was to make women better companions for their husbands, more qualified teachers for their children, and more efficient managers of their homes.

It was almost universally taken for granted that, whether or not women were actually inferior to men, their greatest fulfillment would be found in marriage; their main purpose was to serve men in some capacity. Though they might not put it as bluntly as Jean Jacques Rousseau did in 1762, most people agreed with his views: "The education of women should always be relative to men. To please, to be useful to us, . . . to educate us when young, and take care of us when grown up, to advise, to console us, to render our lives easy and agreeable: these are the duties of women at all times, and what they should be taught in their infancy. . . . The woman is expressly formed to please the man."

Rousseau's ideas carried immense prestige, coming from a leading political philosopher whose writings on the freedom of the individual and the equality of all men (if not women) provided fuel for the French Revolution. There were other, lesser, writers who were also happy to tell women how to act and what to feel and think. Two of these were especially popular. Dr. James Fordyce's *Sermons to Young Women*, 1765, piously urges women to be meek, docile, and compliant, behaving toward men with "respectful observance . . . studying their humours, overlooking their mistakes, submitting to their opinions . . . giving soft answers to hasty words, complaining as seldom as possible, and making it your daily care to relieve their anxieties."

And in *A Father's Legacy to His Daughters*, 1774, Dr. John Gregory instructs young women to cultivate those "chief beauties in a female character . . . that modest reserve, that retiring delicacy." If a girl has any brains, she should hide them because, he says, "Wit is the most dangerous talent you can possess. . . . Be even cautious in displaying your good sense. . . . But if you happen to have any learning, keep it a profound secret, especially from the men, who generally look with a jealous and malignant eye on a woman of great parts, and a cultivated understanding."

Most devastating of all, as Elizabeth Stanton and Lucretia Mott would point out, was the acceptance of these ideas by so many women. Just five years before the Seneca Falls convention, an Englishwoman, Sarah Stickney Ellis, in *The Wives of England, Their Relative Duties, Domestic Influence, and Social Obligations*, was saying that she did not "attach any high degree of importance to the possession of great intellectual endowments in women, because I believe such natural gifts to have proved much more frequently her bane than her blessing." Intelligence in a woman was not a qualification which led "to her own happiness, or the happiness of those around her." But Mrs. Ellis was willing to forgive such an unfortunate endowment in a woman "where she regarded it only as a means of doing higher homage to her husband and bringing greater ability to bear upon the advancement of his intellectual and moral good." Above all, a woman should cultivate "a respectful deportment, and a complying disposition . . . with a general willingness to accommodate all household arrangements to a husband's wishes, making every other consideration subservient to his convenience."

That was the ideal feminine image: the gentle, patient, unassuming, all-enduring wife and mother, having no strong feelings or needs of her own. Or at least masking her own emotions and carefully hiding whatever intelligence, knowledge, and talents she might have.

3

Mary Wollstonecraft

Women are told from their infancy . . . that . . . cunning, softness of temper, *outward* obedience, and a scrupulous attention to a puerile kind of propriety, will obtain for them the protection of man; and should they be beautiful, everything else is needless, for, at least, twenty years of their lives. . . . How grossly do they insult us who thus advise us only to render ourselves gentle, domestic brutes!

—Mary Wollstonecraft,
A Vindication of the Rights of Woman, 1792

Those who are bold enough to advance before the age they live in, and to throw off, by the force of their own minds, the prejudices which the maturing reason of the world will in time disavow, must learn to brave censure. We ought not to be too anxious respecting the opinion of others.

—Mary Wollstonecraft, 1797

We are told that in the past most women accepted the standard domestic pattern for their lives and lived happily ever after. But did they? The grumblings of women were generally ignored, and the few who managed to express their complaints in writing were largely overlooked.

At least as early as the fifteenth century, women wrote in protest against the unreality of the angelic image and against the narrowness of female existence. But Mary Wollstonecraft, with *A Vindication of the Rights of Woman* in 1792, was the first to exert a lasting influence. Though she was English and born nearly a century before the first organized action of the American woman's rights movement, she represents a starting point and a source for its principal themes.

She vehemently challenged the views of Rousseau, Dr. Fordyce, and Dr. Gregory. Women, she said, should be educated not to serve men but for their own purposes, as rational creatures "who, in common with men, are placed on this earth to unfold their faculties." Their first ambition should be to develop character "as a human being, regardless of the distinction of sex." A girl's training should strengthen her mind and body and produce an independent, self-reliant person who can think for herself and earn her own living, for independence, as Mary Wollstonecraft had discovered through her own experience, is "the grand blessing of life."

She freely admitted that many women were vain, ignorant, shallow, sentimental, irresponsible, childish, deceitful. But how could they be anything else, she asked, when they were denied the education and opportunity to become "rational creatures"? When women were told to hide their true emotions, when they were prevented from dealing with men on an equal basis, what could they be but deceitful? If they were childishly frivolous, it was because men treated them without respect, as backward children. "From the tyranny of man, I firmly believe, the greater number of female follies proceed; and the cunning, which I allow makes at present a part of their character . . . is produced by oppression. . . . Let woman share the rights and she will emulate the virtues of man." Education was the key to the condition of women. "The neglected education of my fellow-creatures is the grand source of the misery I deplore." This neglect was due to men who considered women as "females rather . . . than human creatures."

Her great aim was to reverse this view, to have women considered primarily as "human creatures." As equal humans, girls deserved the same education as boys. They should also have the same opportunities to build up their physical strength and health. She criticized the prevalent tendency to keep girls from athletic activities and in a state of ladylike fragility, which really meant poor health. She urged a national system of free, coeducational day schools where girls and boys alike would have healthy outdoor exercise to build their bodies, basic studies to develop their minds, and vocational training to ensure future employment.

A Vindication of the Rights of Woman was written at a time when all Europe was passionately discussing the rights of man. Mary Wollstonecraft insisted that half the human race must not be excluded from the liberty and equality demanded by men. "If the abstract rights of man will bear discussion and explanation, those of woman . . . will not shrink from the same test." In her discussion of the equal rights of women, she examined and attacked every aspect of marriage and the relationship between the sexes: the false modesty affected by women, the assumption of male superiority, the double standard in morals, the pretension that women do not have "the common appetites and passions of their nature."

Do away with all these errors, she says, allow women to become educated and independent, and men themselves would be better off. Respected and self-respecting women could then become real companions to men, and marriage could be an honest relationship between free, rational adults.

A Vindication of the Rights of Woman created an immense stir. Soon after it appeared in England, editions were printed in Boston and Philadelphia. It was translated into French. Advanced thinkers everywhere praised the book and its author. In America its ideas were later to be repeated in the speeches and writings of the woman's rights movement.

In 1840, Elizabeth Stanton and Lucretia Mott would discuss the book when they met in London. Highly original for its own period, it became one of the foundations for all future thought on the subject. And in her own person as well as in her writings, Mary Wollstonecraft provided proof—at a time when such proof was urgently needed—that women were capable of rational thought, intellectual effort, and independent adulthood. When the first volume of *History of Woman Suffrage* was published in 1881, it was dedicated to nineteen women "Whose Earnest Lives and Fearless Words" had been "a Constant Inspiration." The first name, standing by itself, was that of Mary Wollstonecraft.

But even greater than the admiration was the shock or amusement aroused by *A Vindication of the Rights of Woman*. Horace Walpole called its author "a hyena in petticoats." The tendency of most men was to dismiss it, sometimes without even reading it, as ridiculous or typical of a woman's petulant complaints. Many of its proposals, accepted today without question, seemed outrageously farfetched and unrealistic at the time.

Those who considered it a dangerous and immoral book were disturbed as much by the personal life of its author as by its outspoken ideas on sex and feminine passion. Mary Wollstonecraft had dared to become an independent, self-supporting woman, had lived with two men without marriage, and borne an illegitimate child.

Her objections to formal marriage and the traditional role of women started early. As a child, it was hard for her to believe in the superiority of the male as she watched her father lose his inheritance through inept management and turn into a brutal drunkard. Nor was it possible to look forward happily to a housewife's existence when she saw her mother withdraw into an abject, unhappy submission which Mary felt she could not accept for herself. "At fifteen," she wrote later, "I resolved never . . . to endure a life of dependence." Her dim view of marriage was later reinforced by the marital miseries of her sister Eliza.

By the time she was nineteen, conditions at home had become so painful that she decided to leave. In the eighteenth century, when it was unthinkable for a girl to leave home without the consent and assistance of her father, this was an extreme and daring step. And having taken it, there was very little she could do. A young woman of her class could become either a teacher or a companion. With too little education to teach, Mary Wollstonecraft became a companion, a dreary position which she held for two years until she returned home to care for her dying mother.

She was determined to do more with her life than serve as a companion—a form of higher servant—to difficult old ladies. She put herself through a rigorous program of self-education, and eventually opened a school with the help of her closest friend, Fanny Blood, and her sister Eliza. Mary had helped Eliza escape from her unhappy marriage—another example of scandalously unconventional behavior which was later held against Mary.

At first the school was a great success, and Mary Wollstonecraft had her first happy experience as an independent, self-supporting person. But after several years, and after the death of Fanny Blood, the school began to lose money and had to close.

She decided to try writing, prepared a book, *Thoughts on the*

Education of Daughters, and was able to sell it to the famous London bookseller Joseph Johnson. She moved to London and became a professional writer, turning out children's stories, translations, anthologies, essays, and reviews. Most of these were done for Johnson, whose bookstore was a center for progressive thinkers of the time. She joined the circle that included William Blake, Tom Paine, and William Godwin, the celebrated radical philosopher. Even before *A Vindication of the Rights of Woman* appeared in 1792, she was a prominent member of the group; after its publication her fame spread beyond it.

At the end of that year her life took its most dramatic turn. Drawn by the French Revolution, she went to Paris, arriving at the beginning of its greatest turbulence. During the Reign of Terror she lived in a Paris suburb, virtually in hiding, to escape arrest as a British national. She spent most of her time writing a history of the revolution, which Johnson later published. The climax of this period was her passionate love affair with Gilbert Imlay, a charming American adventurer, followed by the birth of her daughter Fanny and her attempt at suicide when Imlay left her for another woman.

Joseph Johnson persuaded her to resume her literary career in London and her place in his circle. This time she and William Godwin were attracted to each other, and they finally married. Just as she was entering what promised to be the best and most serene period of her life, she died after giving birth to their daughter, Mary. She was only thirty-eight years old.

Her daughter, Mary Godwin, would grow up to become Mary Shelley, the wife of the poet. She would also become the author of *Frankenstein*. In the world at large, Frankenstein's monster is probably better known today than Mary Wollstonecraft's ideas about women. But those ideas helped establish one of the great movements of the modern age.

4

From Colonial Dames to American Ladies

I cannot say that I think you are very generous to the ladies; for, whilst you are proclaiming peace and good-will to men, emancipating all nations, you insist upon retaining an absolute power over wives.

—Abigail Adams, letter to John Adams, 1776

The tender breasts of ladies were not formed for political convulsion.

—Thomas Jefferson

Stimulate the sensibilities of your boys, and blunt those of your girls.

—Advice to a young mother,
Godey's Lady's Book, 1840

Mary Wollstonecraft died in 1797, and from then on the movement toward woman's rights was strongest in America. Most American laws and customs stemmed from England, but the circumstances of life, especially in the early pioneer days and on the frontier, produced a very different framework for female existence.

In colonial times, women were vitally necessary in far more than a narrow domestic sense, and they received a high measure of respect. There could be no nonsense about female fragility and helplessness when women worked alongside men to clear the land, or handled guns to shoot game and enemies on the frontier. Female skills were greatly valued. Most of life's essentials—food, clothing, soap, candles—were produced at home, by women, from materials raised at home often by or with the help of women. A farmer could scarcely function without a wife.

Nor, for that matter, could the townsman. The home, whether in town or country, was the center of production. The family was the basic social and economic unit, and the housewife played an indispensable role. She not only cooked, cleaned, laundered, and tended the children; she made the family clothing from cotton, linen, or wool which she had spun or woven herself; she baked bread, canned or preserved food, prepared most of the simple medicines used in the family doctoring, which she did herself. She was often her children's first teacher; and along with all this, it was not uncommon for her to work with her husband at his trade.

When a man died, his wife and sometimes his daughters took over his business without worrying about whether it was "fitting" for a woman. Running a shop or an inn might be taken for granted, but there were also women butchers, shoemakers, barbers. There were female printers, many of whom also published newspapers. There were women blacksmiths. With the great shortage of labor in colonial days, whoever could do a necessary job did it. And with so many men taking off for the West or getting killed in Indian wars, the women unhesitatingly stepped in to do the work.

Work itself, as a way of life, was highly respected in a country settled originally by Puritans. In their eyes, idleness was a sin, and the frivolous, empty-headed woman so sharply criticized by Mary Wollstonecraft in England scarcely existed in colonial America.

Even in the South, where slaves performed most of the domestic labor, women were not always content to lead traditionally "feminine" lives. There were women who managed large plantations producing tobacco, rice, cotton, and cattle. The rich possibilities offered by southern climate and soil led some women to an interest in botany, which in turn led to the naturalization of many foreign plants.

The most dramatically successful of these women was Eliza Lucas Pinckney. Still in her teens, she ran her father's South Carolina plantation while he was governor of the West Indian island of Antigua. He sent her some indigo seed from Antigua with which she experimented until she was able to grow indigo locally and, even more difficult, to extract dye from it. The blue dye was extensively used by British cloth makers, and, as a result of Eliza Pinckney's work, by the middle of the eighteenth century the leading industry of the South was the manufacture and exportation of indigo.

It was possible, in the freer atmosphere of a new country, for women to become independent settlers. Margaret Brent and her sister came to Maryland in 1638, acquired land, built houses, brought over more settlers. They bought and sold property. Ten years after her arrival, Margaret Brent, now a large property owner and woman of many business affairs, demanded a vote in the House of Burgesses. It was denied, but not without a lively argument. This was probably the first demand for woman suffrage in America.

In some colonies women did have the right to vote, since this was generally based not on sex but on ownership of property. Ironically, it was the arrival of independence and the spread of democracy that removed this right. As states adopted their constitutions or revised their laws under the new political conditions, voting qualifications were more clearly defined, usually spelling out the voter as a free, white, male citizen, in addition to whatever property or tax requirement there might be. Thus New York took the vote away from women in 1777, Massachusetts in 1780, New Hampshire in 1784, and New Jersey, the last to do so, in 1807.

The establishment of an independent United States was, if anything, a setback to women. Or at least a missed opportunity. At this point of new beginnings, while the impulse toward political innovation, toward new and liberating forms of government was still strong, women should have insisted on being included in the benefits of independence. As it was, after a war fought, among other reasons, against the injustice of "taxation without representation," the new lawmakers turned around and proceeded to tax women property owners without giving them representation in the form of voting rights.

Women were given no voice in the making of laws by which they would be governed in the new democracy. They could, however, be prosecuted and convicted under these laws; they were also denied the right to a trial by a jury of their peers, since women were not permitted to serve on juries. And in this period of broadening justice, married women were still denied the legal rights taken for granted by their husbands: the right to control their own property, earnings, and children, the right to sign contracts, to sue or be sued in a court of law. In some states their right to handle money was severely limited: in Massachusetts, for example, before 1840 it was illegal for a woman to serve as treasurer of her sewing society unless a man assumed responsibility for her.

When the war which had been fought against the injustices of the colonial system had been won, the new freedoms were granted to only half the population—much less than half, in view of the thousands of black slaves for whom the revolution, independence, and the new democratic constitution had no meaning whatsoever.

In 1777, Abigail Adams wrote to her husband, John: "In the new code of laws . . . I desire you would remember the ladies and be more generous and favorable to them than your ancestors. Do not put such unlimited power into the hands of the husbands. . . . If particular care and attention is not paid to the ladies, we are determined to foment a rebellion, and will not hold ourselves bound by any laws in which we have no voice or representation."

John Adams believed that women had minds and powers of judgment equal to men's, but felt they were too delicate and too busy caring for their homes to be permitted any political activity. He dismissed his wife's threat of insurrection as a joke, though this was at the very height of the struggle for independence, when he and his colleagues were trying to formulate a new kind of government, with more individual freedom and equality than Europe had ever provided. And though there might have been thousands of American women ready and willing "to foment a rebellion," they were unorganized, with no communication between them, and the opportunity passed.

If women had raised the question of their rights at that time, there is of course no proof that they would have succeeded in getting the vote or in erasing the legal discriminations against them. But there are moments in history when rigid social structures are more open to change, even if the change is brought about by force. With the American and French revolutions forcing such change, this was one of the "open moments" when women might have been listened to more seriously than before or after. Mary Wollstonecraft had sensed this and had written *A Vindication of the Rights of Woman* to take advantage of the open moment.

At the very least, an attempt by women to bring forward their claims would have "raised their consciousness" and given them a seventy-year head start on the woman's rights movement. An expression of female discontent might have made the lawmakers stop and think about the position of women and the contradictions of that position in a democratic society. And it might have stemmed, to some degree, the deterioration of woman's social and economic status under the industrialization which was soon to overtake the United States.

The industrialization of America had a profound effect upon women. Much of the work done at home now moved to the factories. The home was no longer the economic nucleus of life. The housewife was no longer an indispensable linchpin of society. As the need for her declined, so did her value, and so did the respect accorded her.

The factories not only took over much of the housewife's production, beginning with spinning and weaving; they also began to replace the small artisan and the home-based workshop. Men left their farms or closed their workshops and went to work outside the home. Instead of spending most of their time near their families, they were now absent the best part of the day. With them went their farmhands and apprentices. The individual household grew more restricted; the housewife became more isolated. Where she had once presided over a bustling, vital social and economic center which included at least a few adults, she was now left alone with her children and perhaps an aged or ailing parent.

As the demand for industrial labor grew, women went to work in the factories. They were paid far less than men. If a man was dissatisfied with his pay or working conditions, he could leave for a hundred other jobs. He could fill the great demand for farm labor, or go off to the West altogether. A woman had no alternatives and had to work for what she could get. Early factory owners understood this all too well and took full advantage of it. In pre-industrial days a woman had often worked side by side with her husband on the farm or in the workshop; she had been a man's economic partner. Now she was his underpaid employee; or if she remained at home, his complete dependent.

Most of the women who worked in early nineteenth-century factories were either unmarried girls or married women from lower economic groups. The majority of women still remained at home, working as hard as ever. The factories might be making cloth, but the housewife still had to sew it into clothes without the help of a sewing machine (that didn't come till the 1840s), launder the clothing without the aid of a washing machine, mend and iron them. She had to cook, bake, and put up preserves in the most inconvenient of kitchens, and clean up after meals with none of the labor-saving equipment or cleansing materials available later on. She might have a kitchen sink, but it wasn't necessarily attached to a plumbing system.

Keeping her house clean was immensely difficult by modern standards. Spread out over several floors, with no mechanical aids like vacuum cleaners available, early houses required constant sweeping, scrubbing, dusting, and polishing by hand. Rooms were crowded with carved and curlicued furniture, with flocks of small tables and whatnots bearing hundreds of pieces of bric-a-brac that had to be carefully and individually dusted. Good servants were hard to get and harder to keep, since even the most unskilled women could get factory jobs that offered better pay than domestic service. But even with help, the middle-class housewife still did a formidable amount of work herself. It was no wonder that, in Seneca Falls, Elizabeth Cady Stanton found herself overwhelmed and driven to rebellion.

It was no wonder, either, that she and the other woman's rights leaders were irritated by the argument that women were too fragile to take part in public life or to vote. If women could scrub floors and lift massive cooking pots and carry heavy babies around, they could certainly muster the strength to fill out a paper ballot and drop it into a box. And if men were so much stronger than women, why didn't *they* stand over a washboard and do the laundry—a backbreaking job in the nineteenth century? Telling women how weak and fragile they were while at the same time assigning some of the most physically strenuous chores to them was one of the inconsistencies that grated upon Mrs. Stanton and her colleagues.

In the long run, the development of industry, despite the initial dislocations and exploitation, would prove a major step in getting women outside the walls of their own homes. As industry expanded and changed the whole nature of economic life, women would be needed in more capacities than that of factory hands. The tight structure of the family would be loosened when girls were able to earn money of their own and see something of the world, however limited and imperfect that view might be.

But these working girls would not be the founders of the woman's rights movement. Female workers would be active in organizing trade unions and in fighting for economic rights, but the struggle for legal and social rights would be carried on largely by members of the middle class. Middle-class women were more hemmed in by notions of what was "proper" for ladies. They were the ones who wanted laws changed so they could control property inherited from well-to-do fathers. They wanted the vote in order to have a voice in the making or repeal of such laws. Working girls had no property to worry about and cared less about voting than about reducing the long working day and raising their wages.

As life on the eastern seaboard became more settled and less rigorous, the lives of middle-class women grew more restricted: traditional views began to reassert themselves. Where women in pioneer and colonial days had worked alongside their husbands, practicing a wide variety of skills, now they fussed more with their appearance and their homes. Once again, as in Europe, the image of woman became that of a weak, helpless, dependent creature, charming perhaps, but not very bright.

In one sense they were perhaps fragile: the indoor life and tight, corseted clothing, together with the poorly balanced diet of most urban women, greatly undermined their health. They might have worked hard inside their poorly ventilated homes, but healthy physical exercise in fresh air was considered unladylike.

The westward-moving frontier, however, continued to provide a freer, healthier, less traditional atmosphere. Women continued their active pioneer role and retained more of the equality that was being eroded in the East. There was more respect, in the western communities, for women as individuals. When the woman's rights movement finally began to grow, it would be the West that would give it much of its strength and encouragement. And it was in western New York State, at that time regarded as geographically and socially distinct from the older eastern section, that the ladies of Seneca Falls would have the temerity to call their pioneering convention.

5

From Abolition to Woman's Rights: I. The Grimké Sisters

Deeply, deeply do I feel the degradation of being a woman—not the degradation of being what *God* made woman, but what *man* has made her.

—Lydia Maria Child, letter to Angelina Grimké, 1838

How monstrous is the doctrine that woman is to be dependent on man! . . . She has surrendered her dearest RIGHTS, and been satisfied with the privileges which man has assumed to grant her.

—Sarah Moore Grimké, reply to the Pastoral Letter, 1837

To be married is too often held up to the view of girls as the sine qua non of human happiness and human existence. For this purpose more than for any other . . . the majority of girls are trained. . . . This mode of training teaches women to regard themselves as a kind of machinery, necessary to keep the domestic engine in order.

—Sarah Moore Grimké, *Letters on the Equality of the Sexes and the Condition of Woman*, 1838

Before the ladies of Seneca Falls held their convention, the way was prepared for them by some equally intrepid ladies who dared take an active part in the great reform movements of the period.

In the late eighteenth century there arose a deep concern over oppressive social conditions. Tom Paine and Mary Wollstonecraft had written in defense of human rights. The poet Shelley and his father-in-law Godwin had passionately pleaded the cause of reform. The American and French revolutions had been fought over political injustice. The Industrial Revolution would produce monumental struggles for economic justice. Democracy, equality, liberty, freedom were more widely discussed and thought about than ever before.

After the revolutionary ordeals and the efforts to establish new forms of government, there was a lull. But by the 1830s the zeal for reform revived, as strong as ever, in America as elsewhere. Prisons, hospitals, charity, education were all to be improved. Slavery, poverty, and strong drink were to be abolished, as were coffee, tea, tobacco, and snuff. Religion was to be revitalized, universal peace established. Missionaries went all over the globe to convert and "civilize" the heathen. Everyone had his own humanitarian cause, his own formula for remaking the world. Groups of reformers established Utopian colonies like Fruitlands, Brook Farm, New Harmony, Hopedale, and Skaneateles, where their beliefs could be put into practice.

Conventions, lectures, debates, meetings of every kind to promote causes of every kind were regularly held. Aside from their serious aims, they provided one of the chief entertainments of the period. Americans of the nineteenth century attended them with the same enthusiasm and frequency as their descendants would go to sports events and movies in the twentieth.

The earlier wave of reform had produced Mary Wollstonecraft to speak for woman's rights. In the revived movement, one of the first to succeed her was Frances Wright, an educated, attractive young Scotswoman, who defended equal rights and education for women. As a friend of Mary Wollstonecraft's daughter Mary Shelley, she must have absorbed some of the progressive ideas of the Godwin circle. She believed ardently in the broadest possible range of freedom for everyone and in everything: freedom of religion, politics, marriage; freedom from slavery and from the poverty which, in her view, resulted from the institution of private property.

Unlike Mary Wollstonecraft, Frances—or Fanny, as she was generally called—had inherited money of her own. She came to America twice, the second time in 1824. She came as the companion of Lafayette, but stayed on after he left. During this second visit she bought a large number of slaves and about two thousand acres of land near Memphis, Tennessee. Here she set up a colony called Nashoba, where she hoped to prepare the slaves for living as free men. But the colony soon expanded its aims, tried to accomplish too much, and eventually failed.

Fanny turned to lecturing and editing, publishing her own paper, the *Free Enquirer*. Free inquiry was the essence of her philosophy. She wanted people to take nothing for granted, to "examine; enquire. . . . Know *why* you believe, understand *what* you believe."

It was as a lecturer—a female lecturer—that Fanny Wright made her greatest impact on the United States. She was the first woman to speak in public here, and this, as much as her radical ideas, created a sensation.

Her principal subjects were such daring ones as equality for women, emancipation for slaves, the political rights of workingmen, free religious inquiry, free public education for everyone, regardless of sex, race, or economic status. She even advocated birth control and equal treatment of illegitimate children. These topics drew large audiences, both male and female, but aroused immense hostility in the press and pulpits of the nation. She was denounced as a "red harlot," a "fallen and degraded fair one," a "disgusting exhibition of female impudence." She was accused of the twin horrors of atheism and free love, sins made worse because they were expressed by a woman, brazenly airing her views for all the world to hear.

From then on, any woman who dared speak in public was called a "Fanny Wrightist." This was a term of great opprobrium and was supposed to warn women against the immodesty of public speaking. But there were some women who admired and took heart from the example she set, and were soon to go out and commit "Fanny Wrightism" themselves.

In the United States, aside from stirrings in religion, the two most active and widespread movements were temperance and the abolition of slavery. Societies were formed to carry on the good work. Meetings and conventions were held, pamphlets and newspapers issued. Speakers went around the country, addressing rallies, describing the evils of drink or slavery. Listeners were urged to sign no-drinking pledges or petitions to free the slaves.

Women soon became deeply involved in reform, the more so because it was one of the few distractions permitted from domesticity. Almost every one of the ladies who were later to engage in the woman's rights movement started as a participant in either the temperance or antislavery cause.

Male reformers were not always happy about having female colleagues, believing the ladies were best off at home. Some antislavery societies refused to accept them as members. But the need for workers became so great that women were reluctantly admitted by some groups, with the hope that they would confine themselves to suitably feminine roles. They were certainly never to speak in public.

The American Anti-Slavery Society was organized in 1833, in Philadelphia. One of its leaders was William Lloyd Garrison, the New England editor and abolitionist who became the symbol for the whole movement. Garrison himself believed firmly in the rights of women, but his view was not shared by most of the others at the initital meeting. Although four ladies, all Quakers and including Lucretia Mott, were present, they were not invited to join. Rebuffed, they formed their own organization, the Philadelphia Female Anti-Slavery Society. Women in other cities followed their example.

There was strong opposition to these female societies. Abolition itself was highly unpopular, especially its militant Garrisonian branch. Some of the more moderate antislavery men advocated gradual or limited emancipation, with time to prepare the slave for freedom; others wanted to leave slavery untouched in the existing southern states, but opposed its extension to the new western territories. Garrison, the pugnacious editor of *The Liberator*, demanded immediate and unconditional emancipation everywhere in the United States, beginning with the South. The Garrisonian speakers, impassioned and zealous, were often in physical danger from hostile mobs. Eggs and rocks were thrown at them, and meetings often turned into riots.

The combination of abolition and women activists was altogether too much for the angry opponents of both. In 1835 the Boston Female Anti-Slavery Society held a meeting at which Garrison was to speak. A mob broke into the hall. Garrison escaped through a back door while Mayor Theodore Lyman urged the women to leave: "Indeed, ladies, you must retire. It is dangerous to remain." Maria Weston Chapman, leader of the group, calmly replied: "If this is the last bulwark of freedom, we may as well die here as anywhere." But at the repeated pleas of Mayor Lyman, the ladies paired off and walked sedately out of the building.

A few years later a mob in Philadelphia expressed its opinion of the Anti-Slavery Convention of American Women by burning down the hall in which the meeting was being held.

The female antislavery societies proved a good school for the ladies who were later to work for woman's rights. They learned how to organize and work together, and how to handle the vociferous criticism they received. They learned the techniques of circulating petitions and holding conventions. They learned how to take direct and often dangerous action by working with the Underground Railway, sheltering the fugitive slaves in their homes and even, when necessary, driving the wagons to the next station.

Above all, they learned to speak before an audience. It is difficult today to grasp the implications of this. In the early nineteenth century, women simply did not address a public group. It was considered not only beyond their capacities, but was frowned upon as improper, indecorous, unfeminine, irreligious, against both God and nature. To speak, as Fanny Wright had done, before "promiscuous audiences"—that is, composed of both men and women—was downright immoral.

At first the female antislavery workers had simply spoken in private homes to other women, telling them of the need to end slavery and getting their signatures on petitions to be sent to Congress. This activity was acceptable even to those men who would just as soon have women stay out of antislavery work altogether.

The earliest of the women to speak in private parlors were two sisters, Angelina and Sarah Grimké. This pair of southern ladies, daughters of a prosperous South Carolina slave owner, were to bring about a great upheaval in the traditional barriers confronting women.

Sarah Grimké had been an alert, intelligent, discerning child who irritated her elders with embarrassing questions about slavery and with her unorthodox behavior. When she was given a young black girl to be her personal slave, Sarah treated her as a playmate instead. Later, in deliberate defiance of South Carolina law, she taught her serving girl to read. When she was found out, she was shaken by the strength of her father's angry reaction. From then on, she abandoned her open violations of southern behavior, but the episode made her more critical than ever of the "peculiar institution" of the South. The daily incidents of brutality, the beatings, the treatment of the slave as not really human—all taken for granted by those around her—bred in Sarah an increasing distress.

Another, if lesser, source of distress was the impossibility of getting the kind of education she wanted. As a proper southern girl, she was taught only the genteel arts: needlework, music, sketching, a smattering of French, and, above all, the gracious manners and correct deportment required in a young lady of good family. This wasn't enough for Sarah, with whom "learning was a passion," and she managed to supplement these accomplishments with some history, geography, natural science, even mathematics and Greek, self-taught from an older brother's books. She wanted urgently to become a lawyer, and for a time studied law secretly. Beyond this, unusual enough for a girl of that era, she could not go; she had to remain unhappily at home while her brothers were sent off to college or trained for professions.

Sarah was almost thirteen when Angelina was born. She assumed a maternal concern and responsibility for the younger sister which was to last all their lives. Angelina grew up a prettier, more popular, more self-assured young woman than Sarah. But she developed the same revulsion to slavery. More aggressive than Sarah, she expressed her views openly and tried to persuade others to take action against slavery. Her family and friends were by turn indulgent and infuriated, especially when she tried to interfere with the treatment of their own slaves. Both sisters eventually found themselves acutely uncomfortable in the "ungentle, uncongenial air" of South Carolina.

They might have remained there forever, wrangling with their family and neighbors, if Judge Grimké himself had not, inadvertently, revealed a way out. When Sarah was twenty-six, he fell mortally ill and she was chosen to take him first to Philadelphia to consult a famous surgeon, then to a New Jersey seaside resort, hoping the climate would help his condition. It was all fruitless; after several months he died.

During this whole period Sarah was in complete charge, making all their traveling and living arrangements, handling medical and financial details. Father and daughter became very close; Judge Grimké came to regard Sarah as a strong and reliant human being. Sarah, released from the image of the helpless and dependent southern lady, and fortified by her father's openly expressed affection and respect, developed a sense of her own personal worth.

It was this strengthening experience that made it possible for Sarah, at the age of twenty-nine, to leave Charleston for Philadelphia, where she was later joined by Angelina. The sisters became Quakers and, still troubled by the existence of slavery, joined the Philadelphia Female Anti-Slavery Society, where they met Lucretia Mott.

In 1836, Angelina wrote a pamphlet, *An Appeal to the Christian Women of the Southern States*, urging them to work against slavery, to free their own slaves, or at least to educate them. The pamphlet, printed and distributed by the American Anti-Slavery Society of New York, was publicly burned in

37

South Carolina. But it was so warmly received in the North that Angelina was invited to come to New York and work for the Anti-Slavery Society as a speaker, addressing women in private homes. Sarah, unwilling to let her cherished younger sister go alone and unprotected, agreed to go with her.

The Grimkés came to New York in the fall of 1836 as the first female abolitionist agents in the country. Their first assignment was to give parlor talks—for women only, of course. But the audiences soon grew too large for private homes and they began to speak in public auditoriums, principally those provided by churches.

The sisters, especially Angelina, became such effective and successful speakers that they were soon in demand by anti-slavery groups outside New York. In 1837 they made a speaking tour of Massachusetts, addressing meetings of women. But as the tour went on, men began to attend in increasing numbers, until the sponsoring society decided to invite all who wanted to come, men as well as women. From then on, all their audiences were mixed. In July, Angelina went to the extreme of debating with two young men who had insisted that the slaves of the South were no worse off than the farmers and workers of the North, and that the Bible itself sanctioned slavery.

The New England clergy had never approved of the Garrisonian abolitionists. They approved still less of female Garrisonians, especially those who violated social and religious custom so flagrantly. It was bad enough for a woman to speak in a public place, worse for her to address mixed audiences; to engage in open debates with men was going beyond the pale altogether. Even before the debates, some churches had refused permission to hold promiscuous meetings in their buildings. After the debates, more churches were closed to them.

At the end of July the Massachusetts clergy took stronger measures to stop the Grimkés. They issued a "Pastoral Letter of the General Association of Massachusetts to the Congrega-

tional Churches Under Their Care," to be read aloud in orthodox churches throughout the state. "We invite your attention,"
it ran, "to the dangers which at present seem to threaten the
female character with wide-spread and permanent injury." The
appropriate duties of women, as stated in the New Testament,
are "unobtrusive and private." God made woman weak for her
own protection; she should confine her activities to "unostenta-
tious prayers" and to "labors of piety and love."

"But when she assumes the place and tone of man as a public reformer," continued the letter, ". . . her character becomes
unnatural. If the vine, whose strength and beauty is to lean
upon the trellis-work, and half conceal its clusters, thinks to
assume the independence . . . of the elm, it will not only cease
to bear fruit, but fall in shame and dishonor into the dust."

The Pastoral Letter was followed by two "Clerical Appeals."
These were attacks upon Garrison as well as upon female anti-
slavery agents who boldly engaged in public speaking. A split
had been developing within the antislavery movement between Garrison's enthusiastic followers and his opponents,
who felt that his flamboyant rhetoric and radical views were
bringing discredit to the cause of antislavery. The moderate
wing was afraid that Garrison's incendiary language might
make a peaceful solution to slavery impossible; it would "roll a
wave of blood over the land." They felt, too, that the Garrisonians would keep out of the movement many northerners
who were against slavery but would not go along with such
extreme tactics as allowing women to speak in public before
mixed audiences. The storm over the Grimkés helped polarize
the two factions. But Garrison continued to state his unpopular views more strongly than ever, and insisted on woman's
rights as an essential part of his program.

At first the Grimkés were dismayed by the commotion raised
by their promiscuous lectures. They worried that their actions

"may injure that blessed cause" of antislavery. But the hostile comments openly expressed by men—particularly by churchmen—made them realize, as nothing had done before, the low regard in which women were held. Their chagrin quickly changed to indignation: "I must confess my womanhood is insulted, my moral feelings outraged when I reflect on these things," wrote Angelina. They began to respond sharply to their attackers and found themselves involved in a new cause: "We are placed very unexpectedly in a very trying situation, in the forefront of an entirely new contest—a contest for the *rights of woman* as a moral, intelligent and responsible being."

Although Angelina was the far better and more active speaker and was more widely known than her sister, it was Sarah who took the lead in defending woman's rights. She was invited to write a series of letters on "The Province of Woman" for the *Spectator*. These were reprinted in Garrison's *Liberator* and then published in book form as *Letters on the Equality of the Sexes*.

Like Mary Wollstonecraft, she demanded the same educational opportunities for women as for men. She also asked equal pay for equal work, and discussed the legal restrictions which discriminated against women. She urged women to make the most of themselves, to become aware of their own worth as intelligent human beings. If women seem less than men, she said, it is because "our minds are crushed, and our reasoning powers are almost wholly uncultivated."

In responding to the Pastoral Letter and to the religious arguments against the equality of women, she claimed that the Bible had been misinterpreted and mistranslated from the original texts by men who injected their own patriarchal views into the matter. She cited passages from the Sermon on the Mount in which Jesus, defining the duties of his followers, drew no distinctions between the sexes. "Men and women were CREATED EQUAL," she insisted, "they are both moral and accountable beings, and whatever is right for man to do, is right for woman to do."

She totally rejected the Pastoral Letter's emphasis on female passivity and dependence. This is not taught by the Bible, she said, but was invented by man "as a means to keep woman in subjection." It is a device in man's war "against her mind, her heart, and her soul. . . . How monstrous is the doctrine that woman is to be dependent on man! Where in all the sacred scriptures is this taught?" But women have learned their man-imposed lesson all too well: they have learned to be submissive, or at least to pretend submission in order to get what they want—"in other words, study to be a hypocrite." Women have allowed themselves to be reduced to childish inferiority, to be content with trivial rewards, condescendingly granted.

In another letter she used arguments that would appear in both the nineteenth-century woman's rights movement and the twentieth-century women's liberation movement. Women shouldn't have to *ask* men for equal rights; these belonged naturally and morally to women. It was "the lust for domination" that had made men assume the power to grant them. And if women seemed inferior, it was because men had reduced them to that state:

"But I ask no favors for my sex. I surrender not our claim to equality. All I ask of our brethren is, that they will take their feet from off our necks and permit us to stand upright on that ground which God designed us to occupy. . . . All history attests that man has subjected woman to his will, used her as a means to promote his selfish gratification, to minister to his sensual pleasures, to be instrumental in promoting his comfort; but never has he desired to elevate her to that rank she was created to fill. He has done all he could to debase and enslave her mind; and now he looks triumphantly on the ruin he has wrought, and says, the being he has thus deeply injured is his inferior."

While Sarah was writing these letters, Angelina was writing another series, in reply to Catherine Beecher's *An Essay on Slavery and Abolitionism with reference to the Duty of American Females*, addressed specifically to Angelina. Catherine Beecher represented a paradox which would become familiar: she spent a good part of her own life working to improve the education of women and to give them professional training, yet she strongly opposed the woman's rights movement. She attacked Angelina not only for speaking in public, but for belonging to an abolitionist society. She was against any public or organized action by women. "Men are the proper persons" for this kind of work. Women must accept their inferior role: "Heaven has appointed to one sex the *superior*, and to the other the *subordinate* station, and this without any reference to the character or conduct of either."

Angelina's tart responses to Catherine Beecher were printed first in *The Liberator* and *The Emancipator*, and then reprinted as a book. She utterly denied the principle of inequality or the "doctrine of masculine and feminine virtues." This view "has robbed woman of essential rights, the right to think and speak and act; the right to share their responsibilities, perils, and toils; the right to fulfil the great end of her being, as a moral, intellectual and immortal creature."

Though many women agreed with Catherine Beecher, there were others who were delighted by the advent of the Grimkés. Letters of encouragement and invitations to speak came from women's organizations. Ladies expressed their approval when their own concealed grievances were openly defined by the sisters. That the Grimkés spoke in public with such success seemed a vindication of female abilities, and many women took a vicarious pride in this achievement. The public at large was not put off by the disapproval of the church and of women like Catherine Beecher. Though it became increasingly difficult for the Grimkés to find churches in which to speak, their audiences were larger and more enthusiastic than ever.

Opposition still continued from many men, however, and not only from those who were hostile to abolitionists or to independent women. Some of the Grimkés' own friends and associates expressed pained disapproval of their actions on behalf of woman's rights. They urged the sisters to soft-pedal the "woman question," at least for the present, for fear it might injure "the greater work" of antislavery.

One of these friends was Theodore Weld. Garrison may have symbolized the abolitionist movement and provided the dramatic publicity and impetus for the cause, but in many respects its real leader and certainly its great organizer was Theodore Weld. He was a brilliant, spellbinding orator as well as a fanatically dedicated reformer. He described himself as a man of "bearish proportions," and his great strength came in handy when he had to battle hostile mobs. By the time the Grimkés came to know him, he had ruined his magnificent voice through strain and was training others to speak for the cause. The sisters were among those whom he trained. He took a special interest in Angelina: he perfected her lecture techniques and helped her outline a series of effective talks.

He did not object to the Grimkés speaking before mixed audiences, but when their letters defending woman's rights began to appear in print, he grew worried. After assuring them that he advocated full equality for women, including the right to be lawyers, preachers, or political leaders, he wrote: "Notwithstanding this, I do most deeply regret that you have begun a series of articles . . . on the rights of woman."

They were uniquely qualified, he went on, for antislavery work, as southerners, former slaveholders, and experienced speakers. "Now can't you leave the *lesser* work to others who can do it *better* than you, and . . . consecrate your whole bodies, souls and spirits to the *greater* work which you can do far better . . . than any body else. . . . Let us all *first* wake up the nation to lift millions of slaves of both sexes from the dust, and turn them into MEN and then . . . it will be an easy matter to take millions of females from their knees and set them on their feet, or in other words transform them from *babies* into *women*."

Angelina wrote a passionate reply. She questioned the wisdom of deferring woman's rights until a more opportune time or till after freedom had been won for the slaves. She felt the antislavery cause itself would benefit from the establishment of woman's rights. "*The time* to assert a right is *the* time when *that* right is denied. *We must establish this right* for if we do not, it will be impossible for *us* to go *on with the work of Emancipation*. . . . Can you not see that woman *could* do . . . a hundred times more for the slave if she were not fettered? Why! we are gravely told that we are out of our sphere even when we circulate petitions; out of our 'appropriate sphere' when we speak to women only. . . . Silence is *our* province, submission *our* duty. . . . If we dare stand upright and do our duty according to the dictates of *our own* consciences, why then we are compared to Fanny Wright. . . . If we surrender the right to *speak* to the public this year, we must surrender the right to petition next year and the right to *write* the year after and so on. What *then* can *woman* do for the slave when she is herself under the feet of man and shamed into silence?"

Weld replied that the sisters were already doing a great deal for woman's rights just by their superior performances as lecturers. Male opposition to female public speaking arose from the notion that women were incompetent: "It arises from habitually regarding them as *inferior* beings. . . . The majority of men regard woman as *silly*. . . . But let intelligent woman begin to pray or speak and men begin to be converted to the true doctrine, and when they get familiar with it they like it and lose all their scruples." Weld approved of their speaking to mixed audiences as long as they confined themselves to the theme of slavery. What he objected to was their discussion of what he considered the irrelevant, or at least the lesser, subject of woman's rights.

His argument was to become a familiar one: women must wait till more important, more basic rights were won, after which it would be easier to win the lesser rights: "Your womans rights! You put the cart before the horse . . . in attempting to push your *womans* rights, until human rights have gone ahead and broken the *path*."

The Grimkés found the protests from Weld and other friends especially hard to take—"it requires divine assistance to sustain the present pressure of opinion from those we love" —but refused to surrender their right to talk or write about "any great moral subject." Weld apparently gave in; at least he stopped expressing his disapproval, even though the sisters continued their series of letters for *The Liberator*.

In any case, their disagreement over the intrusion of the woman's rights issue into that of antislavery did not prevent Weld and Angelina from falling in love. They were married in May 1838. At their wedding, Weld refused to go through the customary ritual in which the bride promises to obey her husband; he also renounced the usual legal rights of the husband to his wife's property—"the unrighteous power vested in a husband by the laws of the United States over the person and property of his wife."

Sarah lived with the Welds after the marriage, and all three continued their antislavery work with scarcely a pause. But the arrival of three children, accompanied by financial problems, illness, and the sheer physical effort of running a large household, cut seriously into their time and energies. Angelina and Sarah found themselves forced to spend most of their efforts on purely domestic concerns. But regardless of how they spent the rest of their lives, they had already made a large contribution to the world's work. They broke down one of the great barriers to women's participation in that work. They forced a recognition of the ability and the right of women to speak in public and to be accepted as human beings, with "the right," wrote Sarah Grimké, "of all human beings to cultivate the powers which God has given us."

6

From Abolition
to Woman's Rights:
II. Lucretia Mott

We deny that the present position of woman is her true
sphere of usefulness; nor will she attain to this sphere, until
the disabilities and disadvantages, religious, civil, and social,
which impede her progress, are removed out of her way.
These restrictions have enervated her mind and paralyzed
her powers. While man assumes that the present is the original state designed for woman, that the existing differences
are not arbitrary . . . but grounded in nature, she will not
make the necessary effort to obtain her just rights, lest it
should subject her to the kind of scorn and contemptuous
manner in which she has been spoken of.

—Lucretia Mott, "Discourse," 1849

The "woman question" agitated the whole reform movement. Even if the cause was righteous and pure, ran the argument, like antislavery or peace, was it morally acceptable for women to speak in public, work together with men on committees, become officers of organizations that included both men and women? Was it even permissible for women to belong to organizations that included men?

These questions tore the American Anti-Slavery Society apart. In May 1840 it split in two. One reason given for the break was the "insane innovation" of allowing women to serve as speakers and officers of the organization. Some of the anti-women abolitionists had been so busy trying to make women stop talking that they had scarcely any time left for the slaves.

Another reason for the division was the increasing dissension between the followers and the opponents of William Lloyd Garrison. Since Garrison supported the women, the anti-Garrisonians became the anti-woman group. They broke off from the original organization and formed their own, which they called the American and Foreign Anti-Slavery Society. This was an unfortunate pairing-off of viewpoints, for quite a few opponents of Garrison's extremism were at the same time strong supporters of woman's rights.

Theodore Weld, the leading spirit and one of the founders of the original society, was one of these. He disagreed too much with Garrison to remain with his faction, yet could not join the rival group since, he said, "I totally dissent from the *foundation principle* on which that society is based—a *denial* of the equal membership of women," and criticized their "persevering attempt to deprive women of what are, in my estimation, their inalienable rights." He withdrew from all organizational work for the antislavery cause, though he continued to do whatever he could on his own.

A month after the split, a World Anti-Slavery Convention met in London. American groups were invited to send delegates. Garrison's society selected five: four men and one woman, Lucretia Mott. Mrs. Mott was also chosen as one of the representatives of the Philadelphia Female Anti-Slavery Society. Other groups, like the Massachusetts Anti-Slavery Society and the Boston Female Society, also sent women.

When they arrived in London, however, they were told that women would not be accepted. Protests were made, and the first day of the convention was completely taken up with impassioned arguments for and against seating the female delegates. It was claimed that women were "constitutionally unfit for public or business meetings," and that their presence would injure the cause of emancipation.

Most of the opposition came from clergymen, who quoted passages from the Bible to prove that the subjection of women was "the will of God." They said it would be better to cancel the convention altogether than to demean it by the unseemly participation of women. When the proposal was made to seat all accredited delegates regardless of sex, the American ministers yelled, "Turn out the women!"

Garrison had been detained in America and would arrive several days late, but other Americans came to the defense of their countrywomen. One of these was Henry Stanton, who, like his friend Theodore Weld, had found himself in the painful position of being anti-Garrison but pro-woman. He had joined the new anti-Garrison society, but nevertheless spoke urgently for the acceptance of the female delegates. Another of their defenders was George Bradburn. When some of the English ministers began hysterically shaking copies of the Bible in the faces of the pro-woman speakers, Bradburn, "exasperated with their narrowness and bigotry," jumped to his feet and said, "Prove to me, gentlemen, that your Bible sanctions the slavery of woman—the complete subjugation of one-half the race to the other—and I should feel that the best work

49

I could do for humanity would be to make a grand bonfire of every Bible in the Universe."

The women themselves were not permitted to take part in the discussion, but had to listen quietly, in what must have been an intensely frustrating silence. Among them were some of the most intelligent and educated women in the United States and Great Britain. To overcome the barriers of prejudice and custom and reach the position of delegate to a convention of this kind, a woman had to be at least twice as qualified as a man. The most mediocre male could take an active role in the reform movements of the period, and get himself appointed as an officer or delegate. For such men to presume the right to reject women like Lucretia Mott appeared both ludicrous and galling to the silent female listeners.

Despite the efforts of Stanton and other supporters of the women, the final vote was against them, and they had to take seats in the curtained gallery. When Garrison arrived on the fourth day, he refused to take his own seat as a delegate and joined the women in their banishment. "After battling so many long years for the liberation of African slaves, I can take no part in a convention that strikes down the most sacred rights of all women."

With Garrison in the gallery, most of the attention and speeches of the delegates were focused in that direction, and the issue of woman's rights remained the most absorbing one of the whole affair. Today the convention is remembered not at all for any help to the slaves, but as the initial spark of the organized woman's rights movement.

The women had been escorted to their gallery with sufficient courtesy, but, wrote Elizabeth Cady Stanton, "the crucifixion of their pride and self-respect, the humiliation of the spirit," was dismissed by the men as "a most trifling matter." Mrs. Stanton was not herself a delegate; she had come as the bride of Henry Stanton and had joined the other women as a visitor. But she felt the full impact of rejection. All women, she said, had been insulted by the rejection of the female delegates.

Of these delegates, the most important American woman was Lucretia Mott. Mrs. Stanton had heard of the Quaker Mrs. Mott as a distinguished but "strong-minded radical," but had never met her until the London Convention. They took to each other immediately, and spent most of their time in London together, discussing, among other things, the ignominious position of women as revealed by the Convention proceedings. Out of this meeting was to grow a lifelong friendship and, in time, the first woman's rights convention.

When Lucretia Coffin was born in 1793, she had three things in her favor: she was born into a family of Quakers, her childhood would be spent on the island of Nantucket, and she had an unusual father who believed in educating girls. The Quakers were the one religious sect to grant women something close to equality with men. Women were allowed to speak freely at Quaker meetings and to become ministers, something unthinkable in almost any other religion. Lucretia Coffin Mott herself became a minister while still in her twenties; by the time she met Elizabeth Cady Stanton she was an accomplished public speaker.

Quaker women never had the humiliating experience of sitting meekly and silently in churches while their ministers fulminated against the daughters of Eve: against woman as temptress, woman as inferior, woman as doomed to suffer and remain in subjection to man. Thus, to begin with, their confidence and self-respect were not eroded as so often happened with women of other denominations. It was almost inevitable that so many early members of the woman's rights movement would be Quakers.

The Quaker view of women was reinforced, in Lucretia

Coffin's case, by the special circumstances of life on Nantucket. The island was a great whaling and fishing center, with the men away at sea for months at a time. In the absence of their husbands, the Nantucket housewives not only managed all the family affairs, but often set up small businesses of their own. With Captain Coffin away so much on his whaleboat, Lucretia's mother—a relative of Benjamin Franklin—ran a small shop. This was a common enterprise on the island, and the women shopkeepers made the difficult trip to Boston, where they exchanged whale oil and homemade articles like candles for the groceries and dry goods with which to stock their shops. They kept their own accounts—there was no talk in Nantucket of figures being too difficult for female heads—and assumed responsibilities generally assigned to men. As a result, wrote Lucretia Mott, they could "mingle with men" and "have intelligent subjects of conversation."

As a child, then, she became accustomed to seeing women in positions of authority and responsibility at a time when, in other parts of the East, women had begun to retreat from these positions. To cap this advantage, she was lucky in having a father who recognized his daughter's ability and encouraged it in every way. After she finished the usual elementary education available, he sent her to an advanced Quaker academy, the Nine Partners Boarding School. She was an excellent student; after a few years she was invited to become a teacher. One of the other instructors was a young man, James Mott, whom she soon married.

Lucretia Coffin's family had moved from Nantucket to Boston and then to Philadelphia, the center of Quaker life. The young Motts came to the same city. James began a business career; Lucretia taught school until the arrival of her third child—she had six altogether. Then she settled down to the arduous routine of a nineteenth-century housewife. Even for that period, when domestic skill was the most significant measure of success for a woman, she became an outstanding housekeeper and hostess, noted for her beautifully kept home and large-scale entertaining. One of her letters casually mentions that after a day of washing and ironing, "We had 40 to sit down & some children at a side table." In later years the Mott home was to become a center for reform leaders, "a resort for people of distinction."

In between household chores, she managed to do a surprising amount of serious reading. Starting with a careful study of the Bible, she proceeded to theological works, then ranged out into philosophy, history, political economy, and, inevitably, woman's rights. Mary Wollstonecraft's *A Vindication of the Rights of Woman* was her "pet book," occupying a place of honor on her table except when it was out on loan to a receptive reader.

She began to take notes on her reading, though with her remarkable memory it was scarcely necessary. She could recall whole passages, especially from the Bible. But memory was the least of her mental qualifications; she also possessed an acute, analytical mind, capable of dispassionate and independent thought.

If any woman of that period could find her way outside the walls of her own home, it would be someone like Lucretia Mott, whose natural intelligence and confidence had been encouraged by her Nantucket and Quaker background and by her uncommon education. As her children grew older and needed less of her attention, she began to speak more often at Quaker meetings. In 1821, at the age of twenty-eight, she was formally appointed a minister in the Society of Friends. She became an experienced and distinguished preacher, highly regarded for the clarity and independence of her views.

When the Quakers split in 1828 between the authoritarian Orthodox Friends and the more liberal Hicksites, Lucretia and James Mott joined the Hicksites. Mrs. Mott believed that religion must be based on "inward spiritual grace," not upon rigid creeds or fixed ceremonial rituals. Each individual should study the Bible and apply his own powers of reason to its interpretation. Men—and women—must think for themselves and act according to their own inner sense of the truth. Furthermore, religion must be based on justice as well as upon reason and "inner light"; it must express itself in "practical godliness."

The reform surge of the 1830s provided many outlets for practical godliness. For the Motts, the principal one was antislavery. Their home was to become an active station in the Underground Railway. James Mott joined the Free Produce Society, refusing to handle slave-produced articles, mostly cotton, in his business. In December 1833, when delegates met in Philadelphia to form the American Anti-Slavery Society, Lucretia Mott was one of the four women invited to attend the convention as observers. But women were not permitted to join the new society. Instead, they formed their own antislavery organization.

Soon afterward a Pennsylvania branch of the national society was established, with James Mott as one of the charter members. Again, women were excluded. But two years later the ruling was reversed and Mrs. Mott joined. She became one of the most influential antislavery workers in Philadelphia. Among those she inspired were the Grimké sisters, whom she advised and encouraged, especially during the difficult period when they were being harassed for speaking before mixed audiences.

When the "woman question" began to ravage the antislavery movement, Lucretia Mott was deeply troubled. She was well aware of the sex discrimination that had always existed in the movement, but the animosity and bigotry which boiled up over the Grimkés was too much. It was only to be expected that the general public would be prejudiced against women and would be scandalized by the idea of women addressing mixed audiences or working together with men in the same organizations. But surely her own male co-workers in a movement whose basic purpose was freedom and justice should have held more enlightened views.

She bitterly regretted the split in the antislavery ranks, but with each new rebuff by the anti-woman faction, her resentment grew. The whole subject of woman's rights began to assume new proportions until it became "the most important question of my life." She mentioned it in almost every sermon and speech.

When she was sent as a delegate to the World Anti-Slavery Convention in London, she was fully prepared for rejection. But though she might have been prepared, she was far from resigned.

7

Elizabeth Cady Stanton

The first event engraved on my memory was the birth of a sister when I was four years old. . . . I heard so many friends remark, "What a pity it is she's a girl!" . . . I did not understand at that time that girls were considered an inferior order of beings.

—Elizabeth Cady Stanton, *Eighty Years and More*

There is not a man in this whole land who wouldn't rather have a boy baby than a gal baby any time. There never was a newly-married man when he learned that his first born was a girl, that didn't try to tear out his hair by the roots because it wasn't a boy.

—Richmond (Kentucky) *Herald*, October 29, 1879

To me there was no question so important as the emancipation of women from the dogmas of the past, political, religious, and social. It struck me as very remarkable that abolitionists, who felt so keenly the wrongs of the slave, should be so oblivious to the equal wrongs of their own mothers, wives, and sisters.

—Elizabeth Cady Stanton, *Eighty Years and More*

Of all the ladies who were to gather at Seneca Falls, of all the leaders and devoted workers in the woman's rights movement, the most interesting and illuminating was Elizabeth Cady Stanton. She was by no means an average person herself, yet in her discontents, her aspirations, her complexities, and even in her personal conflicts, she most clearly represented in one individual what the movement was all about. As a woman whose intelligence far outran the educational and vocational opportunities open to her, as a housewife whose horizons stretched beyond "the making of puddings" and "fine stitchery," as an individual capable of the independence and responsibilities denied by the traditions of femininity, she was typical of a large number of American women.

All of this was in addition to her importance as founder and philosopher, as she has been called, of the woman's rights movement. For years she was its chief writer and speaker, formulating its principles, defining its goals, exploring the nature and causes of woman's subordinate position. Her lively and flexible mind produced ideas and insights that stirred her contemporaries and seem fresh and applicable today. If any one individual could be called a prime mover toward woman's full self-realization, that person would be Elizabeth Cady Stanton.

According to the pattern laid down for girls, especially in the early nineteenth century, she should have followed without question the usual path of a modest education, followed by marriage and total immersion in the domestic concerns of keeping house and raising a family. But it was clear, quite early in her life, that no simple pattern would be able to contain the intellectual energy and immense vitality of Elizabeth Cady.

When she was still a very little girl, she became aware of the repressive elements in her life and refused to accept them quietly, in "obedience and humility." Instead, she angrily complained to her elders, "Everything we like to do is a sin. . . . I am so tired of that everlasting no! no! no! At school, at home, everywhere it is *no!* Even at church all the commandments begin 'Thou shalt not.' I suppose God will say 'no' to all we like in the next world, just as you do here."

The Cady parents imposed a stern regimen upon their children. Judge Daniel Cady was a distinguished lawyer, a member of the New York Legislature, "a man of firm character and unimpeachable integrity." He was also a man of great reserve and impressive dignity. Mrs. Cady had an equally firm character and dignified presence. They loved their children, but controlled them through "fear, rather than affection."

The Cadys lived in Johnstown in upper New York State, where Elizabeth was born in 1815. It was a fairly important town at that time, the cultural center of the Mohawk Valley area. The atmosphere of the Cady home, with its ordered discipline, was probably typical. Parents, teachers, and ministers put fixed limitations on the natural spontaneity of the children.

When she was over eighty years old, Elizabeth Cady Stanton still retained strong feelings about this "crippling" of children's—particularly female children's—lives. One of the chief contributors to the "despair and gloom" of her early years was the Scotch Presbyterian Church, to which her family belonged. The bleak theological dogmas, the endless sermons on predestination and eternal damnation, and the uncomfortable and unattractive church had an intensely depressing and often frightening effect upon Elizabeth as a child. The Scotch Presbyterian devil was a very real entity to her. Convinced of her own wickedness as a rebellious, often disobedient child, she lived in constant fear that he might some day "claim me as his own." As she grew older, these religious fears would change to doubts and finally, as she came to realize the effects of religion on the lives of women, to anger.

The Presbyterian Church of her childhood did, however, have one enormously redeeming feature: the Reverend Simon Hosack, who lived next door to the Cadys. As a minister he may have been the agent of a stern and forbidding religion, but as a warm and affectionate neighbor he was an invaluable source of comfort to the little girl. His sermons may have chilled her soul, but his companionship expanded her mind.

Dr. Hosack was one of the two men, aside from her father, who contributed greatly to the intellectual development of Elizabeth Cady. Despite his important position as a religious leader, he was a lonely man, with little satisfaction in his marriage or personal life. He welcomed the frequent visits of young Elizabeth, and treated her not as a girl, or even as a child, but as a companion. They talked together for hours at a time, while he worked in his garden with Elizabeth helping or looking on, or while he rode around the area on parish business with Elizabeth driving his buggy. When he used words or allusions she didn't understand, he explained them carefully and patiently, until she acquired a superior knowledge of the English language, together with a proficiency in using it, which were to make her one of the finest speakers and writers of the woman's rights movement. She also acquired, from the thoughtful attentiveness of Dr. Hosack, courage and self-confidence in expressing her ideas.

Through her association with him, too, she learned to notice and examine even familiar details with a sensitive eye, and she explored areas of knowledge which might not otherwise have come her way. Her perceptions were sharpened, and her natural intelligence was provided with the kind of exercise not generally available to little girls at that time.

Elizabeth Cady began to discover early in life some of the drawbacks to being a little girl in the nineteenth century—or in any other century, for that matter. There were six surviving Cady children: five daughters and one son. Eleazer was the third child, Elizabeth the fourth. It was clear to the girls that their brother was more important than all of them put together. All of Judge Cady's hopes, his strong sense of family continuity were bound up in his only son. But right after graduating from college, Eleazer became ill and died.

Judge Cady was inconsolable. Eleven-year-old Elizabeth tried desperately to comfort him, but his only response was to sigh heavily and say, "Oh, my daughter, I wish you were a boy!" Instead of resenting the remark, she determined to become "all my brother was," and to replace him in her father's life. But what gave boys their special value? She finally decided that boys were "learned and courageous." The courageous part was relatively easy: she would—and eventually did —become expert at managing a horse. For the learned part, she would study Greek.

She turned to Dr. Hosack for help. He understood her real dilemma and assured her, first of all, that in his eyes, if not in Judge Cady's, girls were as important as boys and equally deserving of both love and scholarship. He began immediately to teach her Greek. She proved an excellent student, advancing more rapidly than even the partisan Dr. Hosack had expected. He repeatedly and pointedly praised her accomplishment to Judge Cady, but, to Elizabeth's intense frustration, her father would only sigh unhappily.

As soon as she had mastered the basic elements of Greek, she became the only girl in a class of boys studying Latin and mathematics, as well as Greek, at the Johnstown Academy. For three years she remained almost at the top of the class, in second place. At the end of that time she received one of the two prizes given for excellence in Greek. She ran home to show her father this tangible proof that girls could do as much and provide the same satisfaction to their fathers as boys. But again Judge Cady, though obviously pleased, repeated his sighed "Ah, you should have been a boy." To the end of her life she would recall her "bitter tears" over this new failure to win her father's unqualified approval and acceptance.

In spite of Judge Cady's view of daughters as being less valuable than sons, he did recognize Elizabeth's ability and probably gave her more encouragement than most fathers of the time. He allowed her to come to his law office, which adjoined the Cady house, and sit in on his discussions of clients' cases. There she was introduced, at an early age, to the legal handicaps of being a woman.

Many of her father's clients were women whose problems arose from the prevailing laws which stripped them of their property and earnings after marriage. Once a woman married, whatever she inherited or earned—money, property, even personal belongings—passed into the unrestricted possession of her husband.

Sitting in her father's office, Elizabeth Cady heard about husbands who spent their wives' money on other women, or dissipated it on drink or gambling. In some cases the husband had willed his wife's own wealth to a son, who now grudgingly gave his widowed mother too little or barely enough to live on. Elizabeth heard about women caught in miserably unhappy marriages who had managed to arrange separations or even divorce, but were not permitted to see their own children or have anything to say about their upbringing. Under the state laws, a father had exclusive rights of guardianship, no matter what kind of man he was or what the cause of separation had been.

Judge Cady was sympathetic to these women and sometimes helped them financially, but he could provide no real solutions to their problems. When Elizabeth urged him to help, he took out his law books and showed her the exact wording of the laws, explaining at the same time the process by which such legislation was created and how it could be changed. "When you are grown up," he said, ". . . you must talk to the legislators . . . and, if you can persuade them to pass new laws, the old ones will be a dead letter."

As an impressionable child, Elizabeth took him seriously. And yet when she did exactly that, when as a grown woman she took a leading part in persuading the legislators to pass new laws governing the rights of married women, her father objected strenuously. He approved the legal changes she helped bring about, but didn't want his daughter, as a woman, to appear in public and "talk to the legislators." "Thus was the future object of my life foreshadowed and my duty plainly outlined by him who was most opposed to my public career when, in due time, I entered upon it."

When she was fifteen, Elizabeth graduated from the Johnstown Academy. The boys who had been her classmates were going on to Union College at Schenectady. Elizabeth learned, to her angry chagrin, that she could not join them simply because she was a girl. She was only partially mollified when her parents agreed to send her to the Troy Female Seminary, the most advanced school for the education of girls then in existence.

It had been founded in 1821 by Emma Willard, one of the pioneers in woman's education. As a girl, Mrs. Willard had shown a talent and liking for mathematics, and her father had encouraged her in this ungirlish tendency. He would have been happy to provide her with a fine education, but at the time there was no institution of higher learning which would accept even such a capable young woman as his daughter.

She became a teacher and spent all her free time mastering such subjects as advanced mathematics and the natural sciences. She finally persuaded the New York Legislature to grant her a charter for a girls' seminary, and raised enough money from public and private sources to establish the first endowed institution for the education of girls.

Advanced as it was for the period, and though it taught mathematics, geography, natural science, and even, to the consternation of some parents, physiology, the seminary was still far below the educational level of men's colleges. There was an emphasis on domestic science and religion. Though Mrs. Willard was an enterprising innovator in woman's education, she was very conservative when it came to other aspects of female life. Like the other two great .pioneers in female education, Mary Lyon and Catherine Beecher, she was opposed to woman suffrage and believed in prescribed limits of proper behavior for her sex.

Elizabeth Cady was not happy during her two years at the seminary. She knew it was only second best and couldn't compare with Union College. She had already covered most of the curriculum in Johnstown, and would add little that was new except French, music, and dancing. And she disliked the atmosphere of an all-girl school, with its jealousies and feuds, its competitive preoccupation with clothes and appearance. Her experience at the seminary led her to become a strong supporter of coeducation.

Moreover, she was disturbed by the heated religious activity going on in Troy. This was the great period of religious turbulence and revivalism, much of which took place in New York State. In 1830, the year Elizabeth entered the seminary, Joseph Smith published *The Book of Mormon* in Palmyra, New York, and would soon organize his Church of Latter-Day Saints. The following year, in Hampton, New York, William Miller founded the Adventist or Millerite sect, which prepared for the Second Coming of Christ, expected on October 22, 1843. Not far from Troy the Shakers were conducting highly emotional services in their religious commune.

The star of the revivalists was the Reverend Charles Grandison Finney, a fiery orator who interlarded his threats of hellfire and doom with diatribes on behalf of temperance and antislavery. He traveled through New York State making converts, including several, like Theodore Weld, who were thereby inspired to organize an antislavery movement. He held six weeks of revival meetings in Troy, with daily prayer sessions at the seminary in addition to the public services, terrifying his listeners with the awful and everlasting punishment awaiting those depraved sinners who failed to repent. One of the most frightened attendants at all the meetings was Elizabeth Cady. Her Calvinistic, Presbyterian background made her especially vulnerable, and she suffered intensely from the religious fears and doubts which were raised but, unhappily, not resolved. No matter how much or how often she repented, she retained the uneasy feeling that she was missing something essential in the religious experience.

The effect on her was so disastrous that her father took her off on a six-week trip to Niagara, together with her oldest sister, Tryphena, and her brother-in-law, Edward Bayard. They spent a good deal of time discussing the new liberal works which were then being published, until "My religious superstitions gave place to rational ideas based on scientific facts, and . . . as I looked at everything from a new standpoint, I grew more and more happy."

Thousands of people went through similar turmoil during the epidemic of religious reform in the early nineteenth century. In Elizabeth Cady's case, the episode shook her free from the usual religious moorings, so that later she was able to examine with a detached and critical eye the effects of the church and its teachings upon the position of women.

Edward Bayard, her brother-in-law, was the second man to have a direct hand in Elizabeth Cady's development. He replaced Dr. Hosack in providing her with lively intellectual exercise. Edward and his brother Henry were two of the many law students who received part of their legal training, according to the custom of the period, in Judge Cady's office. The Cady daughters spent a good deal of time with the students, discussing a wide variety of subjects, going on hiking and horseback excursions with them. The young men made up for the lack of brothers in this female household, and the girls learned to deal with them on a fairly equal footing. Though the boys often started off by condescending to a presumed feminine fragility, the animated, sharp-tongued Cady daughters, with their love of active exercise, soon forced a recognition of their physical and intellectual capabilities.

Elizabeth, especially, loved to argue with the young men about the equality of women and confessed that she often applied herself to books—including those of Blackstone and other legal authorities—and games not so much for their own sake, but "to make those young men recognize my equality. I soon noticed that, after losing a few games of chess, my opponent talked less of masculine superiority."

Edward Bayard was an unusual young man, with no such notions of superiority. He took a special interest in teaching the girls "how to think clearly and reason logically." He introduced Elizabeth to new fields of learning—philosophy, political economy, history, poetry—and taught her to question and closely examine everything, no matter what its source.

He was ten years older than Elizabeth; she was a little girl when he married Tryphena, the oldest Cady daughter. She was still just his young sister-in-law when he opened a law office in Seneca Falls. But by the time Elizabeth came to visit the Bayards, she had become a grown-up, attractive, and stimulating young woman. She was warm and easygoing where Tryphena was severe and critical. Elizabeth in turn now saw him as something other than an older-brother substitute. It was almost inevitable that they should fall in love.

Even today such a triangle involving two sisters would be painful and difficult, but in the 1830s it was cataclysmic. Nineteenth-century views of both marriage and divorce rested on stern foundations of duty and social responsibility. Love was secondary, sexual attraction unmentionable. For Edward and Elizabeth to put their individual happiness first would have been considered scandalously immoral.

It was an impossible and hopeless situation, and one which had to be kept completely hidden. Edward did manage to see her as often as he could; on his frequent business trips to New York City he would stop over in Johnstown, or he would see her in New York when Elizabeth visited another sister, who was married and living in that city. Edward did get to the desperate point of urging her to go away with him, but she refused. The thought of the effect it would have on her own sister was too much for Elizabeth.

She knew divorce was out of the question in this case, but she began to think more closely about the whole problem. After the woman's rights movement started, it was Elizabeth Cady Stanton who introduced the touchy subject of divorce, to the dismay and anger of many workers inside the movement itself. And her acute and realistic views of marriage and love may well have had their beginnings in this early experience.

It was almost a yearly ritual for Elizabeth Cady to pay a long visit to the home of her cousin Gerrit Smith. These interludes contributed more to her real education than her stay at Mrs. Willard's academy. Gerrit Smith was one of the most active reformers of the time; he was also one of the largest and richest landowners in New York State. He contributed generously to the abolitionist movement, devoted much of his time and his writing to it, and made his home a station on the Underground Railway for escaping slaves. He supported other current reforms as well: temperance, liberalized religion, and, soon, woman's rights.

His Peterboro estate was the constantly active meeting

ground for a remarkable range of people: radical reformers, conservative aristocrats, scholars, writers, clergymen, and the local Oneida Indians. Many of the antislavery conventions and meetings were held in the surrounding area, and the speakers enjoyed the openhanded hospitality of the Smith home. The dinner table at Peterboro served as a lively forum for the exchange of every variety of opinion and information.

Judge Cady disapproved of Gerrit Smith's "radical" ideas, but to Elizabeth the long visits at Peterboro were a marvelous experience. She received an intimate, firsthand introduction to the most important reforms and reformers of the day; she sat in on discussions of explosive subjects like abolition, virtually unmentioned at home. At Peterboro, too, the "Calvinistic gloom" of the family's early religious beliefs had given way to a broader, freer theology, producing "an atmosphere of love and peace . . . and good cheer" to which her own ebullient nature warmly responded. And, not least, the fact that Gerrit Smith's only daughter, Elizabeth, was her closest friend made a stay at Peterboro one of the highlights of Elizabeth Cady's existence.

In 1839, on one of these visits, she met Henry Stanton, who was staying at Peterboro while attending a number of antislavery conventions in nearby towns. Stanton was one of the most eloquent speakers of the abolitionist movement, and one of its capable and courageous leaders. Representing an unpopular group, he was repeatedly attacked by violent mobs. As financial secretary of the American Anti-Slavery Society, he collected thousands of dollars for the cause. A charming and attractive man, ten years older than Elizabeth Cady, who was now twenty-four, he was a natural replacement for Edward Bayard. In no time at all, he asked her to marry him and she accepted.

Everyone opposed the marriage. The conservative Judge Cady disapproved of abolitionists, especially a non-affluent one who presumed to marry his daughter. He felt that a professional, full-time antislavery lecturer would never earn enough money to support a wife properly, and sternly lectured Elizabeth on the importance of a firm financial basis for marriage. Gerrit Smith approved very much of abolitionists and especially of Henry Stanton, but he knew Judge Cady would blame him for allowing Elizabeth, while in his home and under his care, to enter what in Cady eyes was an unsuitable engagement. He sternly lectured her on the unwisdom of hasty and ill-considered marriages. Edward Bayard was even more disapproving than the others, but for very different reasons. He wanted her for himself, and again urged her to go off with him.

Confused by arguments and pressures she could not quite dismiss, she broke off her engagement. She refused, however, to break off completely with Henry Stanton, and continued to correspond with him. The following spring he wrote to her saying that he was going to London very soon, as a delegate to the World Anti-Slavery Convention. He asked her one final time to marry him, and go to London with him.

She suddenly decided that she had yielded enough to the opinions of others; she must make up her own mind. Her answer was an unshakable yes. Her father had to give his assent, though reluctantly. The only remaining difficulty was to persuade the conventional Scottish clergyman to omit the word "obey" from the ceremony. She insisted that her marriage was going to be one between equals, and she would not submit to the indignity of that word. The minister yielded, and the marriage took place on May 10, 1840.

For the same reason that she would not allow the word "obey," she objected to being called "Mrs. Henry Stanton." It was a symbol, she said in a letter, that women—like slaves, who also had no names of their own—were "mere chattels, with no civil or social rights. . . . The custom of calling women

Mrs. John This . . . is founded on the principle that white men are lords of all. I cannot acknowledge this principle as just; therefore, I cannot bear the name of another." This was written the year before her marriage. When she married, she compromised: she took the name Stanton, but not Henry, and was always called Elizabeth Cady Stanton.

Before sailing for London, the Stantons spent several days at the home of Theodore and Angelina Weld and Sarah Grimké. They were close friends of Henry Stanton, but had never met Elizabeth. They responded to her warmly, and were pleased with the marriage. But Angelina commented in a letter to Gerrit Smith and his wife: "I could not help wishing that Henry was better calculated to mould such a mind."

In that era it was automatically assumed that the husband, better educated and presumably better equipped mentally, would be in a position to "mould" the mind of his wife—an attitude that not even the Grimkés were wholly free of. But there was little that Henry Stanton could contribute to a mind like Elizabeth's. In recognizing this, Angelina Weld was not putting Henry down. She liked and respected him, but she saw that Elizabeth was already his equal at the very least. Henry Stanton was a very able, intelligent man, but he was not, as Angelina put it, "calculated to mould" the unusually fertile and strongly independent mind of his wife.

8

Margaret Fuller

We would have every path laid open to Woman as freely as
to Man. . . . Inward and outward freedom for Woman as
much as for Man shall be acknowleged as a *right*, not yielded
as a concession. . . . Man cannot by right lay even well-meant
restrictions on Woman. . . . What Woman needs is not as a
woman to act or rule, but as a nature to grow, as an intellect
to discern, as a soul to live freely and unimpeded, to unfold
such powers as were given her.

—Margaret Fuller,
Woman in the Nineteenth Century, 1845

While Elizabeth Cady in New York was discovering what it meant to be a girl, another future feminist was developing her own views on the subject in Massachusetts. This was the highly intelligent and altogether remarkable Margaret Fuller, born in Cambridge in 1810, five years before Elizabeth.

Like so many of the woman's rights leaders, Margaret Fuller's early life was shaped and dominated by her father. Timothy Fuller was a difficult man, brilliant and eccentric, the very essence of unbending New England Puritanism. He was a lawyer and politician, a member of the Massachusetts Senate and of the United States Congress.

As soon as Margaret emerged from infancy, her father took complete charge of her, while her mother faded into the background. He had received a thorough classical education at Harvard and planned to pass on his learning to his first child. He would have preferred a boy, but the fact that it was a girl did not change his fixed purpose. When she was six, she began reading Latin. In the next few years she added French, Italian, and Greek. She learned German in her late teens, and read extensively in the literature of all these languages.

Timothy Fuller was imbued with a rigid New England work ethic. He drove himself, and he drove his precocious little daughter. He trained her rigorously to examine and organize her ideas, to express them clearly and with detailed accuracy. There were long hours of study and virtually no play at all. Margaret was not only her father's pupil, but his companion, whom he treated almost as an equal, replacing his weak, self-effacing wife.

It became too much for the high-strung little girl. She began to suffer from nightmares and depression. When she was thirteen, her father admitted that perhaps she needed young friends, and sent her away to a girls' school. It was a disaster. She had no previous experience with children her own age, knew nothing of how to play or get along with them. The daughter who was born to the Fullers two years after Margaret, and who could have provided companionship, died in early childhood. The seven children who followed were too young for Margaret's needs.

After two unhappy years at school she returned to the Fuller home in Cambridge, near Harvard College. She was now old enough to associate with the students, and life became easier and happier. The boys did not find her physically attractive, but enjoyed her wit, her impressive learning, and her great conversational skill, the results of her father's extraordinary training. In spite of her unpolished manners and ruthless intelligence, and in spite of her earlier failure to get along with the girls at school, she now developed a talent for friendship. Even people who couldn't stand her at first were eventually won over by her intellectual exuberance. She was never upset if people didn't like her; her own interest in another person was enough to make her pursue the relationship, and in the end a firm friendship would be established.

When she was twenty-three, she was forced to leave her increasing circle of friends. Her father, disappointed in both law and politics, decided to try farming in an isolated rural area. It was a mistake for the whole family. The unaccustomed work was too hard for all of them. Mrs. Fuller's health broke down, and Margaret had to run the household. She also spent long hours every day teaching her younger brothers and sisters, in addition to pursuing her own studies of European history and literature, and architecture. As a final strain, she hated farm life and resented being cut off from the intellectual life of Boston and Cambridge. After two years, exhausted by work and discontent, she became seriously ill. Before she was fully recovered, her father, also worn out by excessive and unfamiliar labor, came down with cholera and died.

With her father gone and her mother unable to cope, Margaret became the head of the family. She continued to run the farm, but it didn't pay enough. She turned to teaching school, first in Boston, then in Providence. She was successful as a teacher, but found the classroom too tame for her explosive vitality. "I must die," she said, "if I do not burst forth in genius or heroism." But there was her family to support. In 1839 she moved them to the outskirts of Boston and, in order to earn money with work closer to her intellectual ambitions than teaching, began her famous "Conversations." She was twenty-nine.

Margaret herself, because of her father, had never suffered any educational disadvantages in being a girl. She also had had outlets for her education and intelligence. She realized, however, that most women, even when well educated, lacked the opportunity or need to use their brains and knowledge. Men, she said, must constantly use their learning in their daily lives: in their business or profession, and in exercising their political rights. Women, especially housewives, had few such occasions to apply their minds.

Margaret Fuller proposed to remedy this waste of human capacities. She would teach women to use their learning, to think analytically instead of in vague generalities, "to systematize thought and give a precision and clearness in which our sex are so deficient, chiefly, I think, because they have so few inducements to test and classify what they receive."

Conversation, in this period, was considered an important art, and Margaret Fuller was one of its most skilled practitioners. It was claimed that she talked better than she wrote. Her quick, impulsive mind, scintillating in conversation, was too impatient for careful, disciplined organization when it came to writing. "Conversation," she said, "is my natural element." Her plan was to hold a series of meetings or "Conversations" for the educated women of Boston, where they would discuss a variety of subjects and, on occasion, read prepared papers.

The first series consisted of thirteen two-hour sessions. Margaret opened each session with a brief description of the selected topic and then guided the discussion which followed. Everyone had to speak, and speak to the point, with no holds barred. This itself was an innovation: in a day when women were supposed to speak, if at all, with modesty and reserve, Margaret insisted on the relentlessly honest expression of one's real opinions, however unpopular. She forced her pupils to think and talk not as "ladies," but as intelligent human beings.

The Conversations continued for five years and were successful from the start, though at first they were ridiculed as "female pedantry." Margaret never lacked for participants, even though she charged a substantial fee. The Conversations made her famous as the most learned woman in the United States. More than that, they raised female prestige by demonstrating that women could organize ideas and express them forcefully and effectively. It was another step in preparing women to speak in public, and in weakening the opposition to their doing so. It is not known whether Elizabeth Cady Stanton, who was living in Boston at this time, ever took part in the sessions, but many of the women who attended regularly were soon to become active in the woman's rights movement.

In 1840, several months after the Conversations began, a new magazine appeared, called *The Dial*. Margaret Fuller was selected as its chief editor. *The Dial* was published by an extraordinary group of New Englanders who came to be known as Transcendentalists. They were not in any way organized, nor did any two of them think alike; one of the few beliefs held in common was the importance of a highly developed individualism. It was an informal collection of writers, scholars, and ministers who enjoyed meeting together and carrying on intellectual discussions.

Many of these discussions centered on the new idealistic and romantic philosophies coming out of Germany by way of England and France. The word "transcendental" had been applied to these philosophies since they dealt with intuitive, nonmaterial qualities that were believed to go beyond, or transcend, the limitations of logic and the material senses. Ralph Waldo Emerson, Henry David Thoreau, Bronson Alcott, George and Sarah Ripley, Margaret Fuller, Sophia and Elizabeth Peabody were among the members of this group. Margaret Fuller, one of the few Americans at the time who could even read German, probably had a better firsthand knowledge of the foreign writers than any of the others. For this reason, and for her conversational brilliance, she was a highly valued member of the circle.

The New England Transcendentalists, despite their differences, shared certain general ideas. They were idealistic and open-minded, "hopeful and liberal spirits." They were convinced that through the application of intelligence and practical ideals, man could create a better society. They felt there was a stream of creative energy in the universe, an "over-soul," to which man was linked by his divinely inspired intuition. This intuitive perception, a form of divine guidance, was one of the basic themes of the Transcendentalists.

They also stressed freedom and tolerance, and rejected the old Puritan demands for strict, uncritical conformity to religious or social creeds. They were strong believers in the worth of individual men—and women. The Transcendentalists contributed greatly to the improvement of female status. They unconditionally accepted women as the intellectual equals of men, and would later support the woman suffrage movement. There were several notable women in the group besides Margaret Fuller. Among them were Elizabeth Peabody, whose bookstore became a center for Transcendentalist literature and activities; her sister, Sophia, who later married Nathaniel Hawthorne; and Sarah Ripley, who with her husband, George, founded Brook Farm, the Utopian colony linked to the Transcendentalist movement.

The Transcendentalists were a striking example of the new spirit of reform, individualism, and intellectual invigoration taking place in America. They were part of the changing atmosphere which would make it possible for the woman's rights movement to get under way.

They were also, like any new and original movement, very unpopular. They were called the "Boston zanies," who "transcended" common sense. Members had difficulty getting their ideas published. The conservative magazines refused to print their essays. It was for this reason that they decided to publish their own magazine, *The Dial.*

The Dial lasted four years. For the first two, Margaret Fuller poured her best energies into it, though she was conducting a full program of Conversations at the same time. Ralph Waldo Emerson, with whom she had established a close friendship, was coeditor, but he left most of the work to Margaret until she resigned and turned it over to him for the last two years. Even then she continued as associate editor and contributor. During her editorship she encouraged new writers and published some of the best and most original literary work done in New England.

Material for *The Dial* was sometimes slow coming in, since authors received no payment; Margaret Fuller and Emerson had to fill many pages with their own work. One of the articles written by her for *The Dial* was "The Great Lawsuit: Man *versus* Men, Woman *versus* Women," dealing with the feminist ideas which she kept introducing into her Conversations. She expanded the article into a book, *Woman in the Nineteenth Century*, the first full-length feminist work in the United States.

It became, along with Mary Wollstonecraft's *A Vindication of the Rights of Woman*, one of the gospels of the woman's rights movement. Margaret Fuller recognized its importance, feeling "as if I had put a good deal of my true life into it, and as if, should I go away now, the measure of my footprint would be left upon the earth."

The book deals largely with the question of women's true nature and the need for women to explore and develop their real selves, as men do, unhampered by misconceptions or prejudice. In her preface she says "it is the destiny of Man . . . to ascertain and fulfill the law of his being. . . . By Man I mean both man and woman; these are the two halves of one thought." Her "highest wish" is that "the conditions of life and freedom" should be recognized as the same for men and women. Every opportunity open to men must be equally open to women. They must be considered not as females with limited and closely defined spheres of activity, but as persons with the right to develop whatever talents and capacities they might possess.

This insistence on the right of women to be regarded as completely rounded, full-dimensional people, rather than as one-sided, limited domestic creatures, runs through most feminist writing. "It is a vulgar error," she writes, "that love, *a* love, to Woman is her whole existence." The law of human growth demands "a complete life" for women as well as for men.

To have this complete life, women must cultivate their minds and not confine themselves to the traditional areas of emotion and domestic routine. She is sharply critical of many aspects of marriage and of loveless unions of convenience; but she is not against the institution of marriage itself, and she is all for motherhood. "Earth knows no fairer, holier relation than that of a mother." But women should not be restricted to this single activity. Human beings have "infinite scope" and "must not be treated with an exclusive view to any one relation." Nor should it be taken for granted that all women must become mothers. Some women make very poor mothers; in any case, women must be given freedom to choose how they want to spend their lives. All occupations should be open to them: "Let them be sea-captains, if you will."

Women needed "a much greater range of occupation than they have, to rouse their latent powers." She wanted women to explore their own capacities, and vigorously opposed the prevailing idea that the purpose of educating girls was to make them better wives and mothers. "Too much is said of women being better educated, that they may become better companions and mothers *for men*." She was certainly for improved companionship between men and women, but the main purpose of female education should be to develop a whole person. A woman should be an entity in herself, with the independence and dignity of any human adult. "Now there is no woman, only an overgrown child."

Men are rigidly locked into their view of the relationship between the sexes. Not one man in a million, "no, not in the hundred million, can rise above the belief that Woman was made *for Man*." Nor can men, because "their minds are so encumbered by tradition," change their set notions of women. Even men whose wives are intelligent, rational, and highly competent can be heard saying, "You cannot reason with a woman," or will link "women and children" in a "contemptuous phrase."

Men never, "in any extreme of despair, wished to be women." It is considered an insult to tell a man that he is behaving like a woman. But women, on the other hand, are supposed to be flattered by being compared to men. If a man recognizes the rationality or intelligence of an individual woman, he will regard her as an exception, "above her sex." Margaret Fuller tells of a male friend who thought he was paying her a high compliment by saying that she "deserved to be a man." When she replied that it was as a woman that she deserved respect and that she preferred to be a woman, he smiled at her incredulously, as though she were just trying to make the best of her situation.

Worst of all, men have infected women with such views and have made women distrust their own minds and impulses. She states one of the chief problems that would confront the woman's rights movement throughout its history: "The difficulty is to get them to the point from which they shall naturally develop self-respect, and learn self-help."

She ends her book with a plea for women to develop "self-reliance and self-impulse." Women must take the responsibility for improving their own lot.

"I believe that, at present, women are the best helpers of one another.

"Let them think; let them act; till they know what they need.

"We only ask of men to remove arbitrary barriers."

Woman in the Nineteenth Century appeared in 1845 and made an immediate impact on both the supporters and the opponents of any change in the position of women. Margaret Fuller's outspoken remarks on the relations between the sexes and her critical examination of marriage created shock waves in a society where such things were never mentioned aloud. In conventional circles, Transcendentalists were considered not quite reputable. To be a transcendental feminist went too far indeed.

But others read the book with great interest, in all parts of the United States and in England as well. Women were delighted to find this open expression and reinforcement of what they had believed to be their own singular dissatisfactions. Those who became leaders of the woman's rights movement studied the book closely; its ideas, like those of Mary Wollstonecraft, were echoed throughout the later feminist writings and speeches.

Margaret Fuller herself, though enthusiastic about the organized movement which began three years after her book appeared, never had a chance to become actively involved in it. The rest of her short life was spent away from the center of feminist activities. She lived only six more years. Almost two of these were spent in New York City, as literary editor—and the first woman on the staff—of Horace Greeley's *New York Tribune*. Greeley had been impressed by her as "the best instructed woman in America." She was considered one of the ablest literary critics in the United States, original, acute, and highly objective. In an era when such qualities were not common in either journalism or criticism, she was ruthlessly honest and outspoken, not hesitating to attack the most established writers if she thought their work was second-rate. She felt a responsibility to educate her readers: with her articles on French and German literature, she introduced many foreign writers, particularly Goethe, to Americans.

Horace Greeley was an advocate of reform, and Margaret Fuller took part in the *Tribune*'s social campaigns. She made a detailed, first-hand inspection of prisons and hospitals, and wrote a series of spirited articles exposing the barbarous conditions in these institutions. One of her purposes was to stir the wealthy female readers of the *Tribune* into taking the kind of public action of which she believed women capable.

All of this increased not only her own reputation and prestige but, like the Conversations, that of women in general. It was a prime example of what they could achieve, given the opportunity.

The last four years of her life were spent in Europe, mainly in Italy, where she became involved in the short-lived Roman Republic under the great liberal patriot Mazzini. They were intensely crowded and dramatic years: she fell in love with a young Italian marchese, married him secretly, bore a child, ran a hospital during the three-month siege of Rome, and during all this managed to contribute articles to the *Tribune* and write a book on the history of the Roman Revolution.

In the spring of 1850 she decided to return to the United

States. With her husband and child, she sailed in May. On the last night of the voyage, a heavy gale blew up and the ship grounded on a sandbar about fifty yards off the coast of Fire Island, New York. The lifeboats were washed away before the passengers could use them, and the raging waves made it impossible for help to get through from the shore.

In an attempt to save themselves, each of the passengers lay down on a plank, which was then pushed through the water by a sailor swimming beside it. But Margaret, who had been deeply troubled by premonitions before the voyage, refused to be separated from her husband and child. She said, "I see nothing but death before me—I shall never reach the shore." At that moment, in a great upsurge of the waters, the mast fell. The ship's steward took the child from Margaret's arms and jumped into the sea. Their bodies were washed ashore a few minutes later. Margaret and her husband disappeared into the water; they were never found.

Margaret Fuller died just as the woman's rights movement was getting under way. Plans had been made to invite her, upon her return to the United States, to become an active leader in the developing cause. It is hard to say what part she would have played if she had lived, but she had already made a vital contribution. According to Elizabeth Stanton, she had influenced "the thought of American women" more than "any other woman previous to her time." And in her life, perhaps even more than in her work, Margaret Fuller had not only shown what a woman could accomplish, but had revealed that a woman was indeed the complete person for whom she had pleaded in her book, with the needs, complexities, and endowments common to all human beings.

9

The Road to Seneca Falls

I pined for that freedom of thought and action that was then denied to all womankind. I revolted in spirit against the customs of society and the laws of the State that crushed my aspirations and debarred me from the pursuit of almost every object worthy of an intelligent, rational mind. . . . I read, with intense interest, everything that indicated an awakening of public or private thought to the idea that woman did not occupy her rightful position in the organization of society; and, when I read the lectures of Ernestine Rose and the writings of Margaret Fuller, and found that other women entertained the same thoughts that had been seething in my own brain, and realized that I stood not alone, how my heart bounded with joy!

—Emily Collins, "Reminiscences," 1881

But it will be said that the husband provides for the wife, or in other words, he feeds, clothes, and shelters her! I wish I had the power to make every one before me fully realize the degradation contained in that idea. Yes! he *keeps* her, and so he does a favorite horse; by law they are both considered his property. . . . Again, I shall be told that the law presumes the husband to be kind, affectionate, and ready to provide for and protect his wife. But what right, I ask, has the law to presume at all on the subject? What right has the law to intrust the interest and happiness of one being into the hands of another?

—Ernestine Rose, 1851

When Elizabeth Cady Stanton and Lucretia Mott met in London for the first time, at the World Anti-Slavery Convention in 1840, Mrs. Mott was forty-seven, Mrs. Stanton twenty-five. They were both small: Mrs. Stanton was five feet three inches, with very small hands and feet. At this age her curly hair was black; it would turn white quite early, and her white curls would become almost a trademark. Also notable were her clear blue eyes, usually described as "twinkling" or "sparkling." Anna Howard Shaw, one of the later woman's rights leaders, said that when Mrs. Stanton woke up from the afternoon nap she generally took when attending conventions, "her blue eyes always had an expression of pleased and innocent surprise, as if she were gazing on the world for the first time."

She radiated a buoyant optimism, and had a vivacious sense of humor that she never hesitated to apply to herself. Her health was excellent, and her supply of energy seemed boundless. A tendency to plumpness would turn her later into a frankly stout woman, but she was very light on her feet and a graceful dancer.

Lucretia Mott, by contrast, was slender and always remained so. She had a high forehead, straight brown hair, and lambent dark eyes. Her extraordinary composure and intelligence were revealed in the strong, serene lines of her face, yet it was not at all severe; the overall impression was that of a warm and sympathetic woman. Her natural air of dignity was enhanced by the simple gray and white Quaker dress and cap she always wore. She was attentive and responsive as a listener, lucid and quietly persuasive as a speaker.

The two women spent hours in each other's company. Many of the delegates to the convention were staying at the same lodging house and took their meals together. After the women were denied their official seats and ignominiously relegated to the gallery, the subject of woman's rights and equality was energetically debated around the dinner table. Both segments of the American antislavery movement, pro- and anti-woman, had representatives at the lodging house as well as at the convention, so that the arguments often became personal and acrimonious. The Stantons were in an anomalous and embarrassing position. As a member of the anti-Garrison society, Henry Stanton was officially part of the anti-woman delegation, though he had urged the convention to accept the female delegates. Elizabeth Cady Stanton, however, stood wholeheartedly with the pro-female Garrisonians.

These discussions and the women who took part in them were a revelation to Mrs. Stanton. "These were the first women I had ever met who believed in the equality of the sexes and who did not believe in the popular orthodox religion. . . . It was intensely gratifying to hear all that, through years of doubt, I had dimly thought, so freely discussed by other women."

She and Mrs. Mott took long walks together, on which the older woman opened to the younger "a new world of thought," while Mrs. Mott recorded in her diary, "Elizabeth Stanton gaining daily in our affection." They talked about religion and Mrs. Mott, with her theological experience, was able to help Mrs. Stanton with her last remaining doubts and questions. "When I first heard from the lips of Lucretia Mott," wrote Mrs. Stanton many years later, "that I had the same right to think for myself that Luther, Calvin, and John Knox had, and the same right to be guided by my own convictions, and would no doubt live a . . . happier life than if guided by theirs, I felt at once a new-born sense of dignity and freedom; it was like suddenly coming into the rays of the noon-day sun, after wandering with a rushlight in the caves of the earth."

They also discussed the social theories and reform movements of the day. Most of all, they talked about women. The humiliating rejection of the female delegates by a convention called for the purpose of "liberation" had thrown the unliberated position of women into a new and sharper focus. Though not a delegate herself, Mrs. Stanton shared in the rebuff to someone of Mrs. Mott's caliber: here was an intelligent, experienced, capable adult who had as much to contribute to the convention as any man present, yet she had been dismissed as a childish incompetent. Or if her worth were recognized but she had been denied her place solely because of a presumed Biblical injunction, that was even worse. That would mean a deliberate subjugation of one sex by the other, regardless of what the difference between them might—or might not—be.

Elizabeth Stanton recalled how college doors had been closed to her and to all girls; she remembered her encounters, in her father's office, with the legal disabilities of being a woman. Discussing this unhappy and irritating state of affairs, Mrs. Mott and Mrs. Stanton agreed that women must not continue their meek passivity. Walking arm in arm through London, "we resolved to hold a convention as soon as we returned home, and form a society to advocate the rights of women."

The woman's rights movement may have been conceived at this moment in 1840, but its actual birth was delayed for eight years. During this time Mrs. Mott was preoccupied first by illness and family responsibilities, and later by her continued antislavery work and by her preaching in a period of increasing dissent within the Quaker church. But she did not for a moment forget the subject of woman's rights. She thought and spoke about it often. In 1845, at a meeting of Quaker women in Ohio, she made what many in her audience felt was "the first public Suffrage speech by a woman." Some of her listeners dated their involvement in the woman's rights movement from that moment.

Mrs. Stanton, in her turn, was caught up with the novelty

and excitement of her new life. Henry Stanton decided to study law with Judge Cady, and the young couple spent two pleasant years living in the Cady home, where the main domestic cares were handled by Elizabeth's capable mother. Even after her first baby was born, Elizabeth Stanton had plenty of time for "reading law, history, and political economy, with occasional interruptions to take part in some temperance or anti-slavery excitement." At the end of two years the Stantons moved to Boston, where Henry began to practice law.

Boston was the perfect city for Elizabeth Cady Stanton. It was the center of every kind of reform movement, of intense literary activity, of great religious ferment. She became involved in it all: she attended everything, met everyone, went everywhere. She met Emerson and Hawthorne; the Quaker poet John Greenleaf Whittier and William Lloyd Garrison became her close friends. She spent a few days at Brook Farm, the most famous of the Utopian colonies, where she met another group of writers, reformers, and ministers. She enjoyed it all tremendously; it was an atmosphere in which she flourished. "My mental powers," she wrote, "were kept at the highest tension."

Her life was rich, her marriage happy. The disadvantages of being a woman did not in any way press upon her. The indignation aroused in London subsided. She corresponded with Lucretia Mott, but there was no attempt to call a convention to protest against the lot of women. There was really, at the time, not much in the personal lot of Elizabeth Stanton to protest against.

But, like Lucretia Mott, Elizabeth Stanton did not altogether lose sight of the problems confronting women. Shortly before the Stantons settled in Boston, Judge Cady moved his family temporarily to Albany. Mrs. Stanton made several long visits there and, while in Albany, became involved with the effort to pass a Married Woman's Property Act.

In 1836 a bill to protect the property of married women was introduced in the New York Legislature. Under the existing law, any money or property acquired by a woman before or during marriage was turned over to her husband. Even her jewelry and the clothes she wore were not legally her own, and could be sold by her husband or claimed by his creditors in payment of his debts.

Ideally, this was all part of "protecting" women and keeping them safe from the coarse arena of business dealings. It was also a reflection of the low estimate of female abilities. A woman's incapacity to understand figures and her general inexperience presumably made it advisable for her more capable and worldly husband to handle her land and money. Even if this were true, and even if most husbands were not irresponsible or reckless or greedy, even in the best of all possible marriages a wife was still reduced to utter and often humiliating dependency upon her husband.

If the marriage were less than perfect, if it were intolerable, escape would be extremely difficult, no matter how much wealth she had originally possessed. She couldn't take a penny of it with her if she left her husband; she would even have to leave behind all the clothes not actually on her back. If she did manage to leave and was able to go to work and earn enough to support herself, he could collect her earnings, because these too legally belonged to him.

The life of an unmarried woman was not easy in those days: a spinster was scorned, pitied, ridiculed, ignored. Many hotels would not accept an unescorted woman as a guest; there were restaurants that would not serve her. When one of the woman's rights leaders, traveling with a group of speakers, tried to order her own breakfast, the waiter refused even to listen. Proper usage was for one of the male members of a party to order for the silent women. Yet there were some women, with inherited or earned money, who preferred the disadvantages of spinster-hood to marriage under the existing law.

In the spring of 1836, several months before the introduction of the Married Woman's Property Act, a highly untypical European woman came to the United States. She was Ernestine Potoski Rose, daughter of an orthodox rabbi in Piotrkow, Poland. As a child she had insisted on learning Hebrew and studying the Torah, an occupation reserved for males. She had protested against the daily prayer of orthodox men which included the line, "I thank thee, Lord, that Thou hast not created me a woman." Her final rebellion, at sixteen, was against a marriage arranged by her father. She sued for recovery of her dowry, inherited from her mother, and won the case in a Polish court.

Soon afterward, with some of her dowry money, she left home. This was a bold move for a young girl in 1827, particularly for one of her background. She went first to Germany and eventually to England. There she met the reformer Robert Owen and became his devoted disciple. Owen believed that people were entirely the products of their environment, and spent his life trying to provide ideal environments through labor reform, "rational" education, Utopian colonies, and a series of social organizations. Ernestine learned English and became a speaker for Owen's theories. She married another young Owenite, William Rose, and with her husband came to the United States.

She remained in the United States for almost forty years, devoting her time to reform movements, especially to anti-slavery, religious freedom, and, above all, woman's rights. Facing hostility as a woman, a foreigner, and an "infidel," she nevertheless gave many public lectures. She had "a rich musical voice," to which her foreign accent added an exotic note. A Boston newspaper described her as "an excellent lecturer, liberal, eloquent, witty, and decidedly handsome." She was called "Queen of the Platform."

When the Married Woman's Property Act was proposed, she drew up a petition in its support and went on a house-to-house campaign to collect signatures. She was turned down, as might have been expected, by men who said that women already had too many rights. But women also refused to sign; some said they had enough rights already, others were afraid they would be ridiculed or criticized if they signed. In five months she was able to get only five signatures.

The bill was reintroduced almost every year and on each occasion Ernestine Rose went after signatures for her petitions. At the same time, in the western part of New York, a wealthy young woman named Paulina Wright was trying to collect names on a similar petition for the Married Woman's Property Act. Around 1840 the two women began to work together, and not long after that Mrs. Stanton joined them. Besides circulating petitions, they made speeches and appeared before legislative committees. While Mrs. Stanton was staying with her family in Albany, she met many of the Assemblymen socially and used such occasions to promote the bill.

One of the arguments against giving married women control of their own property was that it would destroy the institution of marriage and bring about a weakening of morality. In spite of this awful prediction, the number of signatures collected on the petitions increased steeply from year to year until there were thousands. Other states began to consider comparable laws—Maine passed the first in 1845—and the chances for passing the New York State bill grew stronger.

What finally brought success was that wealthy fathers of the state, particularly among aristocratic Dutch landowners, realized that here at last was a way to prevent profligate sons-in-law from squandering the family fortunes inherited by daughters. Some husbands, too, saw an advantage in permitting wives to own property in their own names. By putting home and land in his wife's name, a man could prevent these from being seized to pay his debts in case of severe business losses. He might be bankrupt and his business ruined, but the family property would be saved. This appeal to self-interest won the support of men who might otherwise have ignored or opposed the bill.

The Married Woman's Property Act was passed in April 1848. It gave married women full control over their own real estate and personal property, and over any rents or profits from these. It had, however, a serious defect: it still left husbands with the legal right to whatever money their wives might earn by working. The act benefited middle- and upper-class women who were likely to inherit land and money, but it gave no protection to thousands of workingwomen. Husbands could still collect their wives'—and children's—wages, and spend the money any way they pleased.

Still, it was an advance: the law itself had recognized, however reluctantly, an old injustice, and had taken steps to correct it, however incompletely. It gave many women their first inkling that it was possible to change their status, and prepared them for the woman's rights movement, which would begin three months after the passage of the act. And it provided experience and encouragement for Elizabeth Stanton and the other ladies who had worked for the act. They would need the experience and all the encouragement they could get for the strenuous years ahead.

Elizabeth Stanton found Boston an eminently satisfying city in which to live, but her husband's health began to suffer in its severe winters and damp climate. In 1847 they moved with their three sons to Seneca Falls, where Judge Cady owned some property. He let Mrs. Stanton have the use of a house on the outskirts of the town. Here, two more sons and two daughters would be born.

Life in Seneca Falls was very different from the stimulating rush of activity in Boston. There was still a rush of activity, but now it was domestic rather than social or intellectual. In Boston the Stantons' house had been new and efficiently arranged; there were good servants to take care of the house and children, and easy access to the heart of the city. Now they lived in an old, inconvenient house, with a long road, uncomfortably dusty or muddy according to the season, between Mrs. Stanton and the center of the town, and there wasn't as much to do in the small town when she got there.

The difficulty of getting good household help was as common a complaint in the nineteenth century as it is today. It had been easier in Boston, but in Seneca Falls Mrs. Stanton found herself with a succession of incompetent or inexperienced servants. She had to take over or closely supervise much of the household work herself. With three children, and more on the way, there was a good deal of such work.

Running a household was no longer the challenging novelty it had seemed during the first years of her marriage. Now she felt oppressed by the hundreds of details which demanded her unremitting attention: cooking, cleaning, laundering, providing and caring for the elaborate nineteenth-century clothing, taking the children to assorted schools, dentists, doctors, shoemakers. In addition to all this, Seneca Falls proved to be a malarial region, and she spent months nursing the children through bouts of fever and chills.

Hardest of all to bear was the narrowing of her life into the small focus of domestic routine. In Boston she had attended "all the lectures, churches, theaters, concerts, and temperance, peace, and prison-reform conventions within my reach." Now she felt cut off from the world, reduced to endless household chores, "none sufficiently exhilarating or intellectual to bring into play my higher faculties. I suffered with mental hunger, which, like an empty stomach, is very depressing."

Henry Stanton had to be away on business a good deal. She

was left alone to cope with three hyperactive—or restively sick —boys, and with no adult companionship. She felt overwhelmed by the work and depressed by its monotony.

After more than a year of this, she was filled with a rising sense of indignation and resentment over the life mapped out for women. She remembered her childhood discoveries that girls could not get the same education or respect as boys; remembered the legal dilemmas of the women who had come to her father for help; remembered the indignities suffered by the female delegates to the World Anti-Slavery Convention. All of this "swept across my soul," intensified now by her immediate experience.

It was at this moment, when she had reached "this tempesttossed condition of mind," that she received the invitation to the reunion with Lucretia Mott at the home of Mrs. Jane Hunt in the nearby town of Waterloo. Over the tea table on the afternoon of July 13, 1848, she expressed the "long-accumulating discontent" which moved the ladies to action.

They had no specific program. All they could think of was to follow the reform pattern of the day, to call "a public meeting for protest and discussion." In doing this, they became part of a great wave of dissent and revolt moving across the western world.

1. Mary Wollstonecraft

2. Harriet Martineau

3. Margaret Fuller

4. *Frances Wright*

5. *Abby Kelley Foster*

6. Some form of woman suffrage had existed in America before the ladies of Seneca Falls took the daring step of asking for it; this Howard Pyle illustration shows women voting in New Jersey, 1790–1807

7. Ernestine Rose

8. Sarah and Angelina Grimké

9. Lucy Stone

10. Susan B. Anthony at the age of 48

11. Martha Wright

12. Antoinette Brown

13. *Elizabeth Cady Stanton and her son Henry in 1854*

14. *Mary Ann McClintock*

15. *James and Lucretia Mott, about 1842*

16. *Horace Greeley*

17. *Frederick
Douglass*

18. *William
Lloyd Garrison*

10

The Convention

This meeting, as I understand it, was called to discuss Woman's Rights. Well, I do not pretend to know exactly what woman's rights are; but I do know that I have groaned for forty years, yea, for fifty years, under a sense of woman's wrongs. I know that even when a girl, I groaned under the idea that I could not receive as much instruction as my brothers could. I wanted to be what I felt I was capable of becoming, but opportunity was denied me. . . . I rejoice that so many women are here; it denotes that they are waking up to some sense of their situation.

—Mehitable Haskell, 1851

A woman is nobody. A wife is everything. A pretty girl is equal to ten thousand men, and a mother is, next to God, all powerful. . . . The ladies of Philadelphia, therefore . . . are resolved to maintain their rights as Wives, Belles, Virgins, and Mothers, and not as Women.

—Philadelphia *Public Ledger and Daily Transcript,* 1848

The year 1848 was marked by revolutions and reform, by popular stirrings and new beginnings. It started with riots and insurrection in Sicily, the discovery of gold in California, and the overthrow of kings in France and Bavaria. It ended with the abdication of the Austrian Emperor, the election of Louis Napoleon as President of France, and the westward movement of vast numbers of people as Americans rushed to California in search of gold, and Europeans swarmed to America in search of food and freedom.

Toward the end of the eighteenth century there had been powerful impulses against political tyranny and toward personal freedom, leading to the American and French revolutions. With the rise of Napoleon, a reaction had set in; the spirit of protest and rebellion subsided for almost a generation. It reappeared in the 1830s when antislavery and temperance efforts got under way, when social and political theorists drew up programs for new and better ways to live. Most of the reformers were romantic idealists, believing it possible to create a perfect society, with justice and equality for all. The worker and farmer, the average, ordinary citizen long neglected by rulers and overlooked by history, were now being considered. The Age of Reform also saw the rise of the common man.

It came to a head in 1848. In France, after the fall of Louis Philippe, slavery was abolished in the French colonies, the vote was extended to wide sections of the population, and freedom of assembly and of the press was established. Inspired by the events in Paris, revolutions and insurrections erupted in Vienna, Berlin, Prague, Budapest, Cracow, Milan, and Venice. The ironhanded Chancellor of the Austro-Hungarian Empire, Prince von Metternich, who for forty years had been the most powerful man in Europe, was forced to resign his office and flee to England for safety.

In England itself, 10,000 Chartists, members of the working-class movement agitating for the right to vote and the secret ballot among other goals, tried to hold a demonstration in London. They were unsuccessful, but later in the century virtually all their demands were granted. In London too, early that same year, the *Communist Manifesto* of Marx and Engels was published, offering a blueprint for revolution.

The United States had long since accomplished its revolution, but the spirit of reform and idealism was as potent on this side of the Atlantic as in Europe. The campaign against slavery, the temperance movement, the burgeoning Utopian colonies were all at their height. A new political party was formed in 1848, the Free Soil Party, whose slogan of "Free soil, free speech, free labor, and free men" reflected the spirit of the times.

The reform of prisons and insane asylums can be dated from this year, thanks to the efforts of Dorothea Dix. After ten years of working entirely alone, investigating and publicizing the terrible conditions in these institutions, she finally persuaded Congress, in 1848, to introduce the first bill of its kind, providing Federal support for mental hospitals. The bill later passed, but was vetoed by the President. Nevertheless, it was the forerunner and inspiration for much of the reform legislation that followed.

In New York the Married Woman's Property Act was passed in 1848, bringing women into the great reform tide of the year. It was also the year in which anesthesia was first used in childbirth despite opposition, mostly from clergymen who accused doctors as well as women of disregarding God's decree that "in sorrow shalt thou bring forth children." But perhaps the greatest manifestation of the "year of revolutions," as far as women were concerned, was the Seneca Falls convention on July 19th and 20th.

It had taken Elizabeth Cady Stanton and Lucretia Mott eight years before they carried out their plan for a woman's convention; but, having started, they proceeded rapidly. Sitting around the tea table in Waterloo, Mrs. Stanton, Mrs. Mott, and the other ladies drew up an announcement, or call, for a "Woman's Rights Convention," to meet the following week in the Wesleyan Chapel at Seneca Falls. It would last two days: the first day would be for women only, the second for "the public generally." There would be speakers, said the call, but only Lucretia Mott was mentioned by name. It was hoped that her reputation would attract an audience.

The announcement was sent off to the *Seneca County Courier*. The next morning they met at the home of another of the five ladies, Mary Ann McClintock. Seated at a mahogany table (now in the Smithsonian Institution), they drew up an agenda for the convention. The first item would have to be a Declaration of Sentiments and Resolutions. They ran into difficulties immediately: they had plenty of ideas, but they wanted to organize these into one clear and dramatic statement which would establish the guidelines for future action. It wasn't until Mrs. Stanton, looking for possible models, turned to the Declaration of Independence that they found their solution. They would use the same form for their own Declaration.

The opening paragraphs are a symbolic adaptation of the original. Like Mary Wollstonecraft, who insisted that the Rights of Man must include the Rights of Woman, the ladies wanted to emphasize the fact that the rights demanded in the Declaration of Independence must be extended to women as well as to men. To one of the key sentences in the Declaration, they added the words "and women," so that it begins: "We hold these truths to be self-evident: that all men and women are created equal; that they are endowed by their Creator with certain inalienable rights. . . ." Many of these rights, for which a war had been fought, had not been extended to women after independence. This was the glaring exclusion that the ladies wanted to bring before the public conscience.

Using the same phraseology as the original Declaration, the

ladies' statement claimed that "The history of mankind is a history of repeated injuries and usurpations on the part of man toward woman, having in direct object the establishment of an absolute tyranny over her." This was followed by a list of injuries and usurpations: man has denied woman the inalienable right to vote; compelled her to submit to laws she had no voice in making; made her, if married, civilly dead in the eyes of the law; taken from her all rights in property, even to the wages she earns. He has compelled her to promise obedience to her husband, who then becomes, to all intents and purposes, her master, with legal power to deprive her of her liberty and to administer chastisement; and has framed divorce and separation laws entirely to the advantage of the man.

He has monopolized nearly all profitable employments; given woman scanty payments for those she is permitted to follow; and denied her facilities for obtaining a thorough education, since colleges are closed against her. He allows her only a subordinate position in church as well as state, excluding her from the ministry and, in most cases, from public participation in church affairs. He has established a different code of morals for men and women, so that delinquencies which would exclude women from society are tolerated in men as of little account. He has usurped the prerogative of God, claiming the right to assign for woman a sphere of action.

The final paragraphs charged that man has endeavored "to destroy her confidence in her own powers, to lessen her self-respect, and to make her willing to lead a dependent and abject life." Because of the disfranchisement and the social and religious degradation of half the country's population, and because women "feel themselves aggrieved, oppressed, and fraudulently deprived of their most sacred rights, we insist that they have immediate admission to all the rights and privileges which belong to them as citizens of the United States."

They concluded this portion of the Declaration by saying

they anticipated "misconception, misrepresentation, and ridicule," but would nevertheless work for their goals through tracts, petitions to legislatures, appeals to the pulpit and press, and more conventions.

This was followed by a list of resolutions, drawn up principally by Elizabeth Stanton, who took the draft of the document home to Seneca Falls and worked on it almost up to the last minute. The resolutions denounced laws which discriminated against women, and demanded that women be recognized as the equals of men, with the same capabilities and responsibilities. They asked for the abolition of a double standard of morality, and that women be given the same right as men to speak and take part in all public and religious affairs.

The need to rouse women to an awareness of their true condition was emphasized: "The women of this country ought to be enlightened in regard to the laws under which they live, that they may no longer publish their degradation by declaring themselves satisfied with their present position, nor their ignorance, by asserting that they have all the rights they want." Both Mrs. Stanton and Mrs. Mott realized that their efforts to improve the lot of women would have two distinct aspects: the external one of removing legal, educational, and vocational barriers to equality; and the more difficult and subtle problem of breaking through the reluctance of women to face the reality of their inferior status.

In drawing up the resolutions, Elizabeth Stanton had consulted her husband, whose legal knowledge helped in listing the barriers confronting women. He had been very sympathetic to the whole undertaking, but when he came to the ninth resolution, he balked. It read: "It is the duty of the women of this country to secure to themselves their sacred right to the elective franchise."

This was going altogether too far, he said. Mrs. Stanton insisted that the vote was essential; with it, women would find it infinitely easier to gain their other demands. Henry Stanton angrily rejected this argument. He said the very mention of such a preposterous idea would make their whole project ridiculous. If she persisted with this farfetched notion, he wanted nothing to do with the convention and would leave town rather than attend it. Mrs. Stanton did persist, and he left.

Lucretia Mott, with her husband and sister, Martha Wright, arrived shortly before the convention was to open. She went over the resolutions prepared by Mrs. Stanton, approving them all until she was jolted to a stop by the ninth, calling for woman suffrage. Her reaction was almost the same as Henry's. "Oh, Lizzie," she cried, "thou will make us ridiculous! We must go slowly." But again Mrs. Stanton refused to withdraw the resolution.

Early on the morning of July 19, 1848, carriages and wagons began to converge upon Seneca Falls. A young woman, Charlotte Woodward, came with a group of her friends: "At first we travelled quite alone . . . but before we had gone many miles we came on other waggon-loads of women, bound in the same direction. As we reached different cross-roads we saw waggons coming from every part of the county, and long before we reached Seneca Falls we were a procession."

Some had come out of curiosity, but many had been impelled by the same need as Charlotte Woodward. She was one of the large number of women employed by the glove industry of Seneca Falls. Since it was considered unfitting for women to work outside their homes, they did piecework in the seclusion of their own bedrooms. The money they earned was collected —and kept—by their husbands or fathers. "Most women," she wrote, "accepted this condition of society as normal and God-ordained and therefore changeless. But I do not believe that there was any community anywhere in which the souls of some women were not beating their wings in rebellion. . . . Every fibre of my being rebelled, although silently, all the hours that I sat and sewed gloves for a miserable pittance which, after it was earned, could never be mine. I wanted to work, but I wanted to choose my task and I wanted to collect my wages."

When she and her friends reached the Wesleyan Chapel, they formed part of a crowd of three hundred, including about forty men. Men were not supposed to attend the first day's sessions, but since they appeared to be sincerely interested, they were admitted.

At first, however, it looked as though no one would be admitted. The chapel, which was supposed to be opened for the convention, was locked. But Mrs. Stanton's nephew climbed through a window and opened the door from the inside. The waiting crowd entered and took their seats, and the first concerted action to improve the condition of women began.

Although this was to be a convention of and for women, it was unthinkable for a woman to serve as chairman. The most exclusively female organizations had men to chair their meetings. When the Philadelphia Female Anti-Slavery Society held its first meeting some years earlier, a black man had been asked to conduct it. Lucretia Mott commented that "Negroes, idiots and women were in legal documents classed together; so that we were very glad to get one of our own class to come and aid in forming that Society."

In this case, James Mott, Lucretia Mott's husband, served as chairman. If the convention had to be conducted by a man, Mr. Mott was an excellent choice. Impressively handsome and dignified, he gave the proceedings an air of respectability and authority that no woman could have commanded in that era. His wholehearted belief in the equality of women and in the rightness of what the ladies of Seneca Falls were doing added to the sincerity of his manner. The only other participating husband of the five was Thomas McClintock. His wife, Mary Ann McClintock, was appointed secretary.

The first speech, explaining the purpose of the convention, was made by Mrs. Mott, the only one of the organizers who had any experience in public speaking. She was invaluable to the fearful Seneca Falls ladies. She bolstered their failing courage, kept the sessions from wandering off the main issues, and gave the whole proceeding just the right emotional tone. She was followed by Elizabeth Stanton.

During the preceding week, Mrs. Stanton had been filled with increasing terror. It was a combination of stage fright at the prospect of making her first public speech, and consternation at having initiated this unprecedented action by women. A housewife in any period might have quailed at such a formidable undertaking; for a woman in 1848 it was outrageously rash and untraditional, which made it practically earth-shaking.

Nevertheless, she stood up before the audience and, with her confidence growing every minute, read the Declaration of Sentiments. Afterward she delivered a remarkably polished speech, the first of hundreds which were to impress her future listeners. When she had helped write the Declaration and prepared the Resolutions, she had found that she had both competence and pleasure in writing; now she discovered an equal satisfaction in speaking.

On the second day, the convention voted on the Declaration and the Resolutions. Everything was unanimously accepted until the suffrage resolution was proposed. This was too extreme not only for many in the audience but even for the other ladies who, with Mrs. Stanton, had organized the convention. It was argued that so excessive a demand would arouse such antagonism and derision that the movement would be killed before it even got under way.

Mrs. Stanton made an impassioned speech, explaining that through the power of the vote women would be able to win their goals much more quickly. She was warmly supported by Frederick Douglass. Just ten years earlier Douglass, then twenty-one, had escaped from slavery in Baltimore. He made his way first to Massachusetts, where he met William Lloyd Garrison and became an active abolitionist, then moved on to England to avoid being captured and restored to his owner. In 1847, with money raised by British abolitionist sympathizers, he returned to the United States, bought his freedom, and settled in Rochester, New York, where he established the *North Star*, the first newspaper published by a black man in this country.

Elizabeth Stanton had met him when she lived in Boston, and he had long been a friend and frequent visitor of the Motts. Douglass, a firm believer in woman's rights as part of the freedom of all people, had come to lend his assistance to the convention. A highly intelligent and experienced speaker, he made a stirring speech claiming that suffrage was an indispensable basis for winning freedom and equality.

After further debate, some of it acrimonious, a vote was taken. The resolution passed by a small margin. At the end of the final session, one hundred men and women signed the Declaration of Sentiments and Resolutions. Among the signers was young Charlotte Woodward. Of all the women in Seneca Falls that day, she would be the only one alive to cast her first vote seventy-two years later, when the Federal woman suffrage amendment finally granted the vote to the female citizens of the United States.

Elizabeth Stanton called the convention a "grand success." There was so much to talk about that two days weren't nearly enough; the women decided to continue the sessions two weeks later in Rochester. The success at Seneca Falls gave them the courage to try for a more ambitious gathering in a large city, in the hope that it would reach a wider audience.

But even this first small venture in Seneca Falls had some

surprisingly large and tangible results. It gave shape to a dissatisfaction that some women hadn't been able to take hold of or express in concrete terms. The Declaration of Sentiments clearly outlined their dependent legal and economic status, and pointed up their educational and vocational handicaps. Women realized that they were not alone in their frustrations; this lessened the awful self-doubts of many, and gave them courage to look closely at their lives. The convention gave them hope: it was a form of action, however vague. It was at least a beginning; something might possibly come of it.

Even women who were satisfied with their lives, who had no sense of being "oppressed," responded to the idea of a woman's movement. Many of these women, generally middle- or upper-class, had taken up one of the reform causes, sometimes out of conviction, sometimes for lack of anything better to do. Now they had a cause much closer to their own lives than abolition or prison reform. For many it promised to be a rallying point, a center of interest outside the humdrum routine of their daily existence.

By itself, the Seneca Falls convention could not reach very far, despite the excellent attendance. Three hundred people meeting in an upper New York State town was not exactly a national event. But the venomous reaction of the press took care of that. Most newspaper editors were so infuriated by the convention that they gave it the kind of publicity the ladies could never have managed, or even thought of arranging, for themselves.

A typical editorial called the convention "the most shocking and unnatural incident ever recorded in the history of womanity." Editors were outraged or grieved by the "unwomanly behavior" of those who attended the meeting, "no doubt at the expense of their more appropriate duties." Equal rights would "demoralize and degrade" women, and "prove a monstrous injury to all mankind."

Those editors who weren't convinced that the convention

was the first step toward the breakdown of morality and the destruction of the family simply regarded it as a huge joke. They laughed at the "Amazons" who set forth the preposterous notion that "all men and *women* are created equal." They called the convention a petticoat rebellion, arranged by love-starved spinsters.

Not since the Grimkés had dared appear on a public platform to address listeners of both sexes had women received so much notice in the press. "There is no danger of the Woman Question dying for want of notice," wrote Mrs. Stanton in a letter. "Every paper you take up has something to say about it."

In New York City the two great newspapers lined up on either side of the question. James Gordon Bennett's jeeringly hostile *Herald*, in an attempt to discredit the women, printed the entire Declaration of Sentiments, which was "just what I wanted," wrote Mrs. Stanton. "Imagine the publicity given to our ideas by thus appearing in a widely circulated sheet like the *Herald*. It will start women thinking, and men too; and when men and women think about a new question, the first step in progress is taken."

Horace Greeley's *Tribune*, on the other hand, was one of the very few papers that tried to be objective in their reporting, though Greeley himself had reservations about the wisdom of demanding equal political rights for women: "The great majority desire no such thing . . . they prefer to devote their time to the discharge of home duties." But, he went on to say, "however unwise and mistaken the demand, it is but the assertion of a natural right and as such must be conceded." From then on, Greeley not only published fair and accurate reports of what women were doing, but opened his columns to Mrs. Stanton's letters and articles, giving her the opportunity to spread information about the movement.

But Greeley was an exception; most of the publicity was

unfavorable. Many signers of the Declaration of Sentiments and Resolutions were so upset by this reaction that they withdrew their names. Some even turned against those who had called the convention. "Our friends gave us the cold shoulder," said Mrs. Stanton, "and felt themselves disgraced by the whole proceeding." There were women who were deterred from attending future conventions because they could not face "the trial of seeing one's name in the papers," or stand the ridicule, especially from their husbands. "I am with you thoroughly, but I am a born coward," said the wife of Senator William Seward. "There is nothing I dread more than Mr. Seward's ridicule. I would rather walk up to the cannon's mouth than encounter it."

It was so difficult for anyone to take an unpopular or unconventional step that even Elizabeth Cady Stanton was affected by the outcry against the Seneca Falls convention. It was "with fear and trembling" that she agreed to take part in the next meeting, two weeks later, in the Unitarian Church in Rochester.

The arrangements for this second event were handled by another group of women, who insisted that the sessions be conducted not by a man, as in Seneca Falls, but by a woman, the Quaker Abigail Bush. This was opposed by Elizabeth Stanton, Lucretia Mott, and Mary Ann McClintock. They called it "a most hazardous experiment," and almost walked out of the convention before it started. As it was, when Mrs. Bush took the chair, Mrs. Stanton and Mrs. Mott left the platform and sat in the audience. By the end of the first session, however, they were completely won over by the chairwoman's competence. After that, the women ran their conventions with no assistance from men—a striking innovation at that time.

The second convention was an expanded version of the first. The suffrage resolution, again supported by Frederick Douglass, was adopted this time by a wider margin. Even so, suffrage, which would later become the chief goal of the woman's rights movement, was at this point only a lesser issue, reluctantly accepted by some women and rejected completely by others.

Among the issues raised was one which would forever haunt the woman's rights movement. Whenever the subject of female rights or status came up, someone was sure to ask whether or not women were really equal to or the same as men. Were they mentally inferior and therefore incapable of voting intelligently? Or different in the sense that, even granting that women might have intelligence, there were some subjects—like politics and mathematics—that the female brain wasn't equipped to cope with? And if women were in any sense inferior, or at least weaker, didn't that mean that they needed the care and protection of men? And didn't that protection require that men should be the legal guardians of tender, helpless women? And shouldn't these childlike women be spared the trouble of handling their own money or property?

Lucretia Mott answered these questions "in a speech of great sarcasm and eloquence." She calmly admitted that centuries of repression and lack of education might have caused women to appear mentally inferior, but this was no basis for assuming that the condition was innate and couldn't be corrected. Nor should the results of injustice be used as an excuse to continue that injustice. But suppose, for the sake of the argument, that women weren't on the whole as bright as men. That would still be no reason for denying them their basic human rights. "Does one man have fewer rights than another because his intellect is inferior? If not, why should a woman?"

After this second convention, no formal meetings took place for another year and a half. But as the news of Seneca Falls spread, women were aroused and began to prepare for local conventions in several states. The first of four conventions in Ohio was held in Salem, in April 1850. In October of that year the first National Woman's Rights Convention was held in Worcester, Massachusetts. From then on, until the Civil War changed the nature of women's concerns, national conventions were held every year except 1857, with frequent regional meetings throughout New York, Massachusetts, Pennsylvania, Ohio, and Indiana.

Lucretia Mott and Elizabeth Stanton, and to a lesser extent Martha Wright and Mary Ann McClintock, continued their active leadership, but were soon joined by other women who would become prominent in the movement. Even those who were slow to join were affected by these early conventions. They read the newspaper reports, most of which were violently opposed to such unsuitable or downright comic female antics, listened to their preachers sternly denounce such unseemly and impious female behavior, and became increasingly aware that something of great importance to themselves was taking place.

Some future leaders, while not yet involved in the infant woman's rights movement, were preparing themselves for it through work in other causes. They were busy promoting anti-slavery or temperance. But sooner or later, like the Grimké sisters, they would find themselves hampered in their work by the simple fact of being female. They would realize that, before all else, they must first achieve their rights as women.

11

Susan B. Anthony

I do not believe woman's utter dependence on man wins for her his respect; it may cause him to love and pet her as a child, but never to regard and treat her as a peer.

—Susan B. Anthony, 1897

While I do not pray for anybody . . . to commit outrages, still, I do pray . . . for some terrific shock to startle the women of this nation into a self-respect which will compel them to see the abject degradation of their present position; which will force them to break their yoke of bondage, and give them faith in themselves. . . . The fact is, women are in chains, and their servitude is all the more debasing because they do not realize it. O, to compel them to see and feel, and to give them the courage and conscience to speak and act for their own freedom, though they face the scorn and contempt of all the world for doing it!

—Susan B. Anthony, 1870

*L*iving in and around Rochester was a large group of liberal Hicksite Quakers. They were supporters of reform, especially of abolition, temperance, and liberalized religion. When the second woman's rights convention was held in Rochester, they attended enthusiastically. Among those who listened closely to the speakers and who signed the Declaration of Sentiments were three members of the Anthony family: Daniel, his wife, Lucy, and their daughter Mary. A cousin, Sarah Anthony Burtis, was secretary of the convention.

Another daughter, Susan, was away from home, teaching at the Canajoharie Academy. She had read the newspaper accounts of the Seneca Falls convention and had been amused by the "novelty and presumption" of the Declaration of Sentiments. When she came home on vacation and found her family talking of nothing else except the Rochester convention, she was again amused; she teased her father and sister for their preoccupation with it. Their descriptions of Elizabeth Stanton and Lucretia Mott, how attractive they had looked and how impressively they had spoken, awakened her interest, but it was more in terms of how she would like to meet these women personally, rather than in taking any active part in the movement they were fostering.

For Susan Brownell Anthony, being a girl had not created any great problems, as it had for Elizabeth Cady Stanton. Her father was a sixth-generation Quaker, but even for that sect, with its tradition of equality for women, he was unusually progressive. To him, girls were as valuable as boys. He recognized and respected his daughters' intelligence, and gave them a good education. In a letter to a friend, he said, "What an absurd notion that women have not intellectual and moral faculties sufficient for anything but domestic concerns." He taught his daughters to be self-reliant and encouraged them to become self-supporting. At a time when he was very well off, he allowed Susan and her older sister to spend their summers teaching, to the disapproval of his neighbors who believed that girls should work only if their families were in serious need of their earnings.

Susan's mother was not a Quaker. She was a very quiet woman, overshadowed by the more expansive personality of her husband, and overwhelmed by the endless labor of caring for a large household and managing the family farm. Daniel Anthony, whose ambitions rose beyond farming, opened a store at first, and then succeeded in what was a novel enterprise for that region: he built and ran a cotton mill.

Mrs. Anthony was not only quiet but excessively inhibited. Though she gave birth to eight children, she could never bring herself to tell anyone that she was pregnant, and took pains to conceal the fact. She couldn't discuss it even with her own mother, who would have to wait until her experienced eyes discovered it for herself; then she would quietly make clothes for the new infant and put them in a drawer where Lucy would find them. To Susan Anthony, the image of her mother, silent, worried, worn out from work and childbearing, became the symbol of marriage, even with the best of husbands. It made her less eager to enter that condition herself, and more eager to improve it for others.

Susan Anthony was born in Adams, in western Massachusetts, on February 15, 1820. The six surviving Anthony children were brought up as Quakers, though their mother never formally became one. As a member of the only major religious group that allowed women equal participation in church affairs, Susan grew up hearing women speak freely. Her grandmother and aunt were leading "High Seat" Quakers; her Aunt Hannah was a famous preacher. Like Lucretia Mott, Susan developed self-respect and a sense of dignity not generally encouraged in other churches.

The Quakers were also unusual in their belief that girls

could absorb advanced education. Susan was sent to a boarding school in Philadelphia. It was run very strictly, along rigid Quaker lines, with a heavy emphasis on moral values that often produced bouts of self-guilt in the over-serious young girl. But it provided more science than girls generally were exposed to, and on the whole she had a much better education than most young women of that period.

In 1838, when Susan was eighteen, the great business depression which had begun the year before hit Daniel Anthony's cotton mill. Everything was lost: the mill, their home, even, as Susan discovered, articles which her mother had received from her own parents. The very clothes worn by her mother, sisters, and herself were considered the property of her father and could be sold to pay off his debts.

Susan went to work teaching, and by the time the family property was put up for auction, she had saved a little money with which to buy back some of the household goods. A large part of the rest was bought by Mrs. Anthony's brother, Joshua Read. The family moved to an abandoned tavern, and Daniel tried a variety of enterprises, none of them very profitable, while Susan and her older sister continued to teach.

In 1845, Daniel Anthony, having lost still another mill, decided to return to farming. He had no money of his own left, but Lucy Anthony's parents had died, leaving her a share of their estate. Under current law, if it had been turned over to her, it would automatically have passed to her husband and would have been claimed by his creditors to pay off his business debts. To prevent this, the money had been left in her brother Joshua's care. When Daniel found a farm he wanted, about three miles west of Rochester, Joshua bought it for him, but kept the title in his own name. In 1848, when the Married Woman's Property Act was passed in New York, permitting a married woman to hold on to her own real estate, he transferred the farm to Lucy.

This transaction, together with the earlier discovery that women could not claim possession even of their own clothing, provided Susan Anthony with a first-hand experience of the legal disabilities of women. She was less troubled, at this stage, by the fact that women could not vote. To a Quaker, voting seemed relatively unimportant. The Quakers were pacifists and many of them, including her father, refused to cast their ballots for a government that engaged in war. A vote which would probably not be used wasn't worth getting excited about.

Not long after the move to Rochester, Daniel Anthony once more found farming too restricted for his ambitions, and he became an agent for the recently created New York Life Insurance Company. Of all his business ventures, this proved the most enduringly successful; from then on he divided his energies between insurance and farming. This double occupation, together with his affable, outgoing temperament and his great interest in public affairs, brought him in contact with a wide range of people.

Rochester, flourishing as a result of its location on the Erie Canal, was a center of reform, and many of the abolitionist, temperance, and progressive religious leaders became personal friends of the Anthonys. As Daniel Anthony grew older, he became increasingly liberal and more at odds with the strict Quaker discipline. He began to attend the much freer Unitarian Church; two of its leading ministers, William Henry Channing and Samuel J. May, became his close friends. Another friend was Frederick Douglass, who came to Rochester about two years after the Anthonys arrived, to publish his newspaper, the *North Star*. All of these reformers became close friends of Susan Anthony as well.

Several months after the move to Rochester, Susan was offered a position as head of the female department of the Canajoharie Academy. For the next few years she lived in Canajoharie, New York, away from her family and from any Quaker influence. She dropped both the severe dress and the "plain language" of the Quakers, went in for elaborate, brightly colored clothes, attended parties and dances, and went out with young men.

Susan B. Anthony was often portrayed, especially during the height of opposition to the woman's rights movement, as an angular, sharp-tempered, humorless, and unattractive spinster who devoted her life to the woman's movement because she couldn't find a husband. This was a distorted picture on all counts. She had many acceptable offers of marriage, which she turned down by her own choice; everyone who came to know her remarked on the sweetness and warmth of her personality; and she had a strong and often sprightly sense of humor.

She was not softly or conventionally pretty, but she was attractive, even handsome. She was tall and slender, with a fine, erect carriage, and almost classically regular features framed by smooth, glossy brown hair. She had one physical defect, hardly noticeable, but of which she herself was painfully conscious: one eye was slightly off-center. When she was about twenty, she had a corrective operation, but the inept surgeon left it slightly turned in the other direction. Most people were scarcely aware of it, but she remained unhappy about it and always tried to present her profile, especially in portraits.

One of her outstanding qualities, respected even by her enemies, was her uncompromising honesty. As a young woman, she tended to be intolerant and severe in her moral judgments, but these were increasingly tempered by her sense of humor and her deeply sympathetic view of people.

The big reform movement in Canajoharie was temperance, and it was only natural for Susan to join the local Daughters of Temperance. She became an officer of the organization, and made her first public speech, very successfully, at one of their fund-raising affairs. She kept in touch with other reform movements through her frequent visits to a friend, Lydia Mott, whom she had met while a student at boarding school. Lydia and her sister Abigail, cousins of James Mott, lived in Albany; their home was a gathering place for the reformers who came to that city to present petitions or speeches to the Legislature.

After a few years in Canajoharie, Susan Anthony became dissatisfied with teaching. It paid too little, for one thing: a man doing the same work received four times her salary. The prevailing weekly rate was $2.50 for women, $10 for men. There were also limits to female ambition. As headmistress, she had gone as far as a woman could expect to go, in about the only profession open to an educated woman. She was an excellent teacher and a highly competent administrator, but the work itself had lost its original interest and challenge. A "great weariness" came over her.

Part of this weariness was caused by depression over the death of her married cousin, Margaret Caldwell. Susan had stayed in Margaret's home during the years in Canajoharie, and had gained an intimate view of the difficulties inherent in marriage. There were enough drawbacks, she wrote to her mother, to make a woman content to remain single. Marriage for its own sake, without any compelling emotion—the kind of practical arrangement that most young women would have settled for by their late twenties—had no special appeal for Susan Anthony.

By 1849 she found herself emotionally and intellectually underemployed, a condition not uncommon, though seldom acknowledged, among intelligent and educated young women of her day. When gold was discovered in California, touching off the great gold rush of 1849, she wrote, "Oh, if I were but a man so that I could go!"

If she had been a man, she might not necessarily have gone to California, but she would certainly have tried another kind of work. In the middle of the nineteenth century, with the opening of the West and with the explosive growth of railroads, steamships, factories, the telegraph, new industries and commerce of every kind, there were endless and endlessly varied possibilities open to young men. As a young woman, however competent and ambitious, all Susan Anthony could think of was to quit her job and return home.

Life at home was more interesting than one might expect. Daniel Anthony's insurance work took him away from home a good deal, and he turned the farm over to Susan. For more than two years she directed all the planting, harvesting, and marketing, and found herself enjoying this life of action after the static routine of the classroom.

There was also the bustle of reform all about her. Her father had become a dedicated abolitionist, and his house was a popular gathering place for those with antislavery and generally liberal views. On Sundays, whenever he was at home, as many as twenty guests would assemble around the dinner table. Visiting abolitionist leaders, like William Lloyd Garrison and Wendell Phillips, would stop by when their travels brought them to Rochester. Along with their reports on major reform activities, there was a good deal of shoptalk about the inner workings of the movements and the people involved in them. Susan heard all about the split in the antislavery groups over the "woman question," and about the new stirrings among the women themselves. She became increasingly interested in what they were doing, and in individual leaders like Lucretia Mott and Elizabeth Cady Stanton.

It was not surprising that Susan Anthony, steeped in this atmosphere, decided to devote herself to one of the social causes of the day. Her father encouraged her to go ahead without any concern about money. His business was prospering, and in supporting his daughter he would be supporting the work that was closest to his own heart.

The Ladies of Seneca Falls

There were three causes to choose from: woman's rights, antislavery, and temperance. Woman's rights had barely gotten started, and as yet consisted only of an occasional convention. In October 1850, when the first National Woman's Rights Convention was held in Worcester, Massachusetts, it was reported in the newspapers with the usual derision and hostility. The only New York paper that treated the subject fairly was again Horace Greeley's *Tribune*, with its sympathetic interest in reform. The Anthonys subscribed to it, and Susan read about the Worcester convention with great interest, but still took no positive action in the direction of woman's rights.

The antislavery movement was much more established, though getting more controversial as the Civil War approached. The abolitionists were regarded by many people, even in the North, as radical troublemakers. Led by Garrison, the abolitionists demanded "immediate and unconditional emancipation," but to most people the important issue at this time was not so much the existing slavery in the South, but whether it should or should not be extended into the newly emerging western territories. The Quakers were divided on the slavery question; the Rochester Meeting disapproved of the abolitionists, and it was mainly for this reason that the Anthonys had left the Quakers for the Unitarian Church.

For a woman, antislavery activity was frowned upon. One of the first working female abolitionists Susan Anthony met was the Quaker Abby Kelley Foster, who came to Rochester to speak at antislavery meetings. Abby Kelley had been a young schoolteacher in Massachusetts when Theodore Weld had urged her to become a full-time speaker for the American Anti-Slavery Society. At first she had traveled with the Grimké sisters in 1837, then had continued their work as an abolitionist speaker. She had been jeered at, reviled, pelted with eggs. She was the special target of ministers: people had been expelled from their churches for listening to her talk on Sundays. With the Grimkés, she had been one of the women whose public appearances and presence on committees had led to the split in the American Anti-Slavery Society. Like Lucretia Mott, she had been denied her seat as a delegate to the London anti-slavery convention in 1840. Like Angelina Grimké, she had married another dedicated antislavery worker, Stephen S. Foster. And, like many other women who began as abolitionists, her experiences led her to take part in the drive for woman's rights. She was one of the early storm centers, the "most persecuted" woman abolitionist. It was her "bloody feet," she said, that had worn the path smooth for the leaders of the woman's rights movement.

In 1851 the Fosters held an antislavery meeting in Rochester. Susan Anthony heard them speak, admired them, especially the courageous Abby Foster, and traveled with them for a week of meetings in nearby localities. They pressed her to become an antislavery lecturer, but she was not quite ready to devote her main energies to abolition, though she began to attend the antislavery conventions within reach.

There remained, then, temperance. It was one of the oldest, most extensive, and most respectable of the reform movements in the United States, suitable for ladies, especially if they kept to their own organizations and modestly refrained from joint activities with male temperance workers. Since the only fully approved outlets for the energies of public-spirited women, or of those who were simply bored or dissatisfied with domestic confinement, were the church and temperance, it is not surprising that so many of the most able women in the country took part in the movement. In most communities it was the only organized female activity available. There were no women's clubs, study groups, parents' associations; there was nothing but the local woman's temperance society.

Drinking had long been widespread in the United States. Homemade whiskey, hard cider, beer, and West Indian rum were cheap, easily available, and freely imbibed. Brandy and cider appeared on breakfast tables; beer, wines, and whiskey were a regular part of dinner. Doctors prescribed spirits for a variety of ailments, for children as well as adults. Workers often received whiskey or rum as part of their wages; "rum breaks" were the antecedents of today's coffee breaks. No social or ceremonial event, even a funeral, was complete without something strong to drink. The corner saloon was a favorite meeting place, and one of the few sources of recreation available to the less affluent classes of society.

The first settlers, particularly in Puritan New England, had not been heavy drinkers, and had been curbed, in any case, by strict authoritarian control of their personal habits. But as the number and variety of settlers increased, as social controls lessened, and as alcoholic beverages became more plentiful, there was more drunkenness to be seen. By the nineteenth century, drinking was considered a major social problem.

With the growth of drinking came its countermovement, the temperance drive. The earliest advocates of temperance, beginning with Dr. Benjamin Rush in the 1780s, wanted precisely that: temperance or moderation in drinking, or the restriction of drinking to beer and wine. But it soon came to mean complete abstinence or teetotalism.

The first formal temperance society in the United States, inspired by Dr. Rush's popular essay *Inquiry into the Effects of Ardent Spirits*, appeared in 1808 in Saratoga, New York. The movement spread rapidly and widely. By the 1830s every kind of group—men, women, sailors, merchants, religious societies, even the United States Congress—had its own temperance organization.

Women were especially concerned with the problem. Wives had no legal protection against drunken husbands. The stereotype of the husband who drank away his wages at the saloon while his family went hungry was too often true. So was the portrait of the man who, as the law allowed, collected the factory earnings of his wife and children and used the money to buy liquor instead of food and clothing. Or the man who, brutalized by drink, beat up his helpless wife and children. Temperance workers made full use of such stories, with horrendous descriptions of the evils of Demon Rum. But even discounting the heavy strokes of moral indignation, the problem of the drinking husband was a very real one for the nineteenth-century wife with no legal or economic existence of her own.

Susan Anthony joined the Rochester Daughters of Temperance and soon became its president. She proved highly competent at organizing affairs and raising money. She served as a delegate to the many temperance conventions in upper New York State, where she met the activists in the movement. One of these was Amelia Bloomer, who lived in Seneca Falls.

Mrs. Bloomer had attended the Seneca Falls convention and found herself in agreement with most of its aims. But, following her husband's lead, she had decided that asking for the vote was too radical and had not signed the Declaration of Sentiments. Nevertheless, she admired Mrs. Stanton and was so inspired by the idea of positive action by women that she helped organize a local Ladies Temperance Society in Seneca Falls, and became editor of its paper, *The Lily*.

In the spring of 1851, William Lloyd Garrison and the famous English abolitionist George Thompson were in Seneca Falls to conduct antislavery meetings. Susan Anthony wanted to hear them, so Mrs. Bloomer invited her to stay at the Bloomer home while attending the meetings. Walking home after one of the sessions, they met Elizabeth Stanton walking to *her* home with Garrison and Thompson, who were guests of the Stantons. They all stopped at the street corner, and Mrs. Bloomer introduced Susan Anthony to Mrs. Stanton.

The two women liked each other immediately. "There she stood," wrote Mrs. Stanton years later, "with her good earnest face and genial smile . . . the perfection of neatness and sobriety. I liked her thoroughly." Later that day Susan Anthony and Mrs. Bloomer called at the Stanton home, and they spent several hours discussing what by now had become the three-pronged reform pattern of American women: temperance, abolition, and woman's rights.

That summer there was another meeting in Seneca Falls, this time to discuss the creation of a People's College. Mrs. Stanton invited Susan Anthony, Horace Greeley, and Lucy Stone, the young abolitionist lecturer, to stay at her home. The three women insisted that the college accept women on the same basis as men, but Horace Greeley vehemently opposed the idea. Greeley generally supported reforms and social innovations, or at least helped publicize them in the *Tribune*, but he was far more cautious in his personal actions than in the columns of his paper. He was afraid that the proposal to make the school coeducational would scare off its potential backers. He urged the ladies "not to agitate the question," but they refused to compromise.

Nothing came of the college, but during these discussions the three women established a close relationship which would affect the whole course of the woman's rights movement. They would part later, with Elizabeth Stanton and Susan Anthony taking steps more daring than Lucy Stone could accept. Right now the eager and articulate Lucy Stone was very much a vital part of the scene, but the lifelong friendship of Elizabeth Stanton and Susan Anthony would remain at the heart of the movement.

Susan Anthony was not among the original ladies of Seneca Falls. But she became so close to these ladies, thought so much like them, and worked so intimately with them that she must be considered one of them. Her life was inextricably bound up with theirs for more than half a century; after their retirement or death, she carried on their work in the same spirit in which it was conceived. Susan B. Anthony deserves, at the very least, to be considered an honorary lady of Seneca Falls, in spirit and purpose, if not in literal fact.

12

Lucy Stone

Too much has already been said and written about woman's sphere. . . . Leave women, then, to find their sphere. And do not tell us before we are born even, that our province is to cook dinners, darn stockings, and sew on buttons.

—Lucy Stone, 1855

Women feel just as men feel; they need exercise for their faculties, and a field for their efforts as much as their brothers do; they suffer from too rigid a constraint, too absolute a stagnation, precisely as men would suffer; and it is narrowminded in their more privileged fellow-creatures to say that they ought to confine themselves to making puddings and knitting stockings, to playing on the piano and embroidering bags. It is thoughtless to condemn them, or laugh at them, if they seek to do more or learn more than custom has pronounced necessary for their sex.

—Charlotte Brontë, *Jane Eyre*, 1847

Most of the feminists of the early nineteenth century—women like Lucretia Mott, Susan B. Anthony, Elizabeth Cady Stanton, Margaret Fuller—had fathers who recognized the intelligence of their daughters and gave them the best education available to girls at the time. Lucy Stone was an exception. When her father learned that she wanted to go to college, he asked, "Is the child crazy?"

Lucy's older brothers had been sent to college as a matter of course. For girls, however, in the view of her father, an elementary education was enough. Anything beyond that would unfit them for their proper place in life. Hannah Stone, Lucy's mother, knew all too well what that proper place was. She herself was a prime example of the role women could expect to fill in a rural household of that period. The Stone family lived on a 145-acre farm near West Brookfield, Massachusetts. In addition to caring for the seven children who survived out of nine, she wove all the cloth used in the household, did all the cooking and laundry for the farmhands as well as her own family, and helped with the work of the farm itself. The night before Lucy was born, in 1818, Hannah milked the eight cows, since the men had gone off to save the hay from a sudden shower. Exhausted and dispirited, she said, when she learned her new baby was a girl, "Oh, dear! I am sorry it is a girl. A woman's life is so hard."

She never thought of complaining. Like all the women she knew, she was doing her duty as laid down by custom and Biblical injunction. A husband was the unquestioned head of the family; a wife did whatever she was told to do, even to milking cows at a time when she was clearly not up to it. Her rebellious little daughter felt quite differently. She had already begun to resent the authoritarian manner of her own father and of fathers in neighboring families, when she came across a statement in the Bible: "Thy desire shall be to thy husband and he shall rule over thee." This was carrying it too far. If God himself had commanded the awful subservience of women, what, she asked her mother, was the point of living, if you were a girl?

Hannah Stone, greatly distressed, explained the disobedience of Eve and the curse laid upon women. Hannah Stone took her Bible seriously; like many devout women of her time, she accepted her inferior and submissive role as the just punishment of the daughters of Eve. Lucy, like all women, must obey the words of the Bible: "Wives, submit yourselves unto your husbands."

Lucy, however, had other ideas. As a piously reared child she could not dismiss the Bible itself, but upon learning that the book she read was a translation from the original Hebrew and Greek, she began to wonder whether it had been translated correctly. This, at least, was Lucy Stone's explanation years later for her early decision to go to college. There, she said, she could study the ancient languages and read the Bible in the original texts.

She may not actually have thought this all out as a young girl. But it was the same line of reasoning used by other women whose belief in the Bible conflicted with their reluctance to accept the humiliating position of their sex as laid down by the presumed Word of God. The Bible, after all, had been translated by men who, consciously or not, might have distorted the original words in order to maintain their supremacy.

Whatever led to her determination to go to college, the Biblical injunction for wives to submit to their husbands, combined with the noticeably increasing fatigue of her mother, began to build up in Lucy the resolve never to become a wife herself. She was discovering just what it would mean to get married and have a household of her own to care for.

Like most farm children, she had her share of the chores, to which she added, when she was twelve, the job of doing the family laundry in order to ease the strain on her seriously overworked mother. Besides helping with the farm and housework, the Stone daughters made shoes which their father sold to the local general store for four cents a pair. Lucy was especially fast: she was expected to make nine pairs a day. In whatever time she had left, she picked berries or nuts in the woods which she sold to pay for the schoolbooks her father refused to buy for her. He felt it was unnecessary to buy them for a girl. She could use her brothers' old ones or go without.

It was not that Francis Stone couldn't afford to buy books for his daughters or do without their shoemaking labor. The farm did well enough, but he had an almost excessive belief in the value of thrift and hard work. He had been a teacher in his earlier years, and was a man of strong character and stiff principle. He was rigidly strict and undemonstrative. He undoubtedly loved his wife and daughters, and did his best for them according to his own views, but he left Lucy with no illusions about the "protected" life of a woman.

When it came to spending money on his children's education, Francis Stone was perfectly willing, and apparently able, to send his sons to college. But daughters were different. Like most fathers of that period—and perhaps of most periods—he could not see the use of advanced education for a girl. When Lucy was still in her early teens, he said flatly that she knew as much as a girl needed and must leave school. Lucy appealed to his practicality by explaining that just a few more years of school would qualify her as a teacher, able to earn money. Would he at least *lend* her the money to continue? He agreed, but only on condition that she sign a note for the loan.

At sixteen, she began to teach for a dollar a week and board. She gradually worked herself up to almost four dollars a week. After repaying her father, she began saving up for her next round of education. From then on, until she was twenty-nine, she taught and went to school herself by turns.

Her goal was to attend Mount Holyoke Seminary. It was not at this time a college, but it was the best school available to girls and the first with the expressed purpose of educating women to become more than wives or teachers. Until then, the accepted aim of advanced female education had been to produce better wives and mothers or, failing that, teachers.

Mount Holyoke was created by Mary Lyon in 1837. As a woman, she had to make it seem as though the idea for her school had come from men, and men were sent around New England to collect money for it. As the depression of 1837 gained force, the men found it almost impossible to raise enough money, so Mary Lyon set out herself. She was sharply criticized, even by close friends, for such improper behavior on the part of a woman. She denounced their criticism with equal sharpness: "My heart is sick, my soul is pained with this empty gentility, this genteel nothingness. I am doing a great work, I cannot come down."

On one of her trips through Massachusetts, she spoke to a sewing circle to which Lucy Stone belonged. Here at last was some encouragement for Lucy's hope of a better education. She was twenty-one by the time she had saved enough money to enter Mount Holyoke, two years after its opening. And then, after only three months, she had to leave. About a year earlier her oldest sister had died. Now another sister suddenly died. Her ailing, distraught mother could not be left alone, and Lucy had to give up school once again and return home.

Four years passed before she was able to resume her education. In the meantime she had transferred her goal to Oberlin College in Ohio. It was the first college in America to admit both Negroes and women, and the only school at the time which granted degrees to women. It had opened its doors in

1833, but women were then permitted to take only a simplified course of study considered more suitable for their limited intellectual capacities. By the time Lucy Stone decided to attend, however, women were allowed to take the full course. She went in 1843, at the age of twenty-five, with barely enough money—seventy dollars—to see her through one term.

She went through exhausting privations to stretch her money far enough. She spent only fifty cents a week on food, worked in the kitchen of the girls' dormitory for three cents an hour, scanning her Greek grammar as she wiped dishes, and taught in the college's preparatory school for twelve and a half cents an hour.

She also taught remedial classes established for adult Negroes who had been unable, earlier in their lives, to get enough education to qualify for entrance to the college itself. Some were former slaves who had received their freedom, or had escaped. Many of them could not read or write. The first time she entered the classroom, the black men objected angrily to being taught by a woman. Even a male slave, they felt, was superior to any female. Only by urging them not to allow their prejudices to interfere with their vitally essential education was she able to get their cooperation.

In this way she managed to earn enough to keep herself at Oberlin for two years. At the beginning of her third year her father, impressed by her determination and effort, and perhaps concerned at last over the effect on her health, offered to lend her whatever money she needed. Again she had to sign a note, promising to repay the loan with interest.

This was an act of generosity for a man like Francis Stone, and he still retained a careful distinction between the rights of sons and daughters. Under the terms of his will, each of his two surviving daughters was to receive $200, while his sons were to get the rest of his money and property. This was so customary that even Lucy, who knew about the will, expressed little direct resentment: "I know that Father has not done it because he loves his sons more than he does his daughters, and though there is no justice in it, still I feel it is less Father's fault than it is the fault of the time. . . . He probably is only acting in accordance with what he thinks is right."

Even this small inheritance was to be pared down. Lacking money, she was never able to return home during her four years at Oberlin. When she graduated, her father wanted her to spend some time at home before going off to work. He offered to pay her fare, but explained that he would subtract the amount from her legacy.

However Lucy Stone might understand and condone her father's actions, it must have added to the indignation which had been building up in her since earliest childhood, an accumulation of anger over the hundreds of big and little ways in which women were constantly reminded of their inferiority. This gradual accretion of anger over one humiliation after another was a common theme in the lives of those who joined the woman's rights movement. It was something men found hard to understand. They could appreciate distress over the more glaring injustices and perhaps agree that, yes, something ought to be done about certain legal disabilities; or they might sympathize with flashes of irritation over individual slights; but they could not grasp the effect of the whole long, abrasive process. In some women, like Lucy's mother, this process led to a steady erosion of pride and independence. In others, like Lucy herself, it built up an inflexible core of resistance, to which each humiliating incident added another firm layer.

Her first object lesson in the treatment of women had been the sight of her mother, overworked, subdued, reduced to nonentity by an autocratic husband; her second had been the contrast between her own long and painful struggle for an education and the ease with which her brothers received theirs. The fact that her father and brothers accepted this contrast as natural, and did nothing to prevent it, made it all the worse. And as a teacher, there had been a shocking gap between her wage and that of a man doing exactly the same work.

There were other galling experiences. One of the deacons of her church had been brought up for expulsion because of his abolitionist beliefs. Lucy, as a full member of the Orthodox Congregational Church, took it for granted that she was entitled to vote. On the first vote, she raised her hand in favor of the deacon. The minister instructed the counter not to include her, explaining that women were not considered "voting members." Votes were taken five more times; each time Lucy defiantly held up her hand, and each time she was pointedly ignored. She remembered her anger over this incident for the rest of her life.

A few years later, in 1837, the Pastoral Letter against the Grimké sisters was read from the pulpit. Lucy said her "indignation blazed" when the minister, relishing each word, read the censure of women "who so far forget themselves as to itinerate in the character of public lecturers and teachers." She told her cousin, who was with her, that "if I ever had anything to say in public, I should say it, and all the more because of that Pastoral Letter."

This resolve was to grow stronger; at Oberlin she began to act upon it.

The founders of Oberlin admitted that women were a "misjudged and neglected sex." One of the principal aims of the college was "the elevation of the female character" by giving them "all the instructive privileges" hitherto reserved for men. But they didn't want to carry elevation too far, and carefully referred to men as "the leading sex." Equal education was one thing, equal status was quite another. The female students at

Oberlin were expected to confine themselves to feminine roles, "washing the men's clothing, caring for their rooms, serving them at table, listening to their orations, but, themselves, remaining respectfully silent in public assemblages," and preparing "for intelligent motherhood and a properly subservient wifehood."

The very idea of a woman stepping out of "subservient wifehood" to assume "a public character" was "too unnatural to be dreamed of." On the subject of speaking in public, one of the school's female administrators wrote: "God will not lead me to *speak* in the assemblies because he has told me with other females, not to do so." Oberlin regarded it as its "mission to show that a liberal education does not rob a woman of her nature, divest her of the softer graces and give her a masculine character." The college would be emphatically opposed to the "raving" advocates of woman's rights.

Almost from the beginning, Lucy Stone had run-ins with the established code of female propriety. Every Sunday morning the students had to sit through a long chapel service. Lucy, who suffered from headaches, took her hat off one morning. She was charged by the Ladies' Board, which supervised the manners and morals of the coeds, with violating the Bible's teaching that women must keep their heads covered in church. Lucy explained that if she did so she would get a headache and would be unable to do anything the rest of the day. "What account shall I give to God of my wasted Sunday afternoons?" she asked. She refused to yield until a compromise was arranged: she could take her hat off during certain parts of the service, but had to sit unobtrusively at the very back of the chapel.

Another sin in the eyes of authority was her open devotion to Garrison. Oberlin was staunchly antislavery—it was one of the stations on the Underground Railway—but its leaders belonged to the anti-Garrison wing of the movement. Lucy offended their sensibilities by hanging a picture of Garrison on the wall of her room. "They hate Garrison and women's rights," she wrote home. "I love both, and often find myself at swords' point with them."

At the beginning of Lucy's third year, Oberlin acquired another disturbing female, the intensely religious Antoinette Brown. She was to become the first woman ordained as a minister, and an active worker for the woman's rights movement. In the stagecoach traveling to Oberlin, she was warned by one of the college trustees to avoid the radical Lucy Stone, "a young woman of strange and dangerous opinions . . . a Garrisonian . . . always talking about woman's rights." Antoinette's curiosity was aroused: she was not a supporter of the anticlerical Garrison, but she was on the way to becoming a convinced feminist. She made a point of meeting Lucy Stone as soon as possible, and the two became not only the closest of friends but, later on, sisters-in-law.

Antoinette Brown had been something of a religious prodigy as a child. She began to take part in prayer meetings when she was only nine, and spoke so devoutly that everyone predicted a godly future for her as the wife of a minister or even a missionary. Antoinette, however, had another and, for that time, unthinkable idea: she didn't want to marry a minister, she wanted to become one herself. Her deep religious sentiments were combined with a surprising degree of independence and a concern for woman's rights. She believed that a correct interpretation of the Bible would show that it did not teach the inferiority and submission of women.

She joined Lucy in the effort to obtain equal treatment for women at Oberlin. One of the courses they took together was a class in rhetoric. Every week the male students held a debate. The girls in the class were required to attend, but were forbidden to take part in such an unfeminine activity. Lucy and Antoinette objected. Their purpose in taking a class in public speaking was to get practical experience. Listening to others was no help. Their sympathetic professor saw their point. Though it was out of the question for them to debate with men, he said they could at least debate with each other.

The news of this decision spread outside their class, and on the day set for their debate, a large crowd came to watch this unusual spectacle. The authorities were furious, and banned all future debates by women. Lucy and Antoinette then formed a clandestine female debating society which met secretly in the woods as long as the weather permitted, and at the home of one of Lucy's black students when it grew cold.

The following summer, Lucy Stone was invited to speak at a celebration held by Oberlin's black residents to commemorate the ending of slavery in the West Indies. This was her first public speech, and probably one of the first to be made by a woman in Oberlin. The authorities were unhappy about it, and again she was summoned before the Ladies' Board. She was asked if she hadn't felt terribly "out of place" on the same platform with men. Wasn't she "embarrassed and frightened"? It was inconceivable to the ladies that any woman would not swoon in shame and confusion at finding herself in such a position.

That same year, 1846, Abby Kelley Foster and her husband were among the many antislavery speakers who came to Oberlin. Since the town and college were, on the whole, opposed to both Garrisonians and female public speakers, the Fosters aroused a good deal of violently expressed hostility. Mrs. Foster was held up as a shocking "specimen of what woman becomes when out of her place." After three meetings, they were forbidden by the outraged authorities to hold any more. Lucy Stone had met Abby Foster several years earlier, and now she spent a good deal of time with the Fosters, an association that did not improve her reputation at Oberlin.

She wound up her career at Oberlin with one last grand clash. Each year the graduating class selected its outstanding members to prepare and read essays at commencement. One of those chosen by the class of 1847 was Lucy Stone. As a woman, she would not be permitted to read her paper. A man could present his own essay, but one written by a woman had to be read by a male professor. "It is improper," ruled the faculty and the Ladies' Board, "for women to participate in public exercises with men." Lucy Stone refused to prepare an essay, saying it would be "a sacrifice of principle" unless she could read it herself.

Oberlin's president felt that an exception should be made in her case, but most of the faculty disagreed. They even proposed not to let her graduate unless she conformed to the college rules, submitted a paper, and let a man present it. She refused again. Two of the men and all but one of the women who had been selected with her also refused to submit essays, in sympathetic protest. Substitutes were named, but these too refused.

The Oberlin faculty drew a curious distinction between what was and wasn't proper. Antoinette Brown, graduating from the Young Ladies' Course, would be permitted to read an essay before virtually the same audience, though on a different day from the regular exercises. But at the Young Ladies' commencement only women would be on the platform, except for Oberlin's president, who presumably didn't count. The impropriety, then, consisted not so much in a woman's speaking publicly, but in sharing a platform with members of the opposite sex.

In the end, Lucy was not allowed to speak, but she was permitted to graduate, which might be counted a victory of some sort. She received an A.B., the first Massachusetts woman to do so.

Antoinette Brown, completing the simplified program, did not qualify for the A.B. She had planned to continue in the

Theological Course and earn a divinity degree. But the faculty refused to accept a woman as a candidate for that degree. However, they had to take her as a graduate student under the terms of Oberlin's charter, which said that all courses were open to women. When she finished, she was ordained in a small New York church, despite her lack of a formal degree. She was the first woman to be ordained in the United States, and possibly in the whole Christian world. In 1878, Oberlin gave her a Master of Arts. In 1908, when she was eighty-three years old, the college finally mellowed to the point where it graciously awarded her the divinity degree, fifty-eight years after she had qualified for it.

There were two reasons for Lucy Stone's stubborn insistence upon being allowed to speak and debate at Oberlin. One was her constant battle against "the principle which takes away from women their equal rights, and denies to them the privilege of being co-laborers with men in any sphere to which their ability makes them adequate." She was resolved that "no word or deed of mine" should indicate acceptance of such a principle.

The other reason was her decision, long before graduation, to become a professional public speaker. Both Lucy Stone and Antoinette Brown, who was determined to become a minister, felt they were being denied invaluable training and practice in public speaking. Male students were receiving preparation for future careers as lecturers and ministers; why not females as well?

Lucy's family were horrified by her ambition. It was one thing for a man to become a professional lecturer: in the nineteenth century this was a popular and respectable career for a man, especially if he avoided controversial subjects like abolition. A female lecturer, even on the safest subjects, would be considered ludicrous, outrageous, against nature. An Oberlin professor said that to see a woman in such a public role was "positively disagreeable to both sexes." Speaking for abolition or, even worse, woman's rights was certainly not to be thought of.

Yet Lucy Stone was thinking of doing both. To her mother, who was "dreadfully" upset, she wrote, "I expect to plead not for the slave only, but for suffering humanity everywhere. Especially do I mean to labor for the elevation of my sex." Her mother begged her to consider whether she couldn't do more good by teaching, or if she must lecture, not to appear publicly but go "from house to house." Her sister Sarah also recommended teaching, saying that public lecturing by a woman was against divine law. The only relatives who gave her any support were two of her brothers, Frank and Bowman. Bowman went so far as to allow her to give her first public speech, outside of Oberlin, at his church in Gardner, Massachusetts. It was on woman's rights and given in 1847, a year before the Seneca Falls convention began to publicize the subject.

In the spring of 1848, at Abby Foster's suggestion, the Massachusetts Anti-Slavery Society hired Lucy Stone as a speaker. Her parents said she would "disgrace the whole family" and destroy her own reputation forever. Lucy considered this, decided they were wrong, and went off to Boston to begin a career that brought her a reputation far beyond the imaginations of her parents or of Lucy Stone herself.

Lucy Stone proved to be a superb speaker. It was not so much what she said: her ideas were not original, she had no sense of humor, and her intense earnestness often led her into dogmatism and rigidity. But she had a beautiful voice, soft, clear, melodious, and a delivery that was remarkable in its effect upon the most hostile audiences. Her voice was often described as "silvery" or "like a silver bell." She combined a charming simplicity with a calm air of assurance and authority that beguiled disruptive hecklers into respectful attention.

She was small and bright-cheeked, with a natural, unaffected manner that people found appealing. The fact that she spoke extemporaneously added to her effectiveness, and she made many converts to her twin causes of abolition and woman's rights. At the very least, she reduced the antagonism of many to the point where they were willing to give her ideas the serious consideration other speakers had failed to win.

She also had a good deal of courage, an essential quality when abolitionist speakers were being physically attacked. Endurance was another basic requirement. She was sent by the Anti-Slavery Society on extensive speaking tours throughout the Northeast; poor roads and primitive transportation, bad weather, and especially the harassment by anti-abolitionists made these trips grueling tests of her fortitude and determination. The posters advertising her talks were often torn down; pepper was sprinkled in the auditorium, forcing people to leave. One cold winter day she was drenched with water from a hose put through a window behind her. She was jeered at or denounced by local newspapers and ministers. Her own church expelled her, saying she had "engaged in a course of life . . . inconsistent with her covenant engagements to this church."

She was supposed to speak only about the plight of the Negro and the evils of slavery, but almost from the beginning she introduced the plight of women into her speeches. The Anti-Slavery Society objected; they were paying her six dollars a week to speak about slaves, not women. She offered to resign, saying, "I was a woman before I was an abolitionist. I must speak for the women." The society felt she was too valuable a lecturer to lose, and suggested that she talk for women during the week on her own, and for the slave on weekends, for which the society would pay her four dollars.

She agreed, and organized her own one-woman lecture tours on woman's rights. Her audiences were large. Some came out of curiosity to see their first lady lecturer, or for the deliberate purpose of heckling such a brazen female. But a great many of the women who attended were eager to hear this public expression of their own deeply felt problems. After every talk, they clustered around to tell her about their personal difficulties and experiences, adding constantly to her knowledge of the subject.

Her audiences were pleasantly surprised when she appeared. Hostile newspapers gave the impression that she was a large, bold, loud-voiced woman, a "she-hyena," who wore boots, smoked cigars, and swore freely. Instead, they saw a small, neatly dressed, softly spoken woman whose voice charmed them as soon as she began speaking.

At first she passed a hat around after her talks to collect money for her expenses, but soon she found it better to charge an admission fee. It discouraged the hecklers, but was too small to keep out those who were genuinely interested. She lived and traveled with the greatest simplicity, and managed to save a considerable sum of money.

All this time she had no contact with the ladies of Seneca Falls, though it seems likely that she would have heard something about them from abolitionist leaders like William Lloyd Garrison, Wendell Phillips, and the Fosters. All these were her close associates in her antislavery work, and friends of the Seneca Falls organizers as well. But she wrote later of her "solitary battle for women's rights," and said that she "knew nobody who sympathized with my ideas." She felt she was alone in her effort, the first to carry on any sustained campaign on behalf of women. Others, like the Grimkés, Ernestine Rose, Abby Foster, and Margaret Fuller, had spoken or written about the subject, but as a supplement to their major work. To Lucy Stone, this was her major work, and she deserves the title she received: "the morning star of the woman's rights movement."

It was, of course, inevitable that sooner or later Lucy Stone would join up with the other supporters of woman's rights. In the spring of 1850 she attended an antislavery convention in Boston. At its conclusion an announcement was made, inviting those who were interested in a woman's rights convention to meet in the anteroom. Lucy Stone and Abby Foster were among the nine who appeared. The outcome of this meeting was the first National Woman's Rights Convention, held in Worcester, Massachusetts, in October 1850.

The call to this convention was signed by a large number of distinguished people. Lucy Stone's name was at the head of the list, which included Ralph Waldo Emerson, William Lloyd Garrison, Mr. and Mrs. Wendell Phillips, Gerrit Smith, James and Lucretia Mott, and Elizabeth Cady Stanton. But the convention itself was largely the work of Paulina Wright Davis.

Paulina Davis had been left a wealthy widow by the death of her first husband. She decided to devote herself to improving the condition of women in a variety of ways. To counteract the ignorance on the part of most women with regard to their own bodies, she gave lectures on physiology and anatomy. She used a plaster figure of a female nude as a visual aid; whenever it was uncovered, it was considered so "indelicate . . . that women frequently dropped their veils, ran out of the room or even fainted."

Like Elizabeth Stanton and Ernestine Rose, she circulated petitions for the Married Woman's Property Act in New York State. In 1853 she would establish one of the first woman's rights publications, *The Una*. In a piece written for *The Una*, Mrs. Davis claimed for women the right to limit the number of their children and to have control over their own bodies. She emphasized the central demand of feminists of every time and place: "We ask to be regarded, respected, and treated as human beings, of full age and natural abilities, as equal fellow sinners, and not as infants or beautiful angels, to whom the rules of civil and social justice do not apply."

She was chosen president of the Worcester convention. Lucretia Mott, Lydia Mott, Angelina Grimké, Abby Foster, Ernestine Rose—all the original workers for woman's rights—were there, together with Lucy Stone, Antoinette Brown, the remarkable ex-slave Sojourner Truth—who was called the "Lybian Sybil"—and many others soon to become active leaders. Elizabeth Stanton had been invited to sign the call and take part in the proceedings. The Worcester convention was, after all, a direct outgrowth of Seneca Falls, and it would have been unthinkable to hold it without one of the prime movers of the cause. But Mrs. Stanton found herself unable to come; instead, she sent a letter to be read at the convention.

Margaret Fuller had also been invited, in the hope that she would become a leader of the movement. But her terrible death at sea had occurred as she was returning to the United States, just three months earlier.

The Worcester convention, the first on a national scale, gathered together most of the individuals who had been working on their own toward the same goal. It was Lucy Stone's formal introduction to the existent woman's rights movement. She made an eloquent speech, and emerged from that convention as one of the principal leaders.

The press had had its little joke over the Seneca Falls and Rochester conventions; now it really let loose. The Worcester meeting was called a "hen convention," and one paper quoted an Arabic saying: "When a hen crows like a cock it is time to cut her head off." The worst of all the newspapers was the *New York Herald*, which called the convention "that motley mingling of abolitionists, socialists, and infidels . . . . this hybrid, mongrel, piebald, crackbrained, pitiful, disgusting and ridiculous assemblage . . . may God have mercy on their miserable souls." It accused the "gathering of crazy old women" of wanting to abolish both the Bible and the Constitution.

Again the only major newspaper that gave a fair, unprejudiced report was the *New York Tribune*. Most of the others dismissed the convention as an ineffectual farce, while some saw it as a threat to home, motherhood, virtue, and morality. But the women were not to be stopped.

13

Bloomerism

The woman shall not wear that which pertaineth unto a man,
neither shall a man put on a woman's garment: for all that
do so are abomination unto the Lord thy God.
                                              —Deuteronomy 22:5

Gibbery, gibbery, gab,
The women had a confab,
And demanded the rights
To wear the tights.
Gibbery, gibbery, gab.

Heigh! ho! in rain and snow,
The bloomer now is all the go.
Twenty tailors take the stitches,
Twenty women wear the breeches.
Heigh! ho! in rain or snow,
The bloomer now is all the go.
                    —Street doggerel shouted at bloomer wearers, 1850s

When Amelia Bloomer introduced Susan Anthony to Elizabeth Stanton in the spring of 1851, the two Seneca Falls ladies were wearing a strange outfit. Instead of fitting snugly, their waists were comfortably loose, and their skirts, instead of sweeping the streets according to respectable fashion, ended just below their knees. Under the skirts they wore long pantaloons, ballooning out very full, then gathered closely at the ankles, where they ended in a short ruffle.

The costume had been introduced to Seneca Falls earlier that year by Mrs. Stanton's cousin, Elizabeth Smith Miller. Mrs. Miller, daughter of the reformer Gerrit Smith, had just come back from a journey to Europe. In Switzerland she had seen women in sanatoriums wearing similar costumes, and was so impressed by their practicality and comfort that she had one made for herself. She was encouraged to wear it by her father, who, if anything, was even more enthusiastic about it than she was. Gerrit Smith had always insisted that the cumbersome, restrictive clothing worn by women was a mark of bondage; they would never be really free until they emancipated themselves from ridiculous, uncomfortable, and unhealthy fashions.

He had a valid point: female clothing in the mid-nineteenth century was enough to slow down the most ebullient spirit and reduce her to a state of exhausted resignation. It wasn't just the long, trailing skirt, guaranteed to pick up every piece of dust, dirt, and mud in its path, tripping its wearer on stairs and uneven terrain. Under the skirt came the almost geologically stratified petticoats: first the more or less decorated, sometimes flounced, white, starched muslin petticoat, then two scalloped flannel ones, then a bottom layer, stiffened in some fashion, perhaps with circles of straw sewn into the hems to make the skirt stand out, tentlike. In the late 1840s crinoline, made with horsehair, came into use as the stiffener, and steel hoops began replacing the circles of straw. Underneath the whole structure came a pair of long drawers, edged with lace.

Above the skirts, and again working from the outside in, was the close-fitting bodice of the dress, often enhanced with a wide bertha or a fichu crossed over the bosom. Beneath this came the camisole, daintily embroidered or lace-trimmed. Underneath it all were the redoubtable stays, tightly laced contraptions reinforced with steel and whalebone. These squeezed the waist—and the internal organs—into a fashionable hourglass shape, and forced the wearer into a stiff, upright posture. Any deviation from the perpendicular was virtually impossible. Easy movement and normal breathing were greatly hampered, to say the least. The languor and physical delicacy regarded as typical feminine characteristics must have arisen to some degree from these iron-maiden devices. Doctors were always fulminating against them, but the rigid discipline of fashion and custom kept the stays firmly in place.

The weight of all this paraphernalia was enormous; the dress alone could take twenty or more yards of fabric, and the combination of skirt and petticoats could weigh up to twelve pounds. Of course, in the privacy of her home, working in her house and garden, a woman would go easy on the tightness of her stays and the number of her petticoats. Still, the skirt of even the simplest housedress remained long and full; houses were cleaned, floors scrubbed, gardens weeded, with all that surplus fabric getting in the way.

One of the most difficult feats was to walk up stairs carrying several objects at the same time. One hand had to hold up the skirt and petticoats, so as not to trip on them. In pre-electricity days a woman often had to climb stairs carrying a lamp or candle, which took care of the other hand. But what if she had to carry something else, like a baby, as well? It was precisely this detail which set off a brief revolution in women's clothing.

After her return from Europe, Elizabeth Smith Miller, wearing her new outfit, came to visit Elizabeth Stanton. Mrs. Stanton admired the pants and recognized their convenience and comfort. But it wasn't until she watched Mrs. Miller, carrying a Stanton baby and a lamp, walk easily and safely upstairs that she determined to make such an outfit for herself. It was finished in a few days, and the two women astonished—and no doubt appalled—the residents of Seneca Falls by appearing on its streets wearing pants.

Neither lady was disturbed by the shock waves they created. Mrs. Miller had the backing of her unusually freethinking father to behave rationally instead of conventionally; Mrs. Stanton, an even more untypically independent female, was too delighted with her emancipation to care. "What incredible freedom I enjoyed! Like a captive set free from his ball and chain, I was always ready for a brisk walk through sleet and snow and rain, to climb a mountain, jump over a fence, work in the garden."

On their walk, they stopped at the post office. The postmaster was Dexter Bloomer; his assistant, officially approved and duly sworn in despite public misgivings over a female postal clerk, was his wife, Amelia. Amelia Bloomer took a close look at what the ladies were wearing. She had been urging dress reform in her feminist paper, *The Lily*, and since "it seemed proper that I should practice as I preached . . . a few days later, I, too, donned the new costume."

The next issue of *The Lily* mentioned briefly that she was trying out the pants outfit. She had no intention of permanently adopting it, at least in its present form, and even less intention of starting a new fashion. She was completely unprepared for the amazing reaction. Hundreds of women began writing in, eager for more information about the outfit, and asking for patterns. Mrs. Bloomer obligingly supplied detailed descriptions and sewing instructions for what quickly became known as "the Bloomer costume." The circulation of *The Lily* rose from 500 a month to 4000. Mrs. Bloomer was invited to give lectures. She kept reminding her readers that the credit, and hence the name, belonged to Elizabeth Smith Miller, but "Bloomer" stuck. Although the garments that are known as bloomers today are not quite the same as the pants worn in the 1850s, they are still called by Amelia's name.

Amelia Jenks, after receiving what little education was available to a girl in a small New York town, had become a schoolteacher at seventeen, and then a governess. In 1840 she married Dexter Bloomer, the young Quaker editor and part owner of the *Seneca County Courier*. They settled in Seneca Falls, where, in 1849, Dexter was appointed postmaster as a reward for his support of the winning political party.

1840 was not only the year in which Amelia Bloomer— together with Elizabeth Stanton and Queen Victoria—got married; it was also the year of the Great Washingtonian Temperance Reformation, organized by the Seven Reformed Drunkards of Baltimore. Two of the Reformed Drunkards came to Seneca Falls and stayed with the Bloomers while they held meetings urging total abstinence from alcohol. Amelia, already a teetotaler, became interested in their cause and helped organize the local Temperance Society.

The Bloomers had no children, so Amelia, with time and energy to spare, turned, like so many women of that day, to the temperance crusade as an outlet. She recruited a great many members for the Temperance Society and contributed articles to its paper, *The Water Bucket*, writing under the name of "Gloriana."

In 1847 the Stantons moved to Seneca Falls. The following year the announcement for the woman's rights convention was sent in to the *Seneca County Courier*. Amelia was not at that time a feminist, but she and Dexter were intrigued by the idea of such a convention. So were the readers of the *Courier*. The town could talk of nothing else, the women with eager curiosity, the men with consternation or scorn.

The Bloomers attended both days of the convention. This was the first time Amelia had seen Mrs. Stanton, and she liked what she saw. Even more, she liked what Mrs. Stanton said, and found herself strongly inclined to agree with most of it. But when Mrs. Stanton called for woman suffrage, Dexter said this was too radical and, influenced by him, Amelia did not sign the Declaration of Sentiments.

But she thought about it. She thought about everything that had been said at the convention, and she began to look about her with a new consciousness of the position of women. At the meetings of the Temperance Society, for example, she realized that the women took no part in the proceedings. They never spoke, were never given any important work to do. Together with other female members of the society, she decided the solution was to have a Ladies Temperance Society of their own. Soon after its formation the society began to publish its own newspaper, *The Lily*, with Amelia Bloomer as publisher and editor.

The Lily was planned primarily as a temperance paper; its first issues said little about woman's rights. But in the spring of 1849, soon after *The Lily* began, the Tennessee Legislature decided, after serious deliberation, that women could not be permitted to own property since they had no souls. Mrs. Bloomer was outraged. In the next issue of *The Lily* she ran an editorial explaining that though the paper had not expected to say much about woman's rights, the time had come to change that policy. The Tennessee decision had caused her to "think it high time that women should open their eyes and look where they stand. It is quite time that their rights *should be discussed*, and that woman herself should enter the contest."

The Lily and its editor became increasingly feminist. Several months later the masthead was changed, first to include the words "Devoted to the Interests of Women," and later "The Emancipation of Woman from Intemperance, Injustice, Prejudice, and Bigotry." She also provided a room next to the post office to serve as a woman's center for Seneca Falls. Here the women could meet to discuss common problems and to read the exchange papers and magazines received by *The Lily*.

These activities naturally attracted Seneca Falls' number-one feminist, Elizabeth Cady Stanton. She joined in the discussions in the room next to the post office, and became a frequent contributor to *The Lily*, signing her articles "Sun Flower." In one of her articles she complained about the excessive time and energy spent on unnecessary sewing. She wanted women to eliminate all excess trimming that had to be laboriously hand-stitched. "What use is all the flummery, puffing, and mysterious folding we see in ladies' dresses? What use in ruffles on round pillow cases, night caps, children's clothes?" These were nothing but "a continued drain on sight and strength, on health and life, and it should be the study of every woman to do as little of it as possible."

Mrs. Bloomer also recommended editorially that women's clothing be made more sensible and comfortable. But both ladies disapproved, in these first years of *The Lily*'s existence, of "bifurcated garments" for women. Hardly more than six months before she appeared in her bloomer costume, Mrs. Stanton had written on the subject of women wearing pants: "The gents need have no fear of our imitating them, for we think it is in violation of every principle of duty, taste, and dignity." However, when she saw her cousin, Elizabeth Miller, walking so easily up the stairs carrying both a lamp and a baby, Elizabeth Cady Stanton became converted to the bifurcated garment.

After the Seneca Falls and Rochester conventions, the newspapers had tried to laugh the woman's rights movement out of existence. They succeeded only in giving it a vast amount of free publicity which, if anything, helped the new cause on its way. The press and public were more successful in ridiculing the bloomer costume to death.

At first it seemed as if the pants would take hold. Many seized upon the new costume with relief and gratitude. Farm women and those whose activities required unhampered movement were glad to adopt it. So were the girls working in the New England textile factories. The mill girls of Lowell, Massachusetts, organized a Bloomer Institute to further their "Emancipation from the thraldom of that dictatorial French goddess Fashion." Women everywhere enjoyed the comfort provided by the loose waist and the absence of heavy petticoats. From Ohio, Michigan, Florida, even California came reports of women wearing the new style. And of course the feminists were all for it. Sooner or later many in the woman's rights movement came to wear the bloomer dress. Some cut their hair short, as well.

It wasn't easy. They found the costume wonderfully comfortable, but the ridicule, the stares of the public, the disapproval or embarrassment of relatives, friends, ministers were extremely uncomfortable, especially for a generation brought up on the virtues of female modesty and conformity.When they appeared publicly, small boys would follow them, jeering, or chanting verses like:

> Heigh! ho!
> Thro' sleet and snow,
> Mrs. Bloomer's all the go.
> Twenty tailors take the stitches,
> Plenty of women wear the breeches,
> Heigh! ho!
> Carrion crow.

Henry Stanton had been elected to the New York State Senate in 1849 as a Free Soil Democrat. When he ran for reelection in 1851, his opponents made full use of Mrs. Stanton's bloomer costume. Some members of his own party were disturbed by it, refusing to vote for a man whose wife wore bloomers. He won by only five votes. Right after the election it was rumored that he had lost, and boys went through the streets singing a new version of the original jingle:

> Heigh! ho! the carrion crow
> Mrs. Stanton's all the go:
> Twenty tailors take the stitches,
> Mrs. Stanton wears the breeches.

Henry Stanton himself was not opposed to the outfit, though he sometimes poked a little mild fun at it. He was perfectly willing to be seen with his bloomered wife in public, unlike some of her closest friends and relatives. Her sons, attending the Grimké-Weld school, asked her not to visit them in the bloomer costume. One of her sisters refused to write to her when she heard about it; her oldest sister, the very correct Tryphena, burst into tears when she learned of Elizabeth's disgraceful behavior. Judge Cady sent a letter saying that no woman "of good sense and delicacy" would make such a laughingstock of herself, and expressed the hope that she would not visit the Cady home in Johnstown while dressed so outlandishly.

Many women, even some from liberal backgrounds or within the woman's rights movement itself, disapproved strongly of the bloomer costume. When Lucy Stone paid a visit to Lucretia Mott, wearing her bloomer outfit, Mrs. Mott's daughters refused to be seen in the street with her and begged her to return to conventional dress. Some felt it would harm the cause of woman's rights by giving it a bad name.

The "bloomer girls" were harassed in every way. It was unpleasant enough being followed by jeering little boys. But often men joined the hecklers; objects like eggs and stones were thrown at the bloomer wearers, and they would have to duck into stores for safety. One day Lucy Stone and Susan Anthony, in New York City for a convention, walked along the street dressed in their bloomer outfits. They were followed by a growing number of men and boys, and were soon hemmed in until they could no longer walk in any direction. They had to stand there, listening to the taunts of the crowd until they were rescued by a passing acquaintance.

The worst ridicule appeared in the British press. It was just the subject to inspire the wags and cartoonists of *Punch*, the English humor magazine. The costume had appeared in England almost immediately after Amelia Bloomer described it in *The Lily*; it quickly became a leading topic of the day. Lectures on "Bloomerism" were given by earnest supporters of dress reform, a "Bloomer Ball" was held, farcical plays and a pantomime about bloomerism were presented. It was the theme of popular songs and dance tunes heard all over the country. The makers of the Staffordshire china figurines added some new ones to their collection, of women—supposedly modeled after Amelia Bloomer—wearing the pants outfit.

In *Punch*, week after week, verses and cartoons portrayed the dreadful results to be expected if the ladies took to wearing pants. Women were drawn or described as sprawling about ungracefully, smoking cigars, swilling beer, taking over guard and police duty, driving hansom cabs, while their crushed husbands remained meekly at home, wearing skirts, tending the babies, doing the cooking and housework. As *Punch* put it: "He will have to wear a gown / If he does not quickly make her put her Bloomer shortcoat down."

One of the curious reactions to the woman's rights movement was the constantly expressed fear that the slightest change in female status or customs—even in the kind of clothing worn—would turn women into hard-drinking, cigar-smoking, swaggering, coarse imitations of men. An extension of this fear was the implied reverse threat to men: they would be reduced to weak, ineffectual counterparts of women.

It was more than the quite justifiable anxiety that increasing female independence would reduce male power over women and diminish masculine comfort in many ways. Men were quite right to be anxious on this score: this is exactly what would and did happen. But it was also as though there were only a limited number of rights available, a limited amount of freedom possible, so that whatever was given to women would have to be taken away from men. Or it was assumed that this was the goal of the woman's rights movement. If women were allowed to wear pants, suggested the antifeminists, men would have to wear skirts—symbolically—in exchange. If women were permitted to become doctors or lawyers or bank clerks, men would have to give up their jobs, stay home, and do the housework.

Equally curious, and highly revealing, was the image of the homebound partner as it appeared in the anti-bloomer, antifeminist verses and cartoons. This figure was always drawn as a miserable, subservient, dependent nonentity. However exaggerated, it not only exposed what men really thought of women, or of the lives they led, but implied that such a dreary existence was all right for women but heaven forbid that men should be reduced to such a sorry state.

While the press jeered at the bloomer costume, the church denounced it. Women were commanded by their ministers not to wear it. A bifurcated garment was a violation of the word of God, or at least of Moses: "The woman shall not wear that which pertaineth unto a man, neither shall a man put on a woman's garment: for all that do so are abomination unto the Lord thy God." Amelia Bloomer's response to this was that nowhere in Genesis is it indicated that either the fig-leaf aprons worn by Adam and Eve in the Garden of Eden or the skins worn after the expulsion were differentiated into male and female styles. For that matter, among many nations, including the ancient Israelites, there was little difference between the basic male and female dress: both wore skirts or tunics. And finally, she asked, if ministers were so keen on obeying the law of Moses, why didn't they wear fringes on their clothes as commanded in that same chapter of Deuteronomy?

But logic had nothing to do with it. Whatever the ancients might have done, wearing pants was now a male prerogative, and women must not usurp it. Skirts might be uncomfortable, inconvenient, even dangerous, but the important considerations were propriety and modesty. Skirts concealed the indecent fact that women had legs, and if the multilayered petticoats prevented them from leading more active lives, what of it? Physical activity, after all, was not truly feminine.

At first the wearers of the bloomer costume had adopted it for comfort, then as a matter of principle. It became a symbol of woman's emancipation, an example of her right to make her own choices, even in the relatively small matter of clothing. But the bloomer girls discovered that it was harder to go against convention in these small, obvious matters than in larger but more abstract ways. It was easier, they found, to endure criticism for advanced ideas than to suffer ridicule for unconventional appearance.

Susan Anthony, who showed great courage in facing audiences who were violently opposed to her ideas, flinched under the jeers directed at her bloomers. "Oh, I can not, can not bear it any longer," she said after wearing the pants outfit hardly more than a year. And later: "I found it a physical comfort but a mental crucifixion." Elizabeth Stanton said in a letter to Susan Anthony: "We put the dress on for greater freedom, but what is physical freedom compared with mental bondage?"

As the opposition to the costume continued to rage, Mrs. Stanton began to feel that too much energy was being spent on what was, after all, a very minor aspect of the woman's rights movement. There were goals more important than dress reform. She felt also that many women who would otherwise join the movement were staying away because of their opposition to the bloomer dress or to the kind of publicity it was getting. The male supporters of the movement, men like William Lloyd Garrison and Wendell Phillips, disliked the furor, and probably the costume itself; they urged the women to give it up.

After wearing bloomers for about two years, Mrs. Stanton decided it was doing more harm than good. Though she continued to use the outfit for housework and gardening, she stopped wearing it in public, and urged Susan Anthony to do the same. "It is not wise," she wrote to her, "to use up so much energy and feeling in that way. You can put them to better use."

Mrs. Stanton was the first to stop wearing the bloomer dress, but others soon followed her lead. Mrs. Bloomer held out longer than most, while Elizabeth Smith Miller, who had introduced the costume in the first place, wore it for almost seven years. Then she too gave it up. Bloomers went into limbo until the introduction of the "safety bicycle," with both wheels of the same size, in the 1880s. Women took up the new sport and, in order to ride more comfortably and safely, restored the bifurcated garment, first in the form of a divided skirt, then as a modified version of bloomers called knickerbockers or knickers. Both Mrs. Bloomer and Mrs. Stanton, by then too old to mount a bicycle, were greatly pleased to see their old fashion revived and accepted at last, if only for sports.

Mrs. Stanton's vision had gone even beyond bloomers. She had suggested that women wear only the knee-length dress, with just stockings to cover the legs. For summer, she made the surprising proposal that the legs be left bare.

But in their own day, after the demise of the bloomer costume, the feminist leaders became quite conservative in their dress. They tried to avoid any diversion from their main purpose. Susan Anthony in particular fought against all subsequent attempts at introducing novel reforms in dress or other minor matters. At best, these were distracting: "The attention of my audience was fixed upon my clothes instead of my words." To be successful, women must concentrate on one reform at a time: "By urging two, both are injured, as the average mind can grasp and assimilate but one idea at a time."

14

The Rub-a-dub
of Agitation

This noise-making twain are the two sticks of a drum, keeping up what Daniel Webster called "the rub-a-dub of agitation."
> —Theodore Tilton, speaking of Elizabeth Cady Stanton and Susan B. Anthony

In thought and sympathy we were one, and in the division of labor we exactly complemented each other. . . . While she is slow and analytical in composition, I am rapid and synthetic. I am the better writer, she the better critic. She supplied the facts and statistics, I the philosophy and rhetoric.
> —Elizabeth Cady Stanton, *Eighty Years and More*

If Lucretia Mott typified the moral force of the movement, if Lucy Stone was its most gifted orator and Mrs. Stanton its outstanding philosopher, Susan Anthony was its incomparable organizer, who gave it force and direction for half a century.
> —Eleanor Flexner, *Century of Struggle*, 1959

Lucretia Mott, Martha Wright, and Lucy Stone, along with dozens of others who became involved after that first convention, all made immense contributions to woman's rights. But the driving force, the inspirational center, was provided by Elizabeth Stanton and Susan B. Anthony. Mrs. Stanton articulated the goals, Miss Anthony supplied the organizational skill and the unremitting energy which powered the movement for the next fifty years. William Henry Channing called her the Napoleon of the woman's rights movement.

In 1851, when she first met Elizabeth Stanton, Susan Anthony was still primarily concerned with temperance. But her experience during the next two years not only drew her away from temperance to woman's rights, but made her realize that without those rights women could do very little for any reform. These were also the years in which she first became a public figure, and in which she found the chief purpose of her life.

At the beginning of 1852 she was sent as a delegate from the Rochester Daughters of Temperance to a mass meeting of temperance workers held in Albany by the Sons of Temperance. The women delegates had been accepted and given seats, but when Susan Anthony rose to speak on a motion, the presiding officer stopped her. "The sisters were not invited to speak," he announced, "but to listen and learn."

She immediately walked out of the hall, followed by three or four other women. The rest of the female delegates, disapproving of these "bold, meddlesome disturbers," remained and were obediently silent during the rest of the convention.

The "bold disturbers" held their own meeting, at which they decided to form a state organization for women in which they would be free to speak and act. Susan Anthony was appointed chairman of a committee to arrange a Woman's State Temperance Convention to be held in Rochester in April 1852.

She appealed to Elizabeth Stanton for help. Mrs. Stanton

was for temperance, largely because women had no legal protection against the often brutal or irresponsible behavior of alcoholic husbands. She would have preferred to see women work directly to secure legal protection, but she knew that many women were not yet ready for this. Temperance work, though secondary in her view, would at least provide them with experience and self-confidence, and bring them closer to the movement for woman's rights.

She agreed to attend and deliver a speech at the convention, though she warned Susan Anthony that what she had to say would be quite radical. By now she was more than ever incensed at the position of women, at the church as "a terrible engine of oppression . . . as concerns woman," and at the refusal of men to permit women to speak at conventions. "I am at the boiling point!" she wrote to Susan Anthony. "If I do not find some day the use of my tongue on this question, I shall die of an intellectual repression, a woman's rights convulsion!"

At the convention a permanent organization, the Woman's State Temperance Society, was set up, with Mrs. Stanton as president, Susan Anthony and Amelia Bloomer as secretaries. In her speech, Mrs. Stanton made an astonishing proposal. "Let no woman," she declared, "remain in the relation of wife with the confirmed drunkard. Let no drunkard be the father of her children." The state laws, she continued, should be changed so that "the drunkard shall have no claims on either wife or child."

This open advocacy of divorce plainly disconcerted her conservative listeners. Her remarks seemed even more outrageous coming from a woman wearing the immodest bloomer costume, with her hair cut short. Short hair was not uncommon for women at the time; but, combined with bloomers, it heightened the impression of defiant unconventionality. Men and women alike criticized her severely. Both press and pulpit strongly condemned the "radical Mrs. Stanton."

In June, while reaction to Mrs. Stanton was still strong, the Men's State Temperance Society held a convention in Syracuse. All temperance groups were invited to send delegates. The newly formed Woman's State Temperance Society chose Susan Anthony and Amelia Bloomer. When they arrived, both wearing bloomer dresses and Susan with her hair cut short, the clergymen who formed the majority of those present were indignant. Many threatened to leave if such unseemly females were admitted. But the ladies were allowed to enter the hall, and the convention began. When the secretary closed his annual report by welcoming the formation of the Woman's Temperance Society, one of the ministers burst out with a furious and almost hysterical speech. He fiercely opposed any recognition of the new woman's society, saying its members were a "hybrid species, half man and half woman, belonging to neither sex." This society and the woman's rights movement "must be put down, cut up root and branch."

At this, the whole convention broke into an uproar. There were angry arguments over whether the female delegates should be allowed to take part in the proceedings. A few of the male delegates tried to defend the women, but were shouted down. Only once did a woman, Susan Anthony, try to speak. There were cries of "Hear the lady!" "Let her speak!" and even louder cries of "Never! Never!" She was ruled out of order and peremptorily told to sit down. The debate raged for the rest of the session, with the women remaining silent. At the end, the president ruled against them. Though they had been invited, they would not be allowed to participate.

It was very like what had happened at the World Anti-Slavery Convention in 1840, which had convinced Lucretia Mott and Elizabeth Stanton of the need for a woman's rights movement. Susan Anthony, sitting in enforced silence as they had done, felt the same anger and chagrin. Now she too was convinced that before she could work for any reform, she must first overcome the handicap of being a woman. And the best way to do this was to yield to Mrs. Stanton's urgings and transfer her energies to the woman's rights movement.

That fall, in September 1852, Susan Anthony attended the third National Woman's Rights Convention, held that year in Syracuse. It was her formal introduction to the movement. Mrs. Stanton was not there; she was home waiting for the imminent birth of her fifth child. But Susan met the other activists, the people with whom she would work closely for years to come: Lucretia Mott, who presided, Martha Wright, Ernestine Rose, Antoinette Brown, Paulina Wright Davis, and many others, including male supporters of the movement like James Mott and Gerrit Smith. She had heard about all of them long before the convention, and was delighted to meet them at last. By the end of the sessions, she was fully committed to woman's rights and to the people working for them.

It was the largest and most important woman's rights convention yet held. More than 2000 attended, with delegates from eight states and Canada. Lucretia Mott was elected permanent president. Four years earlier, at the gathering in Rochester, Mrs. Mott had been so disturbed when a woman presided that she and Mrs. Stanton had left the platform. Now, however, she calmly took the chair and conducted the meeting with no hesitation. Susan Anthony and Martha Wright were chosen as secretaries.

One of the problems of the early feminist leaders was to persuade women to stop thinking of themselves as genteel ladies and to get down to serious business as citizens, women, and people. Many of the speakers at the convention had no experience with large groups. They spoke in the same soft, gentle tones that one would use in a parlor. People in the back of the hall couldn't hear a word. After one of these unheard speeches,

Susan Anthony suggested that women with weak voices should have their papers read by someone who could speak loudly. Paulina Wright Davis, who had presided over the earlier Worcester conventions, disagreed. She said, "Ladies did not come here to screech; they came to behave like ladies and to speak like ladies."

Susan Anthony retorted that being ladylike was beside the point; the aim of anyone reading a paper was to be heard. The Reverend Samuel May, one of the few ministers who warmly supported woman's rights, agreed with her and said ladies could adjust their voices to the occasion. When a lady wanted to call a child home, he said, she would not go to the door, modestly lower her head, and call him in a soft, ladylike voice. Instead, "you would fix your eye on him and shout, 'Jim, come home!'" If these same ladies would hold their heads up, he explained, and address their remarks to the people in the last row, they would have no difficulty in being heard.

Susan Anthony herself had what one newspaper called "a capital voice," and no one ever missed a word of what she said, no matter how large the auditorium. She never allowed the trivializing image of "ladylike demeanor" to stand in the way of her serious objectives.

Some who couldn't attend the convention in person, like Angelina Grimké, William Lloyd Garrison, and Horace Greeley, sent letters of encouragement and advice. Mrs. Stanton's letter, read aloud by Susan Anthony, created a great stir. It contained three controversial ideas. The first was the question: "Should not all women living in States where woman has the right to hold property refuse to pay taxes, so long as she is unrepresented in the government of that State?" This was to become a leading argument for woman suffrage. One of the causes of the Revolutionary War was the colonial resentment of "taxation without representation." Now women, without the right to vote, were in the same position. If American men had felt this was reason enough for rebellion, why were they subjecting women to the same injustice?

Her second point was a demand that women should be admitted to the same jobs and professions as men, and therefore should be educated together with men. "We need precisely the same education; and we therefore claim that the best colleges of our country be open to us." Her last and most disturbing comment was that religion, instead of making a woman "noble and free . . . has made her bondage but more certain and lasting, her degradation more helpless and complete."

The question of religion was a touchy one. Mrs. Stanton was convinced that the church, with its teachings of female inferiority and the submission of wives to husbands, was one of the greatest barriers to the free development of women. But many women who believed in and worked for woman's rights were also devout churchgoers. They were upset by Mrs. Stanton's attack on religion. The Reverend Antoinette Brown tried to offset their uneasiness by offering a resolution stating that the Bible *did* recognize "the rights, duties, and privileges of woman as a public teacher, as every way equal with those of man; that it enjoins upon her no subjection that is not enjoined upon him."

An angry discussion followed, during which belligerent ministers, who had come to the convention in an attempt to disrupt it, read aloud passages from the Bible to disprove Antoinette Brown's contention of equality. They read passages like "Let your women be silent in the churches; for it is not permitted unto them to speak, but they are commanded to be under obedience," and "Likewise, ye wives, be in subjection to your own husbands."

Ernestine Rose took the floor and spoke strongly against the resolution, saying the convention should not take any official position on Biblical interpretation. Its concern was entirely with "human rights and freedom, based upon the laws of humanity." Any introduction of the Bible would cause endless dissension. It was enough that the clerical enemies of woman's rights used the Bible as a weapon; for the women to hand them this weapon would be a great error. She was supported by Lucretia Mott and by enough of those present to defeat the resolution.

From then on, Susan Anthony tried to keep religion out of the conventions. She felt that nothing was gained by wrangling over theology. Such discussions only created division, solved nothing, and wasted valuable time.

The newspapers and clergy went to work on this convention as on all the others. It was called the Bloomer Convention, the Tomfoolery Convention, the "silly rant of brawling women." The men who took part in it were called "preachers of such damnable doctrines and accursed heresies, as would make demons of the pit shudder to hear." James Gordon Bennett joined in the attack. "How did woman first become subject to man?" he asked in the *Herald*. ". . . By her nature, her sex . . . but happier than she would be in any other condition, just because it is the law of her nature."

A Syracuse minister was so disturbed about the growing threat of the defiant and independent "new woman" that he ordered the women in his congregation not to wear the bloomer outfit, and preached a strong anti-woman's-rights sermon, which he had printed and distributed to ministers throughout the state. There was an immediate urgency, he said, to "head off this new movement of women." If it was not checked now, it might soon be too late.

But for Susan Anthony the point of no return had already been passed. At this convention she had become irrevocably committed to woman's rights.

For a short time after the convention, Susan Anthony continued to work for temperance. With Amelia Bloomer she traveled through New York State in the spring of 1853, giving temperance lectures. But her original impetus was gone; she now considered temperance a lesser reform. More and more in her talks she stressed, not the generalized virtues of temperance, but the specific problems of women whose marriages were unhappily affected by their husbands' drinking. The way to handle these problems, she said, was to give women the right to divorce alcoholic husbands, the right to keep their own earnings, and, above all, the right to vote for these rights, which men would not, of their own volition, give to women.

Elizabeth Stanton, as president of the Woman's State Temperance Society, was also emphasizing the need for gaining these rights before women could do much about temperance. By the time the first annual convention of the society was held in June 1853, at Rochester, both Mrs. Stanton and Miss Anthony had stirred up a good deal of opposition among the more conservative members.

"It has been objected," said Mrs. Stanton in her opening speech, "that we do not confine ourselves to the subject of temperance, but talk too much about woman's rights, divorce and the church." She went on to explain that it was necessary to talk about woman's rights "because many, instead of listening to what we had to say on temperance, have questioned the right of woman to speak on any subject." Women would not be able to work effectively for temperance until their right to speak was first established.

This was the same point the Grimké sisters had made when male antislavery workers had objected to their speaking in public. It was this frustration over being denied the right to speak publicly for reform that led many women out of the temperance and abolition movements into the battle for woman's rights.

In spite of her explanation, Mrs. Stanton's emphasis on woman's rights was regarded by some women as altogether too radical. They were shocked at her support of divorce on the grounds of drunkenness; they were offended by her attack on the church for its subjection of women. They would have liked to depose her as president of the Woman's State Temperance Society, but they were in the minority and by themselves could do nothing.

They could, however, push through an amendment to the society's constitution which would allow men to participate as full members. Mrs. Stanton was strongly opposed, saying men would take control, which is exactly what they did. Once the men had been accepted, they demanded that the organization have nothing to do with woman's rights. They also printed an opposition ticket, which defeated Mrs. Stanton as president by three votes. She was elected vice president instead, and Susan Anthony reelected secretary; but they refused to serve and resigned from the organization.

It was taken over by a conservative group who felt that the instrument of reform should be prayer rather than woman's rights. Before long it became evident that prayer was not enough, and the society fell apart.

Susan Anthony was distressed over what amounted to a defeat of the progressive forces in the woman's temperance movement; but Elizabeth Stanton was, if anything, relieved. Now she could devote all her efforts to woman's rights. She wrote to Susan Anthony: "Now, Susan, I do beg of you . . . to waste no more powder on the Woman's State Temperance Society. We have other and bigger fish to fry."

Susan Anthony was at last ready to give up temperance work, but there was still a tag end to clear away.

In September of that year, 1853, New York City broke out in a rash of special activities. There were two temperance conventions, an antislavery convention, a woman's rights convention, and the first world's fair to be held in the United States. The first temperance convention and the antislavery meeting passed off without incident, but the second temperance convention ran into trouble.

It started when the Reverend Antoinette Brown, an accredited delegate, tried to speak. She stood on the platform for an hour and a half while a violent argument raged over the propriety of a woman speaking. One minister kept shouting, "Shame on the woman!" Others called out, "She shan't speak!" In the end, she had to leave the hall. The argument continued for three days, with Susan Anthony—who was also a delegate —listening but unable to take any part. The final decision was against women, but Miss Anthony had also come to a decision: if it took her whole lifetime, she resolved, she would never rest until women had the right to speak freely at any public gathering, on any subject.

Drawn by the conventions and the World's Fair, an excitement-seeking mob had been forming. When the woman's rights convention opened, after the other three had ended, the mob descended gleefully upon it. They yelled, bellowed, screamed, hissed, stamped their feet, and carried on so that it was almost impossible to conduct any business in spite of attempts, first by Horace Greeley and then by the late-arriving police, to quiet them. Greeley had a brief fistfight with one of the hecklers.

After the opening session, the *Tribune* and William Cullen Bryant's *Evening Post* were the only New York newspapers to criticize the disrupters, while the others turned their attacks against the women. As usual, the *Herald* was the most venomous; it called the women "unsexed in mind" and "barren fools," and their meeting the "Woman's Wrong Convention."

Horace Greeley had the last word, however, when he said that the hostile mob and the equally hostile press were doing the woman's rights movement a good turn: "Nothing is so good for a weak and unpopular movement as this sort of opposition.

. . . The mass of people throughout the country who might otherwise not know of its existence, will have their attention called and their sympathies enlisted in its behalf." Greeley was right. The entire country became aware of the movement and, even more important, began to take it seriously.

Certainly Susan Anthony and Elizabeth Stanton took it more seriously than ever before. From this time on, the main purpose of their lives was the achievement of equal rights, and of respect for women as fully competent members of the human race.

They worked closely together in a remarkable dovetailing of talents. Mrs. Stanton was an incisive speaker and writer. Her ideas were grounded in years of reading and thinking on a wide range of subjects, with special concentration on law. There is no doubt that if Elizabeth Stanton had been the boy her father so ardently wished she had been, she would have become an outstanding lawyer and probably an able politician as well.

For Susan Anthony, speaking and writing were difficult. She was very good at collecting and organizing facts, at assembling material for speeches; but she lacked the easy assurance of Elizabeth Stanton and Lucy Stone. Her special genius lay in organization. She was a natural executive. She could arrange every detail of a meeting, from getting the handbills printed and hiring the auditorium, to planning the agenda and getting just the right speakers. She had formidable energy and drive, and could inspire others by the very strength of her own dedication to the cause.

Mrs. Stanton admitted that there were times when she needed Miss Anthony's drive to get herself started: "It is often said . . . that she has been my good angel, always pushing and goading me to work, and that but for her pertinacity I should never have accomplished the little I have. On the other hand it has been said that I forged the thunderbolts and she fired them."

This last description applied largely to the early years. Though she was the better speaker of the two, Mrs. Stanton was frequently unable to get away from her increasing family, and Susan Anthony would have to make the speech instead. This was hard for Miss Anthony, who at this time had no confidence in her ability as a speaker. But with the script prepared for her, she managed to deliver it—to fire the thunderbolts forged by Mrs. Stanton.

Later, when Mrs. Stanton could get away from her household, they went on tours together, addressing groups of women. In each new town Susan Anthony spent the day making arrangements while Mrs. Stanton lay down for a nap. By the time the meeting was held, Mrs. Stanton was refreshed and relaxed, with her speech all prepared. Susan Anthony, worn out and with no time even to think about what she was going to say, made a poor showing by contrast. Some reporters said this revealed the difference between a poised, assured married woman and a tense, unhappy spinster.

She was perfectly willing to let Mrs. Stanton have all the glory, feeling it was for the good of the cause. In this, as in most things, Susan Anthony was as selfless as humanly possible. She never allowed her own ego or personal feelings to interfere with the larger goal of woman's rights. She had no trace of vanity or self-importance. Much later, when she had already become a world-famous figure, she entered a convention hall with Carrie Chapman Catt, her successor as president of the Suffrage Association. On Miss Anthony's appearance, the audience began to applaud enthusiastically. She whispered to Mrs. Catt, "I wonder what they are clapping about!"

At another convention, accompanied this time by Anna Howard Shaw, who would also become a president of the association, she arrived late. Again the audience burst into excited applause. "What has happened, Anna?" she asked. "*You* happened, Aunt Susan," was the reply.

Nevertheless, she had to confess her pleasure when, on one occasion, it was she and not Mrs. Stanton who became the star. On this trip, Mrs. Stanton returned home after completing her arranged schedule, leaving Susan Anthony to carry on alone. She wrote to her family: "I miss Mrs. Stanton, still I can not but enjoy the feeling that the people call on *me*, and the fact that I have an opportunity to sharpen my wits a little by answering questions and doing the chatting, instead of merely sitting . . . and listening to the brilliant scintillations as they emanate from her never-exhausted magazine. . . . Whoever goes into a parlor or before an audience with that woman does it at the cost of a fearful overshadowing, a price which I have paid for the last ten years, and that cheerfully, because I felt that our cause was most profited by her being seen and heard, and my best work was making the way clear for her."

In those early years, Mrs. Stanton had one baby after another until there were seven, five boys and two girls, most of them boiling over with energy, always getting into trouble and requiring immediate attention from their harassed mother. She was caught between the demands of her family and her zealous impatience to do something about woman's rights. She wrote to Susan Anthony: "Oh, Susan, Susan! Susan! . . . How much I do long to be free from housekeeping and children, so as to have some time to read, and think, and write. But it may be well for me to understand all the trials of woman's lot, that I may more eloquently proclaim them when the time comes."

It often became too much even for someone as invincible as Elizabeth Stanton. "My ceaseless cares begin to wear upon my spirit," she wrote to Susan. "I feel it in my innermost soul and am resolved to seek some relief. Therefore, I say adieu to the public for a time, for I must give all my moments and my thoughts to my children."

When Susan Anthony received such a letter, she would go immediately to the Stantons', take over some of the domestic chores, and rouse Mrs. Stanton to renewed action by telling her of some fresh injustice to women. She was always successful. "With the cares of a large family I might, in time, like too many women, have become wholly absorbed in a narrow family selfishness, had not my friend been continually exploring new fields for missionary labors." Susan Anthony would arrive with a "little portmanteau, stuffed with facts . . . the statistics of women robbed of their property, shut out of some college, half paid for their work, the reports of some disgraceful trial; injustice enough to turn any woman's thoughts from stockings and puddings."

To relieve the pressure on Mrs. Stanton, Susan would help with the "stockings and puddings." She helped especially with the children, who soon regarded her as a member of the family. Susan Anthony loved young children and was very good with them, but the young Stantons considered her a mixed blessing. Whenever they saw her coming, they knew their unrestrained freedom would be toned down. Their indulgent mother would withdraw her attentions from them and retire to her desk, while they would be left in the sterner care of Aunt Susan. She would keep them from disturbing their mother and enforce some measure of order and quiet while the serious work of winning rights for women went on. The relationship between the Stanton children and Susan Anthony became so close that in later years Mrs. Stanton, writing to Miss Anthony, referred to them as "our children."

When the children were safely occupied or sleeping, the two women would sit down and get to work. In her autobiography, *Eighty Years and More*, Elizabeth Stanton describes this small but vital nucleus of the woman's rights movement, made possible and reinforced by the extraordinary association of the two friends: "We would get out our pens and write articles for papers, or a petition to the legislature; indite letters to the faithful, here and there; stir up the women in Ohio, Pennsylvania, or Massachusetts. . . . We never met without issuing a pronunciamento on some question. In thought and sympathy we were one, and in the division of labor we exactly complemented each other. . . . We did better work than either could alone. While she is slow and analytical in composition, I am rapid and synthetic. I am the better writer, she the better critic. She supplied the facts and statistics, I the philosophy and rhetoric, and together, we have made arguments that have stood unshaken through the storms of long years. . . . Our speeches may be considered the united product of our two brains. . . .

"Night after night, by an old-fashioned fireplace, we plotted and planned the coming agitation; how, when, and where each entering wedge could be driven, by which women might be recognized and their rights assured. Speedily the State was aflame with disturbances. . . . Every right achieved, to enter a college, to study a profession, to labor in some new industry, or to advocate a reform measure was contended for inch by inch. . . . So closely interwoven have been our lives, our purposes, and experiences that, separated, we have a feeling of incompleteness—united, such strength of self-assertion that no ordinary obstacles, difficulties, or dangers ever appear to us insurmountable."

At this time there was still no formal woman's rights organization. The movement so far had consisted of local and national conventions, with a central steering committee carrying over between them. The question of a permanent organization had been raised at the national convention in 1852, but the idea was rejected. It was felt that a formal structure would be too rigid and might prevent the development of new ideas. Ernestine Rose said that organizations were like the bandages used to restrict the natural growth of Chinese women's feet.

Between conventions, individual women did what they

could for the movement. Lucy Stone lectured on woman's rights along with antislavery and temperance. Amelia Bloomer continued to devote *The Lily* "to the Interests of Women," and gave talks on woman's rights. Paulina Wright Davis established *The Una*, whose masthead read "Devoted to the Elevation of Women." Lucretia Mott spoke at local conventions on woman's rights and antislavery. Martha Wright often came to visit Mrs. Stanton and helped with whatever project was going on. But no one worked as doggedly and exclusively for women as Elizabeth Stanton and Susan Anthony.

They wrote articles and letters, made speeches, sent petitions to state legislatures, urged women to attend all kinds of conventions and meetings for the purpose of establishing the right to speak. Susan Anthony herself attended every annual New York State Teachers convention, with the expressed—and ultimately successful—aim of forcing the men to allow women to take equal part in the proceedings. In every way possible they roused the country to an awareness of injustice against women, and roused women to an awareness of their subordinate position and of the steps they could take to improve their lives.

Theodore Tilton, the editor and orator who worked for abolition and woman's rights, described them as sitting together in their parlor, diligently forging "all manner of projectiles, from fireworks to thunderbolts. . . . I know of no more pertinacious incendiaries in the whole country. . . . This noise-making twain are the two sticks of a drum, keeping up what Daniel Webster called 'the rub-a-dub of agitation.' "

15

Who Holds the Purse Strings

He who steals my purse may steal trash, but he who holds the purse strings controls my life.

—Harriot Stanton Blatch,
in *Challenging Years*, 1940

To be poor alone, to have to live without a husband, to look forward to a life in which there would be nothing of a career, almost nothing to do, to await the vacuity of an existence in which she would be useful to no one, was a destiny which she could teach herself to endure, because it might probably be forced upon her by necessity. . . . The lot of a woman, as she often told herself, was wretched, unfortunate, almost degrading. For a woman such as herself there was no path open to her energy, other than that of getting a husband.

—Anthony Trollope, *He Knew He Was Right*, 1868–9

"A man who is a nobody [said Dorothy Stanbury] can perhaps make himself somebody,—or, at any rate, he can try; but a woman has no means of trying. She is a nobody, and a nobody she must remain."

—Ibid.

In 1848 the Married Woman's Property Act had been passed in New York State, giving a married woman the right to hold in her own name any property inherited or received as a gift. Her husband could no longer dispose of it without her consent, nor could it be seized to pay his debts. This was a step forward, gained after a long struggle, but it was only a very short step.

Even after the act was passed, if a wife asked her husband to sell the property for her, he could keep the money received. She couldn't sell it herself, since women were not permitted to sign contracts. Nor could she leave it to someone of her own choice without her husband's approval; a married woman's will was invalid without her husband's signature. If she died without a will, he had the right to all her property; if he died without a will, she received only a third of his. And she still had no right to any money earned by her own efforts. Her husband was allowed to collect her wages and those of his children, and to spend the money as he wished. She had no rights of guardianship over her children. Her husband could apprentice them without her permission; he could even put them to work to pay off his debts. In his will, he could appoint someone other than his wife as guardian of their children. In all cases of divorce or separation, custody of the children was automatically given to the father, no matter how unfit he might be.

There was still a long way to go.

In 1853, after attending the multiple conventions in New York City, Susan Anthony went to Cleveland for the fourth annual National Woman's Rights Convention. In recognition of her talent for raising money, she was made head of the finance committee. When the meeting ended, she went on a three-week tour of New York State, speaking and asking for contributions to help pay the expenses of the conventions, which were becoming larger and more elaborate affairs.

A year earlier she had traveled through the same region organizing women's temperance societies. Now she found that all but one of these had disbanded because the women, as housewives financially dependent on their husbands, had no money of their own with which to carry on the work of temperance.

Susan Anthony had never before fully understood what it meant to be entirely without money of one's own. Her progressive father had never claimed his children's earnings and, when she wasn't working, had always helped her generously. He was an enthusiastic supporter of her efforts for woman's rights. She could count on him not only to advance her own expenses, but to act as security for any bills or debts she might run up in arranging for conventions or printing petitions or handbills. If enough money wasn't collected at lectures or through contributions to cover these bills, Daniel Anthony cheerfully made up the deficit. It wasn't until this fund-raising trip that the full impact of financial dependence was brought home to her.

A passage in her journal written at this time reveals not only the reaction to her new insight but the practical working of her mind: "Thus as I passed from town to town was I made to feel the great evil of woman's utter dependence on man. . . . I never before took in so fully the grand idea of pecuniary independence. Woman must have a purse of her own." Without the right to her own money, "there is no true freedom for woman." She could get this right "only through legislation. If this is so, then the sooner the demand is made, the sooner it will be granted. It must be done by petition, and this, too, of the very next legislature. How can the work be started? We must hold a convention and adopt some plan of united action."

She called a local convention in Rochester as soon as she returned home, and suggested that a state woman's rights convention should be held in February 1854 in Albany, where the

New York Legislature would be in session. She would ask Elizabeth Stanton to address the joint judiciary committee of the Legislature, asking that a law be passed giving married women the right to keep their own earnings, to have the same rights as men regarding the making of wills and inheriting property, and to have equal guardianship with their husbands over their children. One set of petitions asking for these rights and another asking for woman suffrage would be presented to the Legislature at the same time.

These suggestions were accepted, and Susan Anthony put them into effect with her usual efficiency. She selected sixty women and put them in charge, one to a county, of circulating the petitions. She canvassed the Rochester area herself. For ten weeks of a cold winter, these women traveled around the state, holding meetings and walking from house to house to get signatures. In those days, when it was considered not quite respectable for women to travel alone, it was difficult for them to find adequate places in which to sleep or even get a meal. But perhaps the worst discomfort came from the doors slammed in their faces, not by men but by antagonistic women. Many said they had all the rights they wanted; others boasted that "they had husbands, thank God, to look after their interests, and they needed no new laws to protect their rights."

There were enough women, however, who did feel the need of new laws to put 5931 signatures on the petitions for the right of women to keep their own earnings and have equal guardianship of their children, and 4164 on those asking for suffrage. On the basis of this showing, the Legislature agreed to let Elizabeth Stanton speak for the bills.

Mrs. Stanton found this speech especially difficult to prepare. With a large household to care for, she had little time for concentrated effort and no opportunity to do the necessary legal research. She wrote to Susan Anthony, asking her to get a lawyer to look up the required statutes and cases. "You see, while I am about the house, surrounded by my children, washing dishes, baking, sewing, etc., I can think up many points, but I cannot search books. . . . I seldom have one hour undisturbed in which to sit down and write. Men who can, when they wish to write a document, shut themselves up for days with their thoughts and their books, know little of what difficulties a woman must surmount to get off a tolerable production."

Elizabeth Stanton managed to finish her speech and then set off for Albany, taking along her two youngest children. On the way, she stopped off at Johnstown in response to a summons from her father. Judge Cady had been terribly upset when he learned from an Albany newspaper that his daughter was going to address the Legislature. He had been angrily opposed to her part in the Seneca Falls convention and in those that followed; he had thought her out of her mind when she put on the bloomer costume; but this was the worst yet. She would be speaking before an audience of men, most of whom were trained lawyers or politicians. The newspaper account had specifically said that Mrs. Stanton was the daughter of Judge Cady; any failure or humiliation would reflect upon him.

He urged, commanded, pleaded with her not to deliver the speech. She would not yield. The house in which the Stantons were living in Seneca Falls still belonged to the judge; he offered to give it to her in exchange for canceling the address. She refused. He threatened to cut her out of his will, but she refused again. At last he gave up, but asked her to read the speech to him.

They sat in his office while she read it. By this time she was already a fairly experienced speaker, but she had never been more nervous. "On no occasion, before or since, was I ever more embarrassed—an audience of one, and the one of all others whose approbation I most desired, whose disapproval I most feared. I knew he condemned the whole movement, and was deeply grieved at the active part I had taken. . . . I was fully aware that I was about to address a wholly unsympathetic audience."

When she finished, he remained silent a long time. Then he asked how she, with her "happy, comfortable life, with all your wants and needs supplied," could "feel so keenly the wrongs" done to women. To his consternation, she replied that she had first learned of these injustices "here, in your office, when a child, listening to the complaints women made to you."

He had no reply to that, but he commended her on the strength and clarity of her arguments, and proceeded to look up some further legal illustrations for her to use. He suggested a few other improvements, and together they put the finishing touches on the text. He continued to disapprove of her public appearances, though now and then helping her with the legal aspects of her speeches, looking up the pertinent laws, "desirous that whatever I gave to the public should be carefully prepared."

Judge Cady need not have worried. His daughter's address was followed with close attention and respect by the male audience. It was filled with concrete examples of the legal handicaps of women, and specific in the changes women wanted. It demanded "the full recognition of all our rights as citizens, persons, property-holders, tax-payers."

She detailed the legal disadvantages of married women: a wife had "no civil existence, no social freedom. . . . She can own nothing, sell nothing. She has no right even to the wages she earns; her person, her time, her services are the property of another. . . . She can get no redress for wrongs in her own name." If a wife managed, in some way, to have money in a savings bank, her husband had the legal right to withdraw it without her permission and "to use as he may see fit." And she had no share in the guardianship of her children.

To add to her humiliation, a husband had the "right to whip his wife . . . to shut her up in a room, and administer whatever moderate chastisement he may deem necessary to insure obedience to his wishes, and for her healthful moral development," as though she were a child in need of parental discipline. By the same token, he had the right also to prevent her from seeing her own friends.

All of these were specific miscarriages of justice which men were able to understand, even if they preferred, for one reason or another, not to remedy. In her impassioned conclusion, she touched upon another kind of injustice: the psychic wounds inflicted by the demeaning status of women. "Would to God you could know the burning indignation that fills woman's soul when she turns over the pages of your statute books, and sees there how like feudal barons you freemen hold your women. Would that you could know the humiliation she feels for her sex, when she thinks of all the beardless boys in your law offices, learning these ideas of one-sided justice—taking their first lessons in contempt for all womankind—being indoctrinated into the incapacities of their mothers, and the lordly, absolute rights of man over all women, children, and property."

She appealed to her listeners to follow the golden rule: " 'Do unto others as you would have others do unto you.' This . . . is all we ask at your hands." Women were asking for no special laws. They wanted only what American men had asked for themselves "since the *Mayflower* cast anchor beside Plymouth Rock; and simply on the ground that the rights of every human being are the same and identical."

The speech, together with the petitions which had been collected under the direction of Susan Anthony, received the approval of many legislators; but there was angry opposition from others. One Assemblyman accused the women of a "desire to unsex every female in the land, and to set the whole community ablaze with unhallowed fire." Their purpose, he said, was to destroy marriage: "It is well known that the object of these unsexed women is to overthrow the most sacred of our institutions, to set at defiance the Divine law which declares man and wife to be one, and establish on its ruins what will be in fact and in principle but a species of legalized adultery. . . . Are we . . . to give the least countenance to claims so preposterous, disgraceful, and criminal as are embodied in this address? Are we to put the stamp of truth upon the libel here set forth, that men and women, in the matrimonial relation, are to be equal?"

The petitions were referred to a committee which, after hearing addresses by Susan Anthony and Ernestine Rose, drew up a greatly modified version of the women's requests and sent it, in turn, to a specially appointed select committee. This body closed the whole matter by throwing the responsibility back on God: "A higher power than that from which emanates legislative enactments has given forth the mandate that man and woman shall not be equal . . . civil power must, in its enactments, recognize this inequality. We can not obliterate it if we would, and legal inequalities must follow."

This was at least an admission that there were inequalities. Senator William Seward, former governor of New York and later Abraham Lincoln's secretary of state, summed it up when he said to Elizabeth Stanton: "You have the argument, but custom and prejudice are against you, and they are stronger than truth and logic."

The women did not give up. Susan Anthony again organized a large group to canvass the state and collect signatures on new petitions. She arranged meetings, hired speakers, and planned a long-range campaign to secure changes in New York State law. Before her appearance in the Legislature, Mrs. Stanton had given a preview of her speech at the Woman's Rights Convention in Albany. Susan Anthony had had 50,000 copies printed, and had put a copy on the desk of each member of the Legislature. The rest were distributed throughout the state, together with new pamphlets written by Mrs. Stanton and William Henry Channing, the Unitarian minister, who helped the woman's movement in many ways.

Susan Anthony herself made an extended tour through the state, holding meetings, lecturing, getting signatures on the petitions, organizing local woman's rights societies, and collecting money to pay for the expenses of the campaign. She took care of all the advance work: she wrote to local sheriffs, asking them to put up her posters, insert notices in the local newspapers, and prepare meeting places. She planned her meetings for every other day, allowing a day in between for travel and for completing arrangements in each town.

She had one speech: she gave half at an afternoon session, the other half in the evening. After her talk, she would get signatures for the petitions and sell pamphlets to raise money for the expenses of the next meeting. The attendance varied from just a few mildly interested people to a large number from the surrounding countryside, drawn largely out of curiosity to see a female speaker.

She charged a small admission fee for the evening sessions. Careful records were kept of every penny, even to items like "56 cents for four pounds of candles to light the courthouse." At the end of her trip, she found that she had raised $2367, of which she had spent $2291, leaving a balance of $76, which she put aside to pay for the next trip. She received no money for her own efforts, nor did she want any.

She did all this entirely alone, traveling under the most uncomfortable conditions during one of the coldest winters in New York. Some of the towns could be reached only by a long sleighride from the nearest railway line, and the roads were often blocked by high drifting snow. She stayed in unheated hotels, where she literally had to break the ice in the water pitcher in order to wash.

When the Legislature was again in session, she went to Albany to present the petitions. They were turned over to the judiciary committee, which this time did something worse than denounce them or hand the problem over to God. It treated the whole thing as a huge joke, saying in its report that women were already pampered and coddled: "The ladies always have the best place and choicest titbit at the table . . . the best seat in the cars, carriages and sleighs. . . . They have their choice on which side of the bed they will lie." What more did they want? If anything, the "gentlemen are the sufferers."

Such patronizing dismissal was supposed to put women like Susan Anthony, Elizabeth Stanton, and Ernestine Rose in their proper, abashed place, but it had exactly the reverse effect. Whatever respect they might have had for the superior male intellect, the gravity of male purpose, and the dignity of political leaders was eroded by this kind of trivial response. Instead of feeling like childish innocents, as intended by the legislators, the women began to regard politicians with amused contempt or bored impatience.

The ladies hadn't really expected to change the laws the first time around, nor were they discouraged by the second failure. Year after year, they continued to bombard the Legislature with petitions and speeches. When they failed one year, they immediately began preparing for the next year's campaign.

In March 1860 they were at last successful. In that year, Susan Anthony suggested an amendment to the Married Woman's Property Act of 1848 which would broaden its provisions considerably. By then, public, or at least legislative, opinion on the ability of women to handle their own money had advanced so much that her suggestion was taken seriously. More than that, the judiciary committee, which had ridiculed the earlier attempts to change the law, not only accepted the proposed bill, but invited Elizabeth Stanton to speak on the measure before a joint session of the Legislature.

In her speech, Mrs. Stanton disposed of the old cliché about the need to protect women from the "grossness and vulgarity of public life. . . . When you talk, gentlemen, of sheltering woman from the rough winds and revolting scenes of real life, you must be either talking for effect, or wholly ignorant of what the facts of life are." There are women, she said, who face the harshest facts of life right at their own firesides, women who are married to drunkards, to "vile, vulgar, brutal" men. Women were tired of the kind of "protection" which stripped them of everything. "True," she said ironically, "we are not so strong, so wise, so crafty as you are, but if . . . we can by great industry earn fifty cents a day, we would rather buy bread and clothes for our children than cigars and champagne for our legal protectors."

The bill was passed the next day. It declared any property received by a woman to be her own, not subject to control or interference by her husband. It gave a woman the right, at last, to keep her own earnings, to use or invest them in her own name, and to bargain, sell, and carry on any trade or perform any services on her own account. She could enter into contracts, sue, and have joint guardianship over her children. As a widow, she was to have the same property rights as the husband would have at her death.

It is hard today to realize what a tremendous victory this law was for women. It took them out of the legal category of "children, idiots, and lunatics," and went a long way toward abolishing the principle of a woman's "legal death" in marriage, where man and wife became one "and that one is the husband." Aside from suffrage, this law was the most important of the women's goals. It had taken years of the hardest kind of work, years of putting up with ridicule and abuse, not only from men but from the very women who would benefit directly from the new law.

These women soon took their new rights for granted. Only a

few years earlier they had severely criticized the "unladylike" behavior of feminists who had won the rights for them. And when the next step toward full equality was to be taken, they would again refuse to help and again censure those who, inch by painful and humiliating inch, fought to advance the position of all women.

16

Lucy Stone
and the Lucy Stoners

I never perform the marriage ceremony without a renewed sense of the iniquity of . . . a system by which "man and wife are one, and that one is the husband."
> —Rev. Thomas Wentworth Higginson, after officiating at
> the marriage of Lucy Stone and Henry Blackwell, 1855

It is the duty of every woman to resent the cowardly indignity which classes educated, virtuous women as the political inferiors of the meanest and most degraded men.
> —Henry Blackwell, 1871

I would not object to marriage, if it were not that women throw away every plan and purpose of their own life, to conform to the plans and purposes of the man's life.
> —Susan B. Anthony, 1888

New York was not the only state in which there was action. All during the 1850s, conventions and meetings were held in many parts of the country. In 1854 a Married Woman's Property Act was passed in Massachusetts. Lectures on woman's rights were given in Maine and as far west as Wisconsin.

Awareness and activity were increasing everywhere but in the South, where an authoritarian society, "southern chivalry," and the almost complete lack of a reform spirit kept women firmly in their place. That place might be an active one, since there were many women who managed large plantations with competence and assurance, but it was also static and isolated. In a largely agricultural economy, plantations and even small farms were too widely spaced to provide the opportunity, as in the small towns of the North, for women to get together and compare problems or take concerted action.

There was, of course, no antislavery movement to stir women up and send them on to a movement of their own. Change and innovation were avoided; efforts were concentrated on keeping things exactly as they were. "Things" meant slavery, for the most part, but the position of women became immobilized as part of the whole dead weight of rigid southern institutions. And since many of the leaders of the woman's rights movement in the North were also outspoken abolitionists, woman's rights and antislavery became linked. To advocate the first might imply the second, which was enough to throttle any stirring that might have been made toward woman's rights in the South.

A few ripples did manage to reach the area. In 1853, Lucretia Mott spoke in Kentucky on the evils of slavery and on woman's rights. A few weeks later, Lucy Stone spoke on woman's rights in Virginia and Kentucky. One newspaper called Mrs. Mott "this brazen infidel," but most listeners were charmed by the quiet, sincere manner of the speakers, however much they disagreed with what was said. But these were rare incursions into an otherwise untouched region.

Lucy Stone was especially busy, traveling long distances to speak on temperance, abolition, and woman's rights. She had determined never to marry but to dedicate her life, as she had told her mother, to pleading "for suffering humanity," especially for the female portion.

In 1850 she had helped organize the first National Woman's Rights Convention in Worcester, Massachusetts. In the middle of the preparations, Lucy Stone had to break off her work and hurry out to Indiana to nurse her brother, ill with cholera. In spite of her care, he died, and she almost died herself of typhoid. As soon as she could travel, she started back east, hoping to arrive in time to attend the convention. On the way, she stopped at a store in Cincinnati where she had been told the abolitionist owners would cash a check for her.

Henry Blackwell, one of the owners, said he would be happy to cash it. As he talked to her, moved by her charm and "the wonderful melody of her voice," he felt she would be just the wife for his older brother, Samuel. Henry was twenty-five, Lucy thirty-two; it never occurred to him to consider himself as a possible suitor. Instead of giving her the money on the spot, he said he would send it to her. He sent it with Samuel, in the romantic hope that a spark would be struck between them. He was disappointed. Samuel found her pleasant but nothing more, gave her the money, and left.

Henry Blackwell was a member of a remarkable family. In its own way, it contributed a great deal to the reform movements, and especially to the position of women, during the nineteenth century. The father had been an active antislavery worker before his early death. The five older children were girls, the four younger, boys. The most famous of the daughters was Elizabeth, who added immensely to what Lucy Stone called "the elevation of my sex" by becoming the first qualified female physician in the United States, and by forcing the highly reluctant medical profession to open its doors a crack for the admission of woman doctors.

After a long struggle to find a medical school that would accept her, Elizabeth entered the Geneva Medical College, graduating in 1849 at the top of her class. Her younger sister Emily also became a doctor. Overcoming formidable barriers at every step, Dr. Elizabeth Blackwell acquired advanced training abroad, and then returned to America, where, in 1857, she established the New York Infirmary for Women and Children. It had an all-female staff, including Dr. Emily Blackwell. Eight months later, Dr. Elizabeth opened a nurses' training school, a rare institution for that period. In 1868, with most medical schools still refusing to admit women, the Blackwell sisters were instrumental in creating the Woman's Infirmary Medical School, which later merged with the Cornell University Medical College when that institution finally admitted women.

The oldest sister, Anna, became a newspaper correspondent in Paris. The youngest girl was an artist and writer. With sisters like these, and with a mother who had the same independence and abilities as her daughters, Henry Blackwell had advanced views about women long before he met Lucy Stone. And as an active abolitionist himself and the son of an abolitionist, he was just as much at home in the world of reform as she was.

He was not in any way overwhelmed by the accomplishments of his older sisters. He was witty, intelligent, energetic, and self-assured.

Three years after his first encounter with Lucy Stone, he went east to find a publisher for a book of poems he had written, and to attend antislavery meetings in New York and Boston. It was 1853, the year of the multiple conventions in New York City. He heard Lucy Stone speak at one of the antislavery gatherings, and was even more attracted by her than in their first meeting. From New York he went to Boston, where he attended the convention to revise the Massachusetts state constitution. Lucy Stone was the only woman to address the convention, asking that the new constitution extend all civil rights to women. Her speech moved the assemblage to tears. Nevertheless, it rejected equal rights for women on the ground that the gentler sex would lose its "feminine grace" if thrown into the harsh world of public affairs.

It dawned on Henry Blackwell, listening to her, that it was he, not his older brother, who should marry Lucy Stone. After the meeting he went to see his father's friend William Lloyd Garrison and asked him for a letter of introduction to Lucy. Garrison agreed, though he thought it futile. Lucy Stone, he explained, had vowed never to marry. She had already turned down several offers, and there was no reason to believe that Henry Blackwell would be any more successful. Blackwell refused to be discouraged, then or later: "I can wait a good while to get Lucy. . . . Jacob, you know, waited patiently 14 years for Rachel."

It looked, at first, as though he would indeed have to be as patient as Jacob. She was glad to meet him again, she was happy to become his friend, but could never be his wife. Marriage would interfere with the work she had laid out for herself. Besides, she believed that marriage "is to a woman a state of slavery."

When Henry Blackwell returned to Ohio, he continued his courtship by correspondence, all through the summer of 1853. He offered to arrange a western speaking tour for her in the fall. He traveled a great deal through several states for his hardware company, and could make detailed arrangements for such a tour. She agreed. Before starting the trip, she went to

Cleveland as a delegate to the fourth National Woman's Rights Convention. Henry went also, in order to see her, and found himself becoming involved in the movement. He made a speech about woman's rights, and was elected as one of the secretaries of the convention.

The lecture tour, a very successful and profitable one, took her through Ohio, Pennsylvania, Missouri, Virginia, and Kentucky. In Cincinnati she stayed with Henry's family. The Blackwells, especially Henry's mother, liked her immediately. Lucy, in turn, was very taken with them. She knew all about Dr. Elizabeth Blackwell and admired her. She found the atmosphere of the whole Blackwell household, so unlike her own, warmly sympathetic.

By the end of the year, she admitted that she loved Henry. But she still objected to the nature of the marriage institution and the unjust laws governing it. He assured her that he shared her views and would publicly renounce all the privileges conferred upon the husband by law. They argued the subject back and forth for almost a year, until at last she began to accept the idea of marriage.

But now she had new doubts. Was she good enough for him? Was she too old for him? When these questions were resolved, others arose. When should they get married? Where should they live? Should Henry continue in business or become a full-time reformer? Back and forth went the letters, with Lucy raising one problem after another and Henry settling each one.

At last, on May 1, 1855, Lucy Stone and Henry Blackwell were married. Before the minister began the ceremony, Henry read the protest which he and Lucy had prepared: "While acknowledging our mutual affection by publicly assuming the relationship of husband and wife, yet in justice to ourselves and a great principle, we deem it a duty to declare that this act . . . implies no sanction of, nor promise of voluntary obedience to, such of the present laws of marriage as refuse to recognize the wife as an independent, rational being, while they confer upon the husband an injurious and unnatural superiority, investing him with legal powers which no honorable man would exercise, and which no man should possess."

There followed specific protests against laws which gave the husband custody of his wife's person, exclusive control and guardianship of their children, ownership of her personal property and use of her real estate, the right to her earnings, and, as a widower, a much larger share in the property of his deceased wife than a widow received in the property of her deceased husband. And "finally, against the whole system by which 'the legal existence of the wife is suspended during marriage,' so that in most States she neither has a legal part in the choice of her residence, nor can she make a will, nor sue or be sued in her own name, nor inherit property." Marriage, they concluded, should be an equal partnership, recognized as such by the law, and "until it is so recognized, married partners should provide against the radical injustice of present laws, by every means in their power. . . . Thus reverencing Law, we enter our earnest protest against rules and customs which are unworthy of the name, since they violate justice, the essence of all Law."

The protest seemed to cover all contingencies; but there was one which had been on Lucy's mind a long time, going back as far as her student days at Oberlin. This was the assumption of the husband's name by the wife. In giving up her own name, a wife lost her individual identity. It would be bad enough to be called Lucy Blackwell—at least she would still be Lucy—but as Mrs. Henry Blackwell she would disappear altogether.

Henry agreed with this view, and had no objection to having her retain her own name; but at the time of the wedding, Lucy had not yet come to any decision about it. It would be a daring and unconventional step, and might cause all kinds of trouble. People would assume they weren't really married. Traveling together would be difficult and embarrassing. There might be legal difficulties. On the other hand, the name of Lucy Stone was already famous. She was proud of her success and didn't relish the thought of submerging Lucy Stone in Mrs. Henry Blackwell.

At first she compromised. She used the name of Lucy Stone Blackwell, just as Mrs. Stanton had deliberately retained her maiden name, always calling herself Elizabeth Cady Stanton. Mrs. Stanton had also refused to use the word "obey" in her wedding ceremony. Angelina Grimké, too, had left out the word when she married Theodore Weld, and at their wedding Weld had also publicly denounced "the vandal law" which gave the husband control of his wife's property.

She was called Lucy Stone Blackwell for a little over a year. Then she asked that in putting her name on an announcement of a forthcoming convention, the "Blackwell" be dropped. Somehow her request was overlooked, and she was listed as "Lucy Stone Blackwell." When she saw this, her accumulating resentment came to a head. In a letter to Susan Anthony she said that when she first caught sight of the offending signature, "it made me faint and sick." From then on, she dropped the Blackwell completely and insisted on being called Lucy Stone. "A wife," she said, "should no more take her husband's name than he should hers." Her only concession was that she should be addressed as "Mrs." Stone. In 1879, Massachusetts allowed women to vote in school elections. Lucy Stone went to register, but when she discovered that she would have to sign as Mrs. Blackwell, she refused, and so forfeited her opportunity to vote.

Elizabeth Stanton and Susan Anthony were delighted. Mrs. Stanton wrote to Mrs. Stone: "Nothing has been done in the woman's rights movement for some time that so rejoiced my heart as the announcement by you of a woman's right to her name." Susan Anthony wrote that she "rejoiced that you have declared, by actual doing, that a woman has a name, and may retain it throughout her life."

Some women in the movement disapproved, however, and wrote to tell her so. She replied that "A thousand times more opposition was made to woman's claim to speak in public," and continued to use the name of Lucy Stone for the rest of her life. Those who followed her example were called "Lucy Stoners." But in spite of Lucy Stone and the Lucy Stoners, the law has been slow to acknowledge the right of a woman to her own name. More than a hundred years later, in the 1970s, the Supreme Court would uphold an Alabama law which required a woman to use her husband's name.

Some eight months later, Lucy's closest friend, Antoinette Brown, married Henry's brother Samuel, the one he had originally selected for Lucy. Susan Anthony was distressed. She had nothing against marriage, but she suspected that Lucy Stone and Antoinette Brown would now be so occupied with domestic cares that they would be unable to continue working for woman's rights. The loss of such competent and experienced workers would be a serious handicap to the movement. She began to feel abandoned, left to carry on all the work herself.

She wrote to Elizabeth Stanton: "Those of you who have the talent to do honor to poor—oh! how poor—womanhood, have all given yourself over to baby-making; and left poor brainless me to do battle alone. It is a shame. Such a body as I might be spared to rock cradles. But it is a crime for you and Lucy Stone and Antoinette Brown to be doing it."

She was even more upset when she realized that it would be impossible to call a national woman's rights convention for 1857. Too many of the leaders would be unable to come. Mrs. Stanton, Lucy Stone, Antoinette Blackwell were involved with babies, recently arrived or on the way. Ernestine Rose was ill.

Susan Anthony had written some blunt letters to Lucy Stone, expressing her fears that Lucy and Antoinette would now become "like other wives . . . and do nothing." Lucy Stone replied with equal acerbity, saying that Susan need have no fears on that score. Antoinette Blackwell had advised Susan to get married herself. "Get a good husband, that's all, dear." Now, when she learned that Lucy Stone was pregnant, Susan Anthony wrote, "Lucy, *neither* of us have *time*—for much *personal* matters." Mrs. Stanton tried to smooth things over. "Let Lucy and Antoinette rest awhile in peace and quietness," she wrote to Susan.

Lucy Stone later resumed her work for woman's rights, and she and Susan Anthony worked together again, but the original rapport between them was broken. A wariness had been created on both sides. Eventually there would be an open break between them, and a great split in the entire movement.

17

The Radical Team of Stanton-Anthony

I declare to you that woman must not depend upon the protection of man, but must be taught to protect herself, and there I take my stand.

—Susan B. Anthony, 1871

A man in marrying gives up no right; but a woman, every right, even the most sacred of all—the right to her own person. . . . Personal freedom is the first right to be proclaimed, and that does not and cannot now belong to the relation of wife, . . . to the financial dependent.

—Elizabeth Cady Stanton, 1857

The woman is uniformly sacrificed to the wife and mother.
—*History of Woman Suffrage*, Vol. I, 1881

After her first speech before the New York Legislature in 1854, Elizabeth Stanton was invited to deliver lectures, for which she would be paid, before large audiences of both sexes. Her father had been so irritated when she proposed to address the Legislature that he had threatened to cut her out of his will. He hadn't done so, perhaps because he recognized the urgent necessity of changing the laws discriminating against women. But he could see no such urgency in these new lectures she was planning, and renewed his threat. He angrily warned her that "your first lecture will be a very expensive one."

She was bitterly offended by his refusal to accept her at her real worth, and by his insistence that she narrowly limit her life and deny her own talents because of her sex. She also resented her husband's growing complaints that she was spending too much time on outside work. Though he was sympathetic to the idea of woman's rights, Henry Stanton wasn't happy about his wife's absences from home and would no doubt have been relieved if she paid less attention to the woman's movement and more to her domestic duties.

She wrote to Susan Anthony: "I passed through a terrible scourging when last at my father's. I cannot tell you how deep the iron entered my soul. I never felt more keenly the degradation of my sex. To think that all in me of which my father would have felt a proper pride had I been a man, is deeply mortifying to him because I am a woman. That thought has stung me to a fierce decision—to speak as soon as I can do myself credit. But the pressure on me just now is too great. Henry sides with my friends, who oppose me in all that is dearest to my heart. They are not willing that I should write even on the woman question. But I will both write and speak. . . . Sometimes, Susan, I struggle in deep waters."

Soon afterward she gave several public lectures. Her father

immediately disinherited her. But before his death in 1859 he changed his will again, restoring her inheritance. His death reminded her again of her "dwarfed womanhood." After he died, she wrote to Susan Anthony: "When I pass the gate of the celestial city and good Peter asks me where I would sit, I shall say, 'Anywhere, so that I am neither a negro nor a woman. Confer on me . . . the glory of white manhood so that henceforth . . . I may enjoy the most unlimited freedom.' "

These were painful years for Elizabeth Stanton, but they were difficult for Susan Anthony as well. She can hardly be blamed for feeling as though she had been left alone to carry the whole weight of the woman's rights movement on her own back. She felt this keenly at the beginning of 1856, when she made another trip through New York State, holding meetings and collecting petitions for the expansion of the Married Woman's Property Act.

With Lucy Stone and Antoinette Blackwell occupied with their recent marriages, and Mrs. Stanton occupied with the expected arrival of her sixth child, she had turned for help to Frances D. Gage, a writer and woman's rights leader from Ohio. They started on January 4, in another terrible winter of heavy snow and freezing cold. On January 20, Mrs. Gage had to return home because of family illness, and Susan Anthony was left alone. She wrote to Lucy Stone, asking her to help out by making some speeches, but the reply was far from helpful: "I wish you had a good husband; it is a great blessing." Appeals to other speakers were equally unproductive. She carried on by herself, finished the tour, presented the petitions, and had the humiliation of learning that they were received "with roars of laughter."

That summer she was invited to address the New York State Teachers' Association on coeducation, a daring subject since most people, including women, were sure that coeducation

would sully the purity of girls and undermine the sanctity of marriage. She begged Mrs. Stanton to help her prepare the speech. Mrs. Stanton replied: "Come here and I will do what I can to help you . . . if you will hold the baby and make the puddings."

The lecture was a great, if oddly qualified, success. The president of the association took her hand and said: "Madam, that was a splendid production and well delivered . . . but I would rather have followed my wife or daughter to Greenwood cemetery than to have had her stand here before this promiscuous audience and deliver that address."

In the fall of that year, Susan Anthony went to work for the American Anti-Slavery Society. She was put in charge of the work in New York State, arranging meetings, hiring lecturers, seeing to the display of posters. She was paid ten dollars a week and expenses. The slavery issue had come to a breaking point that year with the turmoil in "bleeding Kansas," and Susan Anthony had a personal reason for concern.

The Kansas-Nebraska Act, creating the territory of Kansas in 1854, had left it to the settlers to decide whether Kansas should come into the Union as a slave or a free state. Hundreds of pro- and antislavery settlers rushed into the area in an effort to get a majority in the elections. By 1856 a furious conflict had broken out between the proslavery "Border Ruffians" and the antislavery "abolition crowd."

On May 24, 1856, John Brown led an attack on the hamlet of Pottawatomie Creek, killing five southerners and setting off three months of violence and destruction. Farms were burned and looted, settlers murdered. Open warfare raged until Federal troops were sent in. The news of the "Pottawatomie Massacre" didn't reach New York until September, and then it was learned that John Brown had spent the night before the raid at the cabin of Merritt Anthony, Susan's brother. The first reports claimed that thirty settlers had been killed; the Anthonys were in despair until a letter from Merritt assured them of his safety. But though they were personally relieved, they felt "little solace while the cause of all this terrible wrong remains untouched."

Though northerners were shocked by the events in Kansas, and the number of "Free-Soilers" grew, there was nevertheless vehement opposition to the Garrisonian abolitionists. They were considered immoderate, incendiary troublemakers who preferred stirring up angry passions to working out practical solutions without the use of violence. They were accused, too, of ruining business relations between the southern cotton growers and the northern textile manufacturers. Northern bankers and businessmen had extended millions of dollars in credit to the South; their investment would be lost in case of war.

The abolitionists were also considered anti-Union. If the southern states refused to end slavery, said the abolitionists, the North should refuse to be in the same Union with them—the North should secede. One of their posters read, "No Union with Slaveholders." There must be no compromise with slavery. Garrison burned a copy of the Constitution, saying its acceptance of slavery was immoral.

Susan Anthony, who had learned to deal with the righteous indignation or ridicule confronting her as a woman's rights speaker, now had to face outright hostility as an "abolitionist agitator." Her abolitionist activities and the openly declared Garrisonian sympathies of other woman's rights leaders antagonized some of their early supporters. One of the most important of these was Horace Greeley.

The seventh National Woman's Rights Convention was to be held at the end of November 1856. When Susan Anthony, making the usual arrangements, sent a publicity notice to Greeley, he replied that he could no longer carry announcements for woman's rights in the *Tribune*'s columns.

Greeley had always supported the woman's movement, though he made it clear that he believed "the intellectual, like the physical capacities of women unequal in the average to those of men." But he could see "no reason in this natural diversity for a superinduced legal inequality." He felt women were being treated unfairly and, in the interests of justice, had been very helpful to their cause, opening the pages of the *Tribune* to their notices and articles. He had personally attended earlier conventions, and at the riotous convention of 1853 he had courageously defended the women, to the point of exchanging blows with those trying to disrupt the meeting.

But the radical Garrisonian brand of abolition for which Susan Anthony was now working was too extreme for Greeley. He was afraid of being associated with it, though he was firmly against slavery. He was a reformer of moderate views who took little direct action himself. His great contribution to the reform movements was his honest and unbiased reporting of events and conditions, and his generous provision of space in which the reformers could air their views. He provided the kind of publicity that made it possible for more aggressive reformers to carry on their work.

Now, however, his increasing political ambitions were making him cautious. He was one of the sponsors of the new Republican Party—he, indeed, suggested its name. He would run several times for Congress and, in 1872, for the Presidency of the United States. When association with the unpopular abolitionist views of the woman's rights movement seemed to threaten his political career, he wanted nothing more to do with it. He wrote to Susan Anthony that he could not print her notices because "my political antagonists take advantage of such publications to make the Tribune responsible for the anti-Bible, anti-Union, etc. doctrines, which your conventions generally put forth."

Until the outbreak of the Civil War, Susan Anthony continued to work for the Anti-Slavery Society, with time off to make arrangements for the woman's rights conventions, which resumed after the lapse of 1857. She did an enormous amount of traveling, covering what in those days were great distances. She went from Maine to New York, riding on bone-shaking conveyances, frequently bogging down in snow or mud. Hotels and private homes in the outlying areas were depressingly uncomfortable. There was little hot water and no steam heat; inside plumbing was often lacking. Lighting was by candle or kerosene.

One of the worst hardships was the dreadful food. Many years later, Susan Anthony said that, contrary to sentimental myths, cooking in the "good old days" of one's grandmother was awful. Good ingredients were hard to get or unavailable, and housewives knew very little about the processes which turned raw materials into satisfactory cooked products. Bread and cakes were especially bad, in spite of being home-baked. Like many ingredients in the days before government standards and regulations, flour and sugar were often of poor quality, filled with impurities. There was no baking powder and no commercially produced yeast. Instead, salt, soda, and sour milk were used as leavening agents, with no exact measurements of anything. The results were too often uneven, unpalatable, and indigestible.

To add to the discomfort of Susan Anthony's palate, she was frequently exposed to one of the dietetic regimes zealously followed by many of the reformers of that day. It was difficult and expensive for an unaccompanied woman to stay in hotels, so she often stayed at the homes of abolitionists or supporters of woman's rights. These reformers sometimes carried their principles into their kitchens and dining rooms. The Grimkés, for example, were devout believers in the theories of Dr. Sylvester Graham, father of the graham cracker, and lived almost exclusively on meals of rice and molasses, stewed beans, bread, milk, and raw fruit. They never ate meat, fish, or butter, and had hot food only once a week. After three days of nuts, apples, and bran at one vegetarian home, Susan Anthony fled to New York City for a porterhouse steak.

Money was a big problem for the woman's rights movement. As dependent wives, few women could contribute toward the expenses of preparing for and holding conventions, or of printing petitions and leaflets, or of arranging lecture tours. Some money was raised at meetings and lectures by charging a small entrance fee and by the sale of leaflets; sometimes the women were lucky, collecting enough to pay the costs of that meeting and some of the advance charges for the next event, but they couldn't count on it. Susan Anthony's father was always ready to give them money, but they considered it a debt to be repaid.

In November 1858, Francis Jackson, a wealthy Boston abolitionist moved by the sufferings of his married daughter under existing law, gave $5000 to the cause of woman's rights. Under the terms of the gift, Wendell Phillips, Lucy Stone, and Susan Anthony were named as trustees to decide how to spend it. A few months later, in 1859, another wealthy Bostonian reformer and philanthropist, Charles F. Hovey, died, leaving a fund of $50,000 with the income to be divided among several reform movements, principally antislavery and woman's rights. After slavery was abolished, most of the money went to the women.

In May 1860 the tenth annual National Woman's Rights Convention, with Martha Wright presiding, was held in New York City. It started on a high note of jubilation and harmony. Just two months earlier, New York's Married Woman's Property Act had been amended, giving women much greater legal and economic rights, particularly the right to keep their own earnings. This achievement, after years of strenuous effort against the most discouraging odds, had filled the woman's rights workers with new enthusiasm.

Elizabeth Stanton was warmly applauded when, at the first

session of the convention, she repeated the impressive speech she had delivered before the Legislature in support of the new law. Susan Anthony was warmly thanked for her work in getting it passed. It was happily reported that women now had the right to keep their own earnings in Indiana, Maine, Missouri, and Ohio as well as in New York. A final piece of good news was the donation of $400,000 by Matthew Vassar to establish a girls' college in Poughkeepsie, New York.

When the delegates assembled for the second session, they were still in a mellow and relaxed mood. Elizabeth Stanton abruptly jolted them out of it by introducing ten resolutions recommending that divorce laws be liberalized. Divorce should be made easier, she said, so that unhappy marriages could be dissolved. It was "not only a right, but a duty" to end any "covenant between human beings, that failed to produce or promote human happiness." She expressed her "most profound respect and loving sympathy for those heroic women who, in the face of law and public sentiment, have dared to sunder the unholy ties of a joyless, loveless union."

Her audience was stunned. Was Mrs. Stanton, respectable wife and mother of seven children, proposing to discuss the delicate subject of divorce in public? And suggesting that marriages might be broken up in less than extreme circumstances? Wasn't it better to endure unhappiness than violate the sanctity of marriage? What was Mrs. Stanton thinking of?

Mrs. Stanton was thinking that the time had come for the institutions of marriage and divorce to be closely and freshly examined. They were governed by antiquated laws and customs, devised by authoritarian men, and in all too many aspects grossly unfair to women. It was time for women to take a hand in determining the nature of marriage and divorce, and to work for whatever changes they thought necessary.

Shortly before the convention opened, there had been an acrimonious newspaper debate on divorce. It started when a liberal divorce law was introduced in the New York Legislature, modeled after the progressive Indiana law. Horace Greeley, who was against divorce for any reason, angrily opposed the new bill in the pages of the *Tribune*. Robert Dale Owen, who as a member of the Indiana state legislature had worked to broaden the divorce law, energetically supported the bill in the *Free Enquirer*, of which he was editor, and in letters to the *Tribune*.

Mrs. Stanton followed the debate with particular interest. She had been thinking about the subject for many years. The unhappy marriages of close friends and the situation in her own family involving her sister and brother-in-law, Tryphena and Edward Bayard, had led to her present unorthodox views. She felt that this was an issue which belonged in the woman's rights movement.

For the vast majority of women, said Mrs. Stanton, marriage was the absolute center of their lives. Its success or failure affected a woman far more than it did a man. "Marriage is not all of life to man. His resources for amusement and occupation are boundless. He has the whole world for his home. His business, his politics, his club, his friendships . . . can help fill up the void made by an unfortunate union. . . . But to woman, marriage is all and everything; her sole object in life—that for which she is educated—the subject of all her sleeping and her waking dreams. . . . In the present undeveloped condition of woman, it is only through our fathers, brothers, husbands, sons, that we feel the pulsations of the great outer world."

Until now, she said, all the rules of marriage and divorce had been made by men. Under the divorce laws, a wife lost her home and children even if her husband had caused the breakup of the marriage. The rights and feelings of women were never considered. Now, argued Mrs. Stanton, it was time for women themselves to consider them.

She had exchanged several letters on the subject with Lucy Stone. Mrs. Stone agreed with her about the importance of reviewing the whole question of marriage and divorce. She herself believed that a loveless marriage was immoral, and shortly before the convention had written to Mrs. Stanton: "That is a great, grand question, may God touch your lips." But then she decided that it would be wrong to bring up the subject at a woman's rights convention, "for the simple reason that it concerns men just as much." She urged Mrs. Stanton to call a separate meeting to discuss the question, and to keep it distinct from the woman's rights movement. Mrs. Stanton refused. Lucy Stone finally yielded, or appeared to—an ambiguity which was to put a strain on their relations.

When Elizabeth Stanton finished presenting her divorce resolutions to the convention, an impassioned debate broke out. Antoinette Blackwell, who believed that divorce was morally wrong in any circumstance, offered thirteen resolutions in opposition to Mrs. Stanton's ten. Ernestine Rose, supporting Mrs. Stanton, argued against each of Mrs. Blackwell's resolutions. Wendell Phillips was so opposed to Mrs. Stanton's resolutions that he made a motion to strike them out of the convention minutes altogether. He used the same argument as Lucy Stone, saying the convention should concern itself with laws that affected only women, and have nothing to do with subjects like marriage that concerned men as well as women.

Then Susan Anthony took the floor and asked Phillips to withdraw his motion, saying "the discussion is perfectly in order, since nearly all the wrongs of which we complain grow out of the inequality, the injustice of the marriage laws, that rob the wife of the right to herself and her children." Phillips's motion was defeated; the resolutions were retained in the record, but they were not accepted by the convention.

The argument continued long after the convention ended. Everyone took sides. Lucretia Mott and the more radical feminist leaders supported Mrs. Stanton. Lucy Stone went completely over to Wendell Phillips's point of view. A minister who was active in the antislavery movement told Susan Anthony: "You are not married, you have no business to be discussing marriage." She replied, "You are not a slave, suppose you quit lecturing on slavery."

Horace Greeley wrote furious editorials against the resolutions and against divorce in general. Other newspapers came out against Mrs. Stanton. She was accused of wanting to do away with marriage altogether and substitute free love. She was asked what would happen "when men changed their wives every Christmas." "So alarming were the comments . . . that I began to feel," wrote Mrs. Stanton, "that I had inadvertently taken out the underpinning from the social system."

Some newspapers accused the woman's rights leaders of being "unsexed," frustrated, "mannish" spinsters, too unattractive to get husbands, or else "badly mated viragos" taking out their spleen by trying to stir up discontent among normal, happily married women.

This portrait of the movement's leaders as "dried-up old maids," or as "mummified and fossilated females, void of domestic duties, habits and natural affections," appeared with predictable regularity as the years passed. Susan Anthony was a special target. She was called "Spinster Susan," a "shrewish maiden" who couldn't possibly know "of the thousand delights of married life," and held up as a typical example of a woman's rights advocate. She finally drew up a marital status report: of all the early leaders she was the only one who never married, while sixteen of those who did had sixty-six children among them. Elizabeth Stanton had seven children, Lucretia Mott six, and both were famous for their housekeeping and domestic skills.

Every advance suggested or supported by Elizabeth Stanton had produced shock waves, followed by predictions of moral disaster. Votes for women would destroy the home; education for women would unfit them for marriage; speaking in public would unsex them; wearing bifurcated garments would threaten their husbands' masculinity; admitting them into professions would unravel the fabric of society; giving them equal guardianship of children would undermine the family; granting them control of their own money would weaken the moral fiber of the nation. As for easier divorce, with women allowed to institute proceedings themselves and to receive child custody and support, that would indeed, as Mrs. Stanton said, crumble the underpinning of society altogether.

One by one, these horrifying propositions gradually seemed less outrageous. They became accepted as reasonable goals; as some of them were won, they were taken as right and natural. Women like Mrs. Stanton, willing to face the first onslaught of ridicule and denunciation, were largely responsible for educating the public to this acceptance.

In her autobiography, Mrs. Stanton wrote: "What I said on divorce thirty-seven years ago seems quite in line with what many say now. The trouble was not in what I said, but that I said it too soon, and before the people were ready to hear it. It may be, however, that I helped them to get ready; who knows?"

19. At right, bloomer costume, 1851; below, current styles from which bloomer wearers wanted relief

20. The woman's rights movement as seen by Harper's Weekly, 1859

21. Susan B. Anthony
and Elizabeth Cady Stanton,
about 1892

22. Below,
"Two of the Fe'he Males,"
an 1851 lithograph caricaturing
bloomer wearers

23. *Currier & Ives comment on woman's rights, 1869:*
(top) "The Age of Iron: Man As He Expects to Be";
(bottom) "The Age of Brass: or the Triumphs of Woman's Rights"

24. *"The devil himself,"*
George Francis Train

25. *Victoria Woodhull addresses Congressional committee, 1871*

26. Elizabeth Cady Stanton addresses Senate committee, 1878

27. Sojourner Truth

28. Mary Anthony, 1905

29.
Lucretia Mott

30. Lucy Stone in the 1880's

31. Three generations in the
woman's rights movement:
Elizabeth Cady Stanton
with her daughter,
Harriot Stanton Blatch,
and granddaughter,
Nora Blatch, about 1888

32. Carrie
Chapman Catt

33. Susan B. Anthony at her desk, 1900,
surrounded by photographs of woman's rights leaders

34. As votes for women came closer, suffragists and their opponents intensified their efforts. At right, the window display of an "anti" organization; below, suffragists demonstrate in front of the White House

18

Civil War and After: Who Gets the Vote?

There is a great stir about colored men getting their rights, but not a word about the colored women; and if colored men get their rights, and not colored women theirs, you see the colored men will be masters over the women, and it will be just as bad as it was before.

—Sojourner Truth, 1867

We demand . . . suffrage for all the citizens of the Republic. I would not talk of negroes or women, but of citizens.

—Elizabeth Cady Stanton, 1868

With the coming of the Civil War, all woman's rights activities stopped. The last convention took place in February 1861. It was not a national meeting but a New York State convention, held in Albany while the Legislature was considering the liberalized divorce bill. The usual fervent appeals were addressed to the judiciary committee, but the bill failed to pass by just a few votes. Mrs. Stanton blamed this largely on "the intense opposition of Horace Greeley."

Susan Anthony wanted to call the annual National Woman's Rights Convention as usual, but the other women wouldn't hear of it. They felt that in this time of national crisis they must put aside their own concerns and devote themselves to the war effort. They were sure that when peace was restored, women would be rewarded for their patriotic contributions. An appreciative government would give them the right to vote as a matter of course. Susan Anthony thought this a naïve expectation. Woman's rights, she said, would be lost in the welter of postwar problems. She insisted that the movement should continue without a break, but was overruled.

Though all direct action for the woman's movement stopped, many of its aims were promoted by the war itself. It brought thousands of women out of their little domestic spheres into a larger world, where they acquired training, experience, and self-confidence. As the men went off to fight, large numbers of women had to go to work to support their families. With male workers away, employers had to accept women to fill the vacant jobs. Women became clerks—especially in government offices, where they had rarely been hired before—printers, factory workers, and teachers in greater numbers than ever. They learned how to take care of themselves, how to manage business and family affairs without relying on men to do it for them. These were all goals which the woman's movement had been urging for years.

Those women who didn't have to replace absent breadwinners also went to work, as volunteers to help the war effort. Immediately after hostilities began in the middle of April 1861, thousands of local societies were formed to knit, sew, and cook for the soldiers. At the end of the month the Women's Central Relief Association was established to coordinate the work of these local groups. In May delegates from voluntary aid associations all through the North went to Washington and received official permission to set up the United States Sanitary Commission, to provide for the "comfort, security, and health of the Army." Though its president and general secretary were men, the major services were performed by women, with the Women's Central Association becoming part of the new commission. This extraordinary and purely voluntary organization, acting without any precedent and little experience, took care of virtually every nonmilitary need of the soldiers.

Dorothea Dix, the reformer of prisons and insane asylums, became Superintendent of Nurses, providing the army with 3000 trained women to supplement or replace the largely untrained male orderlies. Dr. Elizabeth Blackwell helped recruit and train the nurses. Clara Barton, who would later establish the American Red Cross, and Mary Ann Bickerdyke, the Quaker "tornado" known as Mother Bickerdyke, went directly to the battlefields, bringing supplies and nursing the wounded. The Sanitary Commission established and ran hospitals and convalescent homes, inspected army camps and medical facilities, provided clothing, bandages, medicine, extra food, all of which were inadequately supplied by the poorly provisioned Army. They helped locate men missing in action, wrote letters for soldiers unable to write themselves, and helped them get back to their homes after leaving the hospital. To carry on this work, the 7000 branches of the Sanitary Commission raised $50,000,000, and handled the spending of every cent themselves.

In later wars, almost all of these services and expenses would be borne by the government. But the harried Union forces had neither the money nor the staff, nor, for that matter, the experience or tradition of setting up Army hospitals, nursing services, and personal assistance for soldiers. In providing all of this, and with great competence and efficiency, the women were making an inestimable contribution. Together with the success of those who went to work in offices and factories, it was a clear demonstration that women could be effective and responsible when given the chance.

Elizabeth Stanton, Susan Anthony, and Lucy Stone took little part in this kind of work, but concentrated instead on politics. As abolitionists, they were gratified when Lincoln issued the Emancipation Proclamation at the beginning of January 1863, but they felt it was not enough. The proclamation freed only the slaves in the rebellious states, leaving slavery untouched in the border states of Missouri, Kentucky, Delaware, and Maryland. An amendment to the Constitution was needed, banning slavery in the entire country.

What was also needed was an improvement in northern morale, some new rallying point. With the South winning one battle after another, everyone was sure the North would lose. During that same year the terrible draft riots would explode in New York City as antiwar sentiment turned into anti-Negro violence. Henry Stanton wrote to Susan Anthony from Washington, describing the despair within the government itself. Some men, he said, "have pretty much given up the struggle. . . . You have no idea how dark the cloud is which hangs over us. . . . Here then is work for you. Susan, put on your armor and go forth."

Henry Stanton had joined the staff of the *New York Tribune* as its Washington correspondent; he would later become an editor of the *New York Sun*. The Stantons had left Seneca Falls and moved to Brooklyn in the spring of 1862, and shortly afterward to New York City. After receiving Henry's letter, Susan Anthony came down to the city to confer with Mrs. Stanton. They decided to set up an organization of women whose purpose would be to rally support for the war, "to kindle and sustain the fires of a high enthusiasm." They would emphasize the freeing of the slaves as a major purpose of the war, turning it into a moral crusade. Their principal work would be to collect signatures on a petition asking for an antislavery amendment—the thirteenth—to the Constitution.

The National Woman's Loyal League was established in May 1863, at a meeting presided over by Lucy Stone. Most of the woman's rights leaders were there to address the huge audience. It was agreed that the new organization would support the war as long as its main purpose was to free the slaves, and would collect a million signatures to a petition for the Thirteenth Amendment.

The only real dissension came when Susan Anthony proposed a resolution asking that the "civil and political rights of all citizens of African descent and all women" be established. Some women protested, saying they didn't want political rights. Others said they had come to pledge support to the government, not to work for woman's rights or even abolition. But the resolution was finally adopted.

Elizabeth Stanton was elected president of the new organization. Susan Anthony was made secretary, with a stipend of twelve dollars a week. An office was set up in Cooper Union, where the petitions were sorted and counted before being sent on to Washington. By the end of fifteen months the league had grown to 5000 members and collected 400,000 signatures.

Everyone who signed a petition was asked to contribute one cent to help pay for postage, printing, and office expenses. Through these pennies $3000 was raised; the rest of the necessary money came from a course of lectures which Susan

Anthony arranged at Cooper Union, and from voluntary contributions. When the league ended its work, there was a debt of $4.72, which she paid herself.

The petitions were presented to Congress in installments by Charles Sumner, the outspoken antislavery Senator from Massachusetts. With this strong expression of public sentiment in its favor, the Thirteenth Amendment was formally proposed on February 1, 1865, and ratified that same year, on December 18.

When the war ended, the leaders of the woman's movement were ready to resume their campaign for woman's rights. By this time most women felt that the basic right was suffrage, and that all efforts should be concentrated upon this single goal. They thought they would get suffrage easily. Surely, by their work during the war, women had shown that they had the ability and intelligence to vote; surely they would be given the vote in return for their service to the country.

As Susan Anthony had foreseen, they were wrong. Not only were state and Federal authorities as reluctant as ever to grant suffrage, but the New York Legislature, in 1862, had taken away some of the hard-won rights which had been gained for married women in 1860. With no active woman's rights movement to protest the action, the Legislature had repealed the sections of the law which gave mothers equal guardianship of their children and widows certain property rights.

Male reform leaders had promised that once the slaves were freed, woman's rights would be taken up again. But after the war these leaders wanted women to wait awhile longer while everyone worked to secure full civil rights for the ex-slaves. The Thirteenth Amendment had freed the slaves; it did not assure them citizenship. Reformers such as Phillips, Greeley, and Sumner began working for another amendment, the fourteenth, to establish the citizenship and civil rights of the former slaves.

When Elizabeth Stanton saw the proposed draft of the Fourteenth Amendment, she was deeply disturbed because it would introduce the word "male" for the first time in the Constitution. The first section of the amendment was acceptable, since it read, "All persons born or naturalized in the United States . . . are citizens," and stipulated that no state shall "abridge the privileges . . . of citizens." Under this wording, women could claim the privilege of voting if they too were "born or naturalized in the United States."

But the second section contained the phrase "But when the right to vote . . . is denied to any of the male inhabitants." The word "male" appeared twice more, each time referring to "male citizens." The question could now be raised whether women were included in the term "persons" and therefore considered citizens as described in the first section, entitled to the privilege of voting. This exclusionary use of "male" was a terrible setback to women's efforts to vote. It would take another amendment to give them suffrage and, as Elizabeth Stanton suspected, this would be a slow and difficult process.

She and Susan Anthony began a drive for petitions asking that women be included in the Fourteenth Amendment. They collected 10,000 signatures and sent them to Washington. But the very people on whose support they counted turned them down, saying it would be hard enough to win approval of Negro suffrage without connecting it with the equally unpopular cause of woman suffrage. The women must wait their turn. First the black man must get his vote; then perhaps women, white and black, could start working for theirs.

Charles Sumner, who had expressed his gratitude to the women for their war work and who was supposedly for woman suffrage, said it was "most inopportune" for them to ask for the vote at this time. Sumner was the Republican Senate leader, and the Republicans wanted nothing to interfere with winning two million black votes for their party.

To the bitter disappointment of Miss Anthony and Mrs. Stanton, most of their closest male friends and supporters, men like Wendell Phillips and Gerrit Smith, agreed completely that women should put aside their demand for the vote. Phillips said that to combine the two suffrage movements "would lose for the Negro far more than we should gain for the women."

Many of the women opposed this view. They wanted to work for both Negro and woman suffrage at the same time, in one united effort. In May 1866 they called a woman's rights convention, the first since 1860. At its conclusion, Susan Anthony proposed that the woman's rights movement convert itself into the American Equal Rights Association, which would work for universal suffrage. It would be inefficient, she said, to keep Negro and woman suffrage apart, "since to do so must be at double cost of time, energy and money." The new organization was to include the former Anti-Slavery Society, now that their goals were alike. Her proposition was accepted, and the Equal Rights Association was formed.

Many members of the Anti-Slavery Society had entered the new association with reservations about joining the two suffrage causes. All too soon they revealed their intention of emphasizing black suffrage and going slow on female suffrage. They urged that "This is the Negro's hour." Women should put their claims second. Some women began to go along with this view.

During the Civil War, women who had once rejected the disturbing idea of voting had come to accept it, giving the movement a new impetus which might have produced results. But now, just at the crucial time, when suffrage laws were being reconsidered in the light of postwar conditions, they backed down, saying that women should be generous and wait for their vote until the Negro had his.

The "radical" feminists refused to wait. At the convention of the Equal Rights Association in May 1867, Sojourner Truth, speaking for them as well as for black women, said they must work for universal suffrage now, "while things are stirring; because if we wait till it is still, it will take a great while to get it going again." She was glad to see black men get their rights, but "while the water is stirring," women must step into the pool too. Black women would be no better off than before if they were denied the vote while their men received it, because then "the colored men will be masters over the women."

Lucretia Mott and Elizabeth Stanton warned that if black men were given the vote first, they would join with white men in refusing to enfranchise women. Asking women to work for black male suffrage before their own was asking them to strengthen the opposition to their own suffrage.

Sojourner Truth perceived the dangers of not moving at the opportune time. After the Revolutionary War, women had failed to take advantage of the "open moment," and now, in spite of the warnings of Sojourner Truth and the other "radicals," there were some who wanted to repeat the same error.

Whether the conflict between Negro and woman suffrage was necessary, and whether joining the two would have given women the vote a half century sooner or would have delayed the black man in getting his, is impossible to say. But it became apparent in at least two states, in 1867, that such a conflict did indeed exist.

In that year New York held a constitutional convention. Among the changes suggested in the old constitution was the elimination of the word "white." Elizabeth Stanton and Susan Anthony wanted the word "male" removed as well. Soon after the formation of the American Equal Rights Association, they had suggested that petitions be circulated asking for both these changes. Wendell Phillips and other men in the association objected, saying the women should work just for the Negro. They could ask for their own rights later, at the next constitutional revision.

Horace Greeley also pressed them to wait. He was one of the

leading Republicans in the state and had been elected a member of the constitutional convention. "This is a critical period for the Republican party and the life of the Nation," he said. ". . . It would be wise and magnanimous in you to hold your claims . . . in abeyance until the Negro is safe beyond peradventure, and your turn will come next. I conjure you to remember that this is 'the Negro's hour' and your first duty now is to go through the State and plead his claims."

He warned them that "if you persevere . . . you need depend on no further help from me or the *Tribune*." They went ahead with their petitions anyway. Several months later, in June 1867, Mrs. Stanton and Miss Anthony went to Albany to present the petitions and to address the committee on suffrage. Its chairman was Greeley. By this time, with his political ambitions stronger than ever, his views on woman suffrage were rapidly becoming more conservative. A few months earlier he had said that what a woman really needed was "a wicker-work cradle and a dimple-cheeked baby." Now he claimed that true women didn't want the vote—"The best women I know do not want to vote"—in spite of the fact that his own wife's name was at the head of one of the petitions. In his negative report he said that "public sentiment . . . would not sustain an innovation so revolutionary and sweeping . . . and involving transformations so radical in social and domestic life."

Enough convention delegates accepted his recommendation so that the word "male" was retained in the New York State constitution, and the distinction between Negro and woman suffrage was reinforced.

The same distinction was made a few months later in Kansas, where a referendum was held offering two propositions. One was to remove the word "male" from the voting requirements in the state constitution; the other would remove the word "white." This was the first time woman suffrage was presented directly to the public—or to the male part of the public—for its decision. There would be fifty-five more referendums of this kind. Each time, the women would carry on an exhaustive campaign to win the vote. Women would come from all over the country to help, feeling that every state success would bring national suffrage that much closer. Susan Anthony, in particular, would be present at most of these campaigns, offering assistance and encouragement.

Lucy Stone and her husband spent April and May traveling through Kansas, speaking and distributing leaflets urging acceptance of both propositions. Lucy Stone had done little public speaking since the birth of her child in 1857, and was relieved to find that she had not lost her oratorical skill. The Blackwells sent optimistic reports of their success back east. By summer, however, it became evident that the Republicans, worried about losing Negro suffrage and the new voters the party might thus gain, were going to drop woman suffrage. They not only stopped supporting it, but openly showed their opposition.

At the end of August, Susan Anthony and Elizabeth Stanton went to Kansas to help with the campaign. They went all through the state, with Susan Anthony handling the arrangements and Mrs. Stanton doing most of the speaking. Sometimes, to cover more ground, they separated, and Susan Anthony spoke in the towns to which she went alone.

Alone or together, they found it an uncomfortable experience. Conditions were primitive, the prairie was infested with insects, the food was ghastly: greasy bacon, canned vegetables, in some places no milk or sugar, no fresh fruit. Mrs. Stanton often wished she could stop and teach the housewives on this pioneer frontier how to cook. Bedbugs kept them awake at night and had to be picked out of their clothes in the morning.

And it was all for nothing. When the referendum was held, both Negro and woman suffrage lost. Apparently, separating the two hadn't helped Negro suffrage. Out of 30,000 votes, it received 10,843; woman suffrage, 9070.

Susan Anthony and Elizabeth Stanton, however, were not ready to give up. Instead of returning home, they set out on a lecture tour which lasted a month and brought an amazing development in its wake.

19

George Francis Train and The Revolution

Women learned . . . that it is impossible for the best of men to understand women's feelings or the humiliation of their position.

      —Elizabeth Cady Stanton, *Eighty Years and More*

We must not trust any of you. All these men, who have pushed us aside for years, saying "This is the negro's hour," now, when we, dropped by them, find help in other quarters, they turn up the whites of their eyes and cry out their curses.

      —Elizabeth Cady Stanton, 1868

The ten-year-old boy will say to his women relatives, "Oh you don't know anything, you are only a woman," and when man wishes to insult his fellow man, he calls him a woman.

      —George Francis Train, 1867

The Kansas campaign filled Susan Anthony and Elizabeth Stanton with a deep sense of personal betrayal. Their antislavery and Republican friends had let them down badly. One by one, their former male supporters flatly refused to do anything more for woman suffrage, saying, like Gerrit Smith, that removing "the political disabilities of race is my first desire—of sex, my second."

Everyone wanted the women to put aside their own needs until after the black man was assured of his civil rights. The familiar technique was used of assuring women that the highest feminine ideal was to be self-sacrificing, generous, and patient.

The betrayal by their closest male friends, said Elizabeth Stanton, had taught women the important lesson that even "the best of men" could not fully comprehend the humiliation of a woman's position. Women now realized that they must rely entirely upon themselves. Once they decided on a course of action, "no amount of ridicule and opposition" must have the slightest influence, "come from what quarter it may."

At the moment of greatest disenchantment with the Republicans, a month before the Kansas referendum, the St. Louis Suffrage Association offered to send a Democratic speaker to help win local Democratic votes for woman suffrage in Kansas. To accept help from the Democrats, the "party of slavery," seemed like the worst kind of heresy to abolitionist members of the woman's movement. But the ladies were desperate.

The Democratic speaker was George Francis Train, a rich, erratic, eccentric Irish-American adventurer, whose extreme views disturbed not only the conservative women in the movement but even the former abolitionists, who were considered pretty radical themselves. He believed in such advanced heresies as the eight-hour day, organized labor, paper money, Irish independence, and, of course, woman suffrage. He loved nothing more than a new cause, any daring new field in which to pioneer.

He offered to go on a two-week speaking tour, paying his own expenses. Susan Anthony knew little about him, but was in a mood to welcome any help she could get. If the Republicans weren't going to vote for woman suffrage, maybe the Democrats would. This hobnobbing with a Democrat was regarded as rank desertion by the Republicans, who had been taking the support of women for granted. But Susan Anthony was through supporting the Republicans and getting nothing in return. She made all the advance arrangements for Train's tour. A leading Kansas Democrat was supposed to go along, but when he backed out at the last minute, Miss Anthony went instead.

Train proved to be an effective, highly colorful speaker. He was about thirty-five, the very image of the tall, dark, handsome, romantic hero, "with curling hair and flashing dark eyes," and with "a fine courtliness of bearing toward women." He sported brass-buttoned coats, patent-leather shoes, and lavender kid gloves. He was quick, witty, and lively on the platform, using clever mimicry and dramatic effects to get his points across. Audiences loved him—except for those who distrusted him as an "egotistic clown."

Toward the end of the tour, he made two astonishing offers to Susan Anthony and Elizabeth Stanton: he would give them money to start a woman suffrage paper, and pay all their expenses if they would join him on a lecture tour on the way back east from Kansas. The paper would be called *The Revolution*, with the motto, "Men, their rights, and nothing more; women, their rights, and nothing less."

The ladies were aware of Train's eccentricities. Nevertheless, since their old friends had abandoned them, they were willing to accept help for their cause from any source. They accepted both offers. How could they resist? Especially the chance of their own newspaper, where Mrs. Stanton could at last express all the ideas bursting for release. She wrote to Martha Wright: "Mr. Train is a pure, high-toned man, without a vice. He has some extravagances and idiosyncrasies, but he is willing to devote energy and money to our cause when no other man is. It seems to me it would be right and wise to accept aid even from the devil himself, provided he did not tempt us to lower our standard."

The joint lecture tour was by far the most comfortable, the most deluxe trip imaginable. They had suites of rooms in the finest hotels and traveled by the best conveyances. Train made all the arrangements and paid all the bills, including the printing costs of their announcements and leaflets. This amounted to some $3000. And when they reached New York, he gave them $600 with which to put out the first issue of *The Revolution*, which appeared on January 1, 1868.

It was a sixteen-page weekly. Elizabeth Stanton and Parker Pillsbury, a seasoned reformer and antislavery journalist, were the editors; Susan Anthony, the publisher and business manager. Train, as financial backer, brought in a co-sponsor, David M. Melliss, financial editor of the *New York World*. The two men agreed to pay the bills until the paper could support itself. In return they would be given the back pages in which to express their views on financial and political matters, including a lively, gossipy Wall Street column by Melliss.

Mrs. Stanton was in her element. The period spent as editor of *The Revolution* was, she said, "one of the happiest of my life, and the most useful." She printed "spicy, readable, and revolutionary" articles on universal suffrage, the problems of poverty, prostitution, equal pay for equal work, the opening of new occupations for women, the need for changing the divorce laws, the role of the church in keeping women subordinate. Her editorials urged women to acquire training so that they might be self-supporting, and to take better care of their health by exercising and getting plenty of fresh air, two ideas by no means commonly applied to women in that period.

The Revolution carried news that no other paper did. It told women who had no way of finding out about these things just what was happening to other women: how they were breaking into the professions, what they were doing in industry, in the existing trade unions, and about their efforts to form their own unions. It carried reports of criminal cases involving women, and presented the woman's side with a sympathetic understanding not to be found in most newspapers. It printed stories and articles by female writers, and had foreign correspondents to provide news about women in other countries.

A publication of its own was just what the movement needed, what its leaders had always hoped for. It served as a clearing-house for information, and was a source of reassurance to those who had thought they were alone in their doubts and questions about their position as women. By coordinating efforts going on all over the country to win rights for women, it put the whole movement on a solid professional basis.

And yet, *The Revolution* and the man responsible for it contributed to the great split which tore the movement apart.

When the ladies accepted Train's help during the Kansas campaign, many members of the American Equal Rights Association were incensed. They regarded Train as a charlatan, an anti-Negro copperhead who would willingly sacrifice Negro suffrage in order to gain the vote for women. He was anathema to the abolitionists, who considered him an "enemy and defamer" of the Negro, especially when Train kept saying things like "Woman first, and Negro last is my programme." Garrison wrote to Susan Anthony about his "regret and astonishment that you and Mrs. Stanton should have taken such leave of good sense as to be travelling companions and associate lecturers with that crack-brained harlequin and semi-lunatic,

George Francis Train. . . . He is as destitute of principle as he is of sense. . . . He may be of use in drawing an audience, but so would be a kangaroo, a gorilla, or a hippopotamus." Many others, like Wendell Phillips and Gerrit Smith, agreed with Garrison and angrily denounced Train.

Henry Blackwell, who heard Train speak in Kansas, said it was true that he attracted "immense crowds," but he made the campaign "utterly offensive and ridiculous." Lucy Stone felt that Train's "presence as an advocate of woman suffrage was enough to condemn it." As chairman of the executive committee of the Equal Rights Association, she issued a statement disclaiming all connection between that organization and Train.

It was bad enough when Elizabeth Stanton and Susan Anthony shared the same lecture platform with the controversial Mr. Train, but when *The Revolution*, backed by his money, appeared, that was the absolute end. The very name *Revolution* was an insult to the more conservative members of the Equal Rights Association. Though they couldn't deny the need for such a publication and were willing to concede its effectiveness, they nevertheless felt that its association with a sponsor so notorious was enough to damn it and its editors in the eyes of the respectable world.

They turned against Susan Anthony first, blaming her for the unfortunate involvement with Train, and accusing her of highhanded, dictatorial methods in managing the affairs of the woman's movement. They said she exercised a harmful influence over Elizabeth Stanton. Even close friends urged Mrs. Stanton to have nothing more to do with her or with *The Revolution*. Mrs. Stanton, however, felt that Susan Anthony was absolutely right. At the beginning of the Civil War "they asked us to be silent" on the woman question. Susan Anthony had said it was a great error which would set the woman's movement back for years. Mrs. Stanton now agreed with this and "ever since, I have taken my beloved Susan's judgment against the world." She remained editor of *The Revolution* and the close friend of Susan Anthony. "No power in heaven, hell or earth can separate us."

Triggered by the controversy over Train, the movement began splitting into two wings. The "New York" group, supporting Mrs. Stanton and Susan Anthony, included Lucretia Mott, Martha Wright, and Ernestine Rose, while their antagonists, the "Boston" group, were headed by Lucy Stone and Henry Blackwell.

George Francis Train and *The Revolution* were not the only discordant issues between the two factions. The first coolness had been between Lucy Stone and Susan Anthony, when Susan had complained that Lucy's marriage and motherhood would interfere with her work for woman's rights. Then there had been the argument over whether such subjects as divorce should be discussed at woman's rights conventions. The Boston group said no, the New Yorkers yes. The Bostonians were embarrassed when *The Revolution*, presumed by the public to speak for the whole movement, discussed divorce and, as a result, was attacked as being against marriage.

The Boston ladies considered the New Yorkers too outspoken, too radical, and altogether too willing to sacrifice principle for expediency. Lucy Stone had been especially outraged by the acceptance of money from Train. Like Mrs. Stanton, Susan Anthony said she would "take money from the devil" to help the cause of woman suffrage; Lucy Stone retorted that Susan had taken not only his money "but the devil too."

The greatest divergence was over which came first: Negro or woman suffrage. At first the New York group wanted both together; so did Lucy Stone, for that matter. But when a choice had to be made, the Bostonians were clearly for the Negro, asking women to wait until some indefinite time in the future. The women of this group, commented Elizabeth Stanton, "educated to self-sacrifice and self-abnegation readily accepted the idea that it was divine and beautiful to hold their claims for rights and privileges in abeyance." She herself thought that "If we love the black man as well as ourselves we shall fulfill the Bible injunction. The . . . requirement to love him better is a little too much for human nature."

The New Yorkers started out by feeling, as Mrs. Stanton said in *The Revolution*, that "NOW'S THE HOUR.—Not the 'negro's hour' alone, but everybody's hour." It was the time "to redeem the Constitution from all odious distinctions on account of race or sex." But, asked to choose between women and Negroes, they began to veer away from universal suffrage to educated suffrage, which favored women. Why, they asked, should the illiterate ex-slave be given the vote when it was denied to literate women?

They also stressed the point, brought up earlier, that if black men were given suffrage first, that would increase the total number of men who would vote against woman suffrage. If women were granted the vote first, that would not affect Negro suffrage; if anything, most women activists were for it. But if it were the other way around, the black male voters, "viewing all things from the same standpoint as white men, would be an added power against us."

The antagonism between the two factions grew, and the warm personal friendships which had suffused the whole movement began to unravel. Susan Anthony, going to New England in 1868, was distressed by "the icy faces of Boston." The atmosphere grew even colder when discussion began that year on the Fifteenth Amendment. This provided that the rights of citizens shall not be abridged "on account of race, color, or previous condition of servitude." The New York group wanted the word "sex" included. Otherwise, they would oppose the amendment. When it appeared that the new amendment would omit sex, Mrs. Stanton printed a sharp editorial, "That Infamous Fifteenth Amendment," in *The Revolution*.

The Boston group, which included many of the male anti-slavery leaders, was all for the amendment, arguing that Negro and woman suffrage should be kept separate. Mrs. Stanton wrote in *The Revolution* that such a separation would repeat what had happened in Kansas: it would set up a dangerous rivalry between the two causes, produce a division of strength, and end in defeat for both.

In January 1869 a woman suffrage convention met in Washington, the first of a long series to be held in the capital. By this time the Fifteenth Amendment had been passed by both houses of Congress. Elizabeth Stanton made the opening speech, "with great force and pithiness," criticizing the amendment as "establishing an aristocracy of sex," and proposing that a Sixteenth Amendment be adopted, granting the vote to women.

The heated reaction to her speech revealed the growing division. Her opponents attacked her suggestion of a Sixteenth Amendment as premature. They demanded that the women take no action of any kind toward getting their vote until the Fifteenth Amendment had been safely ratified and the Negroes assured of theirs. Several young black men in the audience made highly critical speeches, claiming that agitation for woman suffrage would weaken the chance for black suffrage. Some of them were altogether opposed to letting women vote, using the familiar argument that God had intended the dominance of men over women, thus reinforcing the New York view that giving the vote to black men first would make it all the harder for women to get theirs.

Right after the convention, Susan Anthony and Elizabeth Stanton left for a tour of the Midwest to address suffrage meetings and "to awaken women everywhere to a proper self-respect," which they regarded as "the special mission of the suffrage movement." They discovered that not only was interest in the vote growing rapidly among women, but that the men of these states were more pro-suffrage than in the East.

This strengthened their conviction that the time to work for woman suffrage was now, while the whole postwar question of suffrage was being considered.

A significant episode demonstrated the value of such speaking tours and of woman's rights conventions. Seated in the audience at a speech given by Susan Anthony in Peru, Illinois, was Esther Morris, who listened intently to every word. Soon afterward, Mrs. Morris moved to the territory of Wyoming, carrying the message of suffrage with her. She went to work immediately, inviting influential legislators to her home and repeating Susan Anthony's speech to them.

As a result, one of her guests introduced a bill in the territorial legislature providing for woman suffrage, married women's property rights, and equal pay for male and female teachers. The bill passed and went to the governor for his signature. He was urged to veto it, but he remembered an experience of almost twenty years earlier. In 1850 he had been living in Salem, Ohio, where the women, inspired by the Seneca Falls convention, had held a convention of their own. Men had not been permitted to take part in it, but he had slipped into a back row and had been so impressed by the ability and determination of the women that, nineteen years later, he was happy to sign the first woman suffrage bill in the country.

Women were also given the right to serve on juries in Wyoming. Esther Morris, a forceful, rugged six-footer, became the first female Justice of the Peace in the country. She was called "the mother of woman suffrage in Wyoming." A few months after Wyoming, the territory of Utah granted the vote to women.

As the New York and Boston groups drew further apart, there appeared still another difference between them, or at least between Susan Anthony and Lucy Stone. This was their attitude toward workingwomen. Lucy Stone had no interest at all in the economic problems of women aside from the rights of wives to control their own property and earnings. Both Lucy and Henry Blackwell had little sympathy with the trade union movement and disapproved of strikes.

Susan Anthony was not only interested, but directly involved in labor organizations. In 1868 she arranged a meeting at the offices of *The Revolution* which resulted in the formation of the Workingwomen's Association. Most of its members were in the printing trades; soon afterward she organized Working-women's Association No. 2, of those in the sewing trades. She urged these groups to work for the right to vote as well as for economic equality with men. They refused, saying that economic rights must come before political rights. They were afraid that including suffrage in their demands would harm their fight for such things as equal pay for equal work, the same opportunities for advancement as men, and the eight-hour day.

Susan Anthony kept up her interest in workingwomen, but the suffrage movement was essentially a middle-class phenomenon. In spite of her insistence that it would be easier for women to gain economic rights if they first had political rights, workingwomen gave priority to higher pay and better working conditions. The vote was something of a luxury, not directly connected with bread-and-butter matters, and so it could wait.

20

Schism

For over thirty years some people have said from time to time that I have injured the suffrage movement beyond redemption; but it still lives. Train killed it, Victoria Woodhull killed it, the *Revolution* killed it. But with each death it put on new life. . . . Reforms are not made of blown glass to be broken to pieces with the first adverse wind.

—Elizabeth Cady Stanton, 1880

Cautious, careful people, always casting about to preserve their reputation and social standing, never can bring about a reform. Those who are really in earnest must be willing to be anything or nothing in the world's estimation, and publicly and privately, in season and out, avow their sympathy with despised and persecuted ideas and their advocates, and bear the consequences.

—Susan B. Anthony, 1860

In May 1869 the woman's movement finally broke apart. At the meeting that month of the Equal Rights Association, a number of attacks were launched against Susan Anthony and Elizabeth Stanton which brought the division to the surface. Stephen S. Foster, husband of Abby Foster, objected to having them serve any longer as officers. He accused them of having "publicly repudiated the principles of the society" by advocating educated suffrage, opposing the Fifteenth Amendment, and bringing into the movement so dubious a character as George Francis Train.

After sharp debate, a vote was taken on the nominations of Mrs. Stanton and Susan Anthony. A majority supported them, but it had been made clear that a large segment disapproved of their views and of their association with Train and *The Revolution*.

The convention then turned to the Fifteenth Amendment. It was proposed that the association officially endorse it. Frederick Douglass, one of the oldest and closest friends of the woman's rights leaders, the man who had defended the original suffrage resolution at the Seneca Falls convention, spoke in favor of endorsement, saying "black men first and white women afterwards." In 1848 he had written an editorial in his newspaper, the *North Star*, saying that women were "justly entitled" to all the political rights claimed for men, and that, politically, women were "on an equal footing" with men. Now he said: "I must say that I do not see how anyone can pretend that there is the same urgency in giving the ballot to woman as to the Negro. With us, the matter is a question of life and death. . . . When women, because they are women . . . are objects of insult and outrage at every turn; when they are in danger of having their homes burnt down over their heads; when their children are not allowed to enter schools; then they will have an urgency to obtain the ballot equal to our own."

Susan Anthony repeated the stand taken by herself and Elizabeth Stanton: they were against having one form of suffrage take precedence over another. Equal rights meant just that: rights for both blacks and women, with the association working for both at the same time and with the same degree of enthusiasm. Women should not be told to "stand back and wait." Douglass said that women should be generous and allow the Negro to get his vote first. A young woman in the audience replied that she did not think it generous "to compel women to yield on all questions . . . simply because they are women."

Lucy Stone, trying to take a middle ground, said she regretted the omission of women, yet was happy to accept the Fifteenth Amendment, "thankful in my soul" to see anybody win the right to vote.

Throughout the discussion, there was an echo of the old split in the Anti-Slavery Society between the pro- and anti-woman forces, with women being told to remain inconspicuously in the background. As Elizabeth Stanton and Susan Anthony listened to the long argument before the pro-amendment resolution was passed, they became convinced that the cause of woman suffrage could expect little help from the Equal Rights Association. It contained too many men and, as Mrs. Stanton had discovered in Kansas, it was "impossible for the best of men to understand women's feelings." What was needed was an association of women, whose central aim would be to win the vote—for women.

Other women at the convention came to the same conclusion. They met immediately afterward and organized themselves into the National Woman Suffrage Association, with Mrs. Stanton as president. Its principal aim was to work for the passage of an amendment, the sixteenth, granting the vote to women.

Lucy Stone and the other members of the Boston group were outraged. They felt they had been deliberately excluded—as they probably were. But, after all, the impetus for the new association had been a fundamental disagreement with the Boston-abolitionist views. In the attack on Susan Anthony and Elizabeth Stanton at the Equal Rights convention, it had virtually been suggested that these ladies, with their heretical beliefs, leave the organization altogether. Which was, in effect, exactly what they were doing, but going one step further and forming their own organization to carry out these beliefs.

The Bostonians particularly resented having the new suffrage association, in which they were given no part, call itself "National." And they felt it was dominated by women whose radical ideas on marriage and divorce, and unfortunate association with men like Train, had already alienated conservative women and might bring the whole movement into disrepute.

The Bostonians decided to form a new group of their own. In November, led by Lucy Stone, they organized the American Woman Suffrage Association, "to unite those who cannot use the methods, and means, which Mrs. Stanton and Susan use." The National was primarily a woman's organization; the American admitted men on an equal basis. No man could hold office in the National; in the American, Henry Ward Beecher, the popular minister, was elected president, with Henry Blackwell as one of the secretaries. In the National, a few top leaders could make and execute decisions, which allowed for quick action. In the American, a slow, cumbersome procedure had to be followed before any action could be taken by the executive committee.

Another difference was that instead of trying, like the National, to get a Federal woman suffrage amendment, the American would work mainly for state and local suffrage. And finally, where the Stanton-Anthony organization concerned itself with anything that in any way affected the lives or freedom of women, Lucy Stone's group confined itself to suffrage, carefully avoiding what they considered "extraneous" or controversial subjects.

The split caused dismay among those who were friendly to both factions, and among the new suffragists of the western states and territories. Lucretia Mott and others tried to bring them together again. Elizabeth Stanton offered to resign if it was her presence that stood in the way of unity. Susan Anthony expressed her own desire for a united organization. But it was hopeless. The two groups—or at least their leaders— were too far apart in temperament and tactics, though their ultimate goals were much the same.

Lucretia Mott and Martha Wright gave their allegiance to the Stanton-Anthony National. So did most of the western women. They were younger, and had not been involved either in the earlier disagreements between Lucy Stone and Susan Anthony, or in the relationship between antislavery and woman's rights, or even, in the Far West, in the conflict between black and woman suffrage. They were interested only in getting the vote, and getting it as soon as possible, which was what the National proposed to do.

To the westerners, Susan Anthony and Elizabeth Stanton had always been the most visible leaders of the movement. *The Revolution* and Mrs. Stanton's outspoken articles on subjects like marriage, divorce, sex, and birth control—regarded as not quite respectable in the more conservative East, especially in Boston—did not at all dismay the women of the freer and less tradition-bound West. In the rough, difficult, frontier conditions of the newer areas, women were neither sheltered from nor unaware of the harsher realities. They responded much more to the pioneering, aggressive spirit that had propelled the ladies of Seneca Falls than to the more decorous tactics of the slower-moving ladies of Boston.

One great source of irritation to the Boston group had been *The Revolution*, with its frank discussions of indiscreet topics and its sympathetic reporting of scandalous criminal cases involving women. One of the first actions of the American Association was to establish its own moderate, uncontroversial paper, the *Woman's Journal*. The first issue appeared in January 1870, with Lucy Stone, Mary Livermore, and Julia Ward Howe as editors.

Julia Ward Howe was a writer and lecturer, active in anti-slavery and woman's movements, but best remembered for writing "The Battle Hymn of the Republic" in 1861. Mary Livermore, the editor-in-chief, was an educated Bostonian of strict Calvinist background. She wanted women to have the vote so that they could fight against drinking, poverty, and prostitution. She had started her own suffrage paper, *The Agitator*, in 1869, but merged it with the *Woman's Journal* the following year. Mrs. Livermore had helped form the National Woman Suffrage Association, and had considered merging her *Agitator* with *The Revolution*. But she had been uncomfortable and even "repelled by some of the idiosyncrasies of our New York friends" and by "their opposition to the Fifteenth Amendment, the buffoonery of George F. Train, the loose utterances of the *Revolution* on the marriage and dress questions." When the American was organized, she went over to the more conservative group with relief.

There were undoubtedly others who joined the American with relief, and perhaps even more who switched their subscriptions from the daring *Revolution* to the less abrasive *Woman's Journal*. *The Revolution*, already in serious financial trouble, began to go under.

Right after the first number had appeared, Train had left for England. He had given Susan Anthony $600, and said that in his absence Melliss would pay the bills. But Train's first act abroad was to make a pro-Irish-independence speech which landed him in a Dublin jail, where he spent the next year. He continued to send articles, but no money. Melliss provided as much money as he could, but it wasn't enough. Susan Anthony went after advertising and new subscribers with her usual energy, but that didn't bring in enough money either. The debts began to pile up.

Train suggested that it might help *The Revolution* to drop his name and writings, since so many people objected to his association with the paper. This was done in May 1869. *The Revolution* continued for another year after that. For a paper of its kind and in that period it had a fairly good circulation, but not enough to keep it going without extra financial backing, especially after the competing *Woman's Journal* appeared.

Susan Anthony did everything possible to save it, borrowing from her family and friends, but it was futile. Even Elizabeth Stanton urged her to give up, saying it was not worth the financial struggle. In May 1870, Susan Anthony yielded. She turned the paper over to a wealthy contributor, who ran it for a while as a literary journal; then it merged with the *Christian Enquirer*.

There remained debts of more than $10,000, all of which Susan Anthony undertook to pay off. Her brother and friends urged her to declare the paper's bankruptcy, which would have relieved her of all financial responsibility, but, she wrote to Mrs. Stanton, "My pride for women, to say nothing of my conscience, says no." It took years of strenuous lecturing and even more strenuous scrimping, but in May 1876 she finally paid off the last debt.

After some preliminary sniping and mutual misunderstandings and recriminations, the two organizations, National and American, settled down to work, if not side by side, at least toward the same general goals. In a way, both organizations were needed. The American was able to draw into the suffrage movement those who felt the National was too radical in its ideas and methods, too broad in its scope. Women who wanted the vote, but didn't want to tamper with traditional views of marriage or divorce, or become involved in controversial issues, found a comfortable place in the American Association. These women, who might otherwise have remained outside the suffrage movement, were able to contribute to it in their own quieter way.

The National attracted the more enterprising, younger women, especially from the West, who were willing to be more daring in their attempts to get the vote, and who were ready to consider other problems of women besides suffrage. After twenty years, however, these bolder maneuvers and less conventional ideas would become domesticated. A new generation would care little about the old quarrels, and insist that a single organization would be more effective.

Lucy Stone's daughter, Alice Stone Blackwell, helped unite the two groups. After two years of negotiations, the National American Woman Suffrage Association was formed in 1890, with Elizabeth Stanton, seventy-five years old but still active and lively, as president; Susan B. Anthony, seventy and even more active, as vice president; and Lucy Stone, seventy-two, as chairman of the executive committee.

With the merger, they would all be back together again. But in the meantime, Elizabeth Stanton and Susan Anthony, with their own organization behind them, had a few more jolts for their more cautious colleagues.

21

Are Women Persons?

The most ignorant and degraded man who walks to the polls feels himself superior to the most intelligent woman.

—Susan B. Anthony, 1894

Disfranchisement says to all women: "Your judgment is not sound; your opinions are not worthy of being counted." Man is the superior, woman the subject, under the present condition of political affairs, and until this great wrong is righted, ignorant men and small boys will continue to look with disdain on the opinion of women.

—Susan B. Anthony, 1891

Abraham Lincoln said: "No man is good enough to govern another man without his consent." Now I say unto you, "No man is good enough to govern any woman without her consent."

—Susan B. Anthony, 1895

By the end of 1869, Mrs. Stanton's three oldest sons had completed their education, but there were still four children left. She insisted that her two daughters, like the boys, must go to college; they would be sent to Vassar, which had opened in 1865. Henry Stanton's income from law and journalism wasn't quite enough to cover all of this, so when the New York Lyceum Bureau asked her to make a western lecture tour for which she would be well paid, she was happy to accept.

The invitation came at an opportune time. The National Woman Suffrage Association had been established and, under the capable management of Susan Anthony, required less of Mrs. Stanton's immediate presence. *The Revolution* was obviously on the way out and Mrs. Stanton's editorial work was coming to an end. Her seven children no longer needed her close attention. Her home was now admirably looked after by Amelia Willard, the Quaker housekeeper who had joined the Stantons and become "the joy of our household." Without her, wrote Mrs. Stanton, "much of my public work would have been quite impossible."

For eight months of every year, during the next twelve years, she lectured all over the country. She spoke on a great variety of subjects, including politics and prison conditions, but tried as often as possible to include something about women. She urged that girls be encouraged to develop their natural talents, receive education and training for self-support, and not be taught to regard keeping house as the main purpose of their existence. She talked about the advantages of coeducation and dress reform, about marriage and divorce, about child care.

She had a special interest in this last subject. When she had her first baby, she read the existing books on child care, listened to doctors, and took note of the prevailing customs, only to find from her own experience that she disagreed with practically all of these. It was the custom in those days to swaddle, or wrap, infants tightly, on the theory that their soft bones needed protection. Infants were also protected from such dangers as drinking water or being exposed to fresh air and sunshine. Mrs. Stanton, after rejecting most of the current shibboleths and raising seven healthy children, carried on a crusade to dress babies loosely and comfortably, give them water to drink, and avoid keeping them in airless, overheated rooms.

She earned between $3000 and $4000 a year. Traveling remained difficult and uncomfortable; on one trip she went through snowbound Iowa on sleighs, covering as much as fifty miles during a single day and delivering her lecture that same evening. She missed her family and suffered from loneliness. But she enjoyed the work, she loved meeting new people, and she welcomed the opportunity to spread the message about woman's rights and suffrage. And she was glad of the money, not only to pay for her children's education, but for the feeling of independence it gave her. It was a sense of personal satisfaction that only a woman who had spent her life as a dependent daughter and wife could fully appreciate.

Susan Anthony, too, spent these years as a Lyceum lecturer. Her purpose was to earn enough money to pay off the $10,000 debt left by the failure of *The Revolution*. She had never thought of herself as a professional lecturer, and joined the Lyceum almost by accident. A sudden illness had made it impossible for Mrs. Stanton to fulfill several engagements in Pennsylvania. A substitute was needed immediately; Susan Anthony was drafted with practically no time to refuse. She did so well that the Lyceum management asked her to make a tour of her own through the West. She accepted, realizing that she would be able to pay off *The Revolution*'s debt and advance woman's rights at the same time, since her principal lecture topic was "Work, Wages, and the Ballot."

Later she added a speech on "Social Purity," dealing with

such taboo questions as prostitution, venereal disease, adultery, bigamy, abortion, and sex crimes. If women were given vocational training, she said, and, like men, "have equal chances to earn a living," they would be able to support themselves without turning to desperate measures like prostitution. The lecture was well received in the larger cities, but small-town newspapers complained that "no modest woman ought to acknowledge that she is so familiar" with topics "that maidenly delicacy should refuse to discuss."

She was not a naturally eloquent speaker like Elizabeth Stanton or Lucy Stone or Anna Dickinson, one of the younger feminists, who was a dynamic orator. But years of addressing conventions and meetings had given her self-confidence and expertise. She had developed the ability to respond quickly and pointedly, and with wit, to questions from the floor. She no longer wrote out her speeches, having learned that written speeches were the least effective. She expressed herself without flourishes of style or emotion, resting her case, as one newspaper put it, on facts rather than oratory.

She was often a surprise to those seeing her for the first time. For years, newspapers had talked about her as a bony, vinegary, aggressive spinster, a die-hard fanatic, as unattractive physically as she was ideologically. A female public speaker was still a rare and curious object, especially in the small towns of America. When the female was the notorious Susan B. Anthony, curiosity became even greater. But when she appeared on the platform, she was found to be nothing like the newspaper cartoons and caricatures. She was slender and well built, rather than angular. As she spoke, she conveyed an innate warmth and friendliness, an engaging sense of humor, and, at the same time, strength of conviction. One listener said: "Her fund of logic, fact, and fun seems inexhaustible."

She was paid $75 for each of her first lectures; she was soon receiving $150 apiece. When she wasn't filling a Lyceum engagement, she arranged lectures on her own. In one six-month period she traveled 8000 miles and gave 108 lectures. Sometimes, on her trips, she would run into Elizabeth Stanton. Once, for several months in 1871, they made a tour together through the Far West. But most of the time she was alone. The work was hard, the constant travel exhausting. But at the end of six years she was able to pay off the last debt of *The Revolution*. "The day of Jubilee for me," she said, "has come."

No matter how busy their lecturing kept them, Elizabeth Stanton and Susan Anthony continued as the active heads of the suffrage movement. Their lectures were considered part of the suffrage effort, since woman's rights was a principal subject for both of them. And in their extensive travels they took advantage of every opportunity to help local suffrage groups.

Susan Anthony, especially, would cancel lecture engagements, though it meant losing money, to attend conventions or take part in new attempts to win the vote. In 1871 and 1872, when a new and dramatic stratagem was tried, creating another explosion of publicity and excited response, Susan Anthony was at its center.

When the Fourteenth Amendment was passed, many lawyers and Congressmen, studying it carefully, came to the startling conclusion that it gave women the right to vote. The first section of the amendment says that "All persons born or naturalized in the United States . . . are citizens. . . . No State shall make or enforce any law which shall abridge the privileges . . . of citizens." It is true that the second section refers to "male inhabitants" and "male citizens," which might imply that voting is restricted to males. But it speaks only of the possible denial of suffrage to such male citizens. The positive right to vote seems to be granted in the first section to all citizens, who are defined as "all persons born or naturalized in the United States."

Well then, ran the argument, aren't women persons? And

therefore, under Section I, aren't they entitled to vote? Section II might link the number of Congressmen to the number of eligible male voters denied the ballot, but that did not necessarily mean that there could not be female voters. It was one of those legal instances where the wording of a law lends itself to conflicting interpretations.

Among those who saw the Fourteenth Amendment as providing grounds for woman suffrage was Victoria Woodhull, one of the most notorious figures to appear on the nineteenth-century American scene. Victoria and her younger sister, Tennessee Celeste ("Tennie C.") Claflin, had come from a raffish family whose members dabbled in spiritualism, the occult, and faith healing. At sixteen, Victoria Claflin had married Dr. Canning Woodhull—the "Dr." based on a small amount of medical training—who joined the nomadic Claflin family in dispensing an "Elixir of Life."

By 1868, when the sisters appeared in New York, Victoria was divorced and their background conveniently obscured. They were sponsored by Commodore Cornelius Vanderbilt, the millionaire famous for his shrewd financial manipulations and his comment, "The public be damned." Vanderbilt, now a sick and superstitious man in his seventies, had been drawn to Tennessee by her supposed skill as a faith healer and her youthful charm and vivacity. To everyone's amazement, he set the sisters up as brokers and bankers on Wall Street.

In 1870 they began to publish *Woodhull & Claflin's Weekly*, a newspaper dedicated to social and political reform. The masthead read "PROGRESS! FREE THOUGHT! UNTRAMMELED LIVES! / Breaking the Way for Future Generations." Its contents were a curious combination of financial news and articles on spiritualism, sex, birth control, and free love. The paper supported woman's rights, vocational training for girls, and votes for women.

Their neighbors in the financial district regarded the "Bewitching Brokers" with mingled amusement and shock. Rumors about their virtue, or lack of it, began to spread. The Claflin girls were free souls and dashing adventuresses in a style generally limited to males at that time. Blessed with beauty, charm, intelligence, and, from all accounts, great personal magnetism, they were able to lead astonishingly unorthodox lives in a period of rigid double-standard morality and rockbound convention. They believed in a single standard of morality for both men and women, but—unlike Susan Anthony, who was also for a single standard—they didn't want that standard to be the one set for women. They wanted it just the other way around: they wanted women to have the complete sexual freedom that men enjoyed. Victoria said openly that it was her "inalienable right" to have as many lovers as she pleased.

It would be hard to imagine today the scandalized reaction to such statements. No one knows for certain how far the sisters practiced their beliefs. Tennessee may well have done so, but Victoria was busy with other things. Victoria had political ambitions, nurtured by her faith in spiritualism. She said she had been informed by Demosthenes, the Greek statesman and orator of the fourth century B.C., that she was destined to become the ruler—or President—of the United States.

First, she had to establish the right of women to vote. She applied for and received permission to present a memorial to Congress on the question of woman suffrage; in January 1871 she addressed the judiciary committee of the House of Representatives. She believed that the Fourteenth and Fifteenth amendments implied the right of women to vote, and she wanted Congress to pass legislation making it possible to exercise that right.

She made her address on the same morning as the scheduled opening of the annual woman suffrage convention in Washington. When Susan Anthony arrived in that city and heard about

Mrs. Woodhull's address, she insisted on postponing the opening session of the convention so that she could attend the congressional hearing. This was the first ever held on Federal woman suffrage legislation, and Susan Anthony, of all people, did not intend to miss it.

She was accompanied by Isabella Beecher Hooker and Paulina Wright Davis, two highly respectable woman's rights leaders, and Albert G. Riddle, a constitutional lawyer whom Miss Anthony had retained to represent the suffrage movement. They had heard something about the notorious Mrs. Woodhull, but had never met her. When she appeared, impeccably dressed, with a refined air and modest manner, her beautiful face filled with an earnest sincerity, all of them were impressed. By the time she had finished speaking in her pleasant, musical voice, they were completely won over. They invited Mrs. Woodhull to repeat her talk at the suffrage convention.

A few months later, in May, the National Woman Suffrage Association held its anniversary convention in New York City. This time it was Elizabeth Stanton who invited Victoria Woodhull to address the convention. Mrs. Woodhull hadn't been well known in Washington, but here in New York the scandalous Woodhull-Claflin rumors were in full cry. Some of the association officers refused to sit on the same platform with the dubious lady. In reply, Mrs. Stanton seated Mrs. Woodhull between herself and Lucretia Mott. That, she said, should provide sufficient respectability.

The effect was sensational, and almost disastrous. For years the enemies of woman suffrage had warned against its deplorable effects upon feminine purity. It would lead, they cried, not only to the decline of marriage and neglect of the home, but to that awful nightmare, free love. Here, in the person of Victoria Woodhull, was their living proof. The newspapers made the most of it, linking the woman's movement with free love and casting the whole cause into outer darkness.

Lucy Stone and her Boston colleagues had warned against the rash impetuosity of Mrs. Stanton—with her insistent discussion of divorce—and against the headstrong fanaticism of Susan Anthony, which led to consorting with unsavory characters like George Francis Train. And now here was the association with Victoria Woodhull to prove them right. This was much worse than the Train episode. He had been simply undesirable; Mrs. Woodhull and her sister were, as Lucy Stone's daughter expressed it, "women of licentious lives."

Susan Anthony herself began to have doubts. The questions raised about Mrs. Woodhull, the gossip, the reaction of the press, the shocked animosity of many women—far greater than anything created by the Train connection—made her stop and think. It was not that she was afraid of criticism or disapproval; she had resisted such pressures when she believed herself right. But the questions raised about Mrs. Woodhull echoed her own doubts and questions.

Was Mrs. Woodhull really a genius, as some people believed? Was she really the dedicated worker for woman's rights she claimed to be? Or was she in truth a self-seeking, completely amoral egotist, and a slightly unbalanced one at that, who might damage or destroy the suffrage movement in the pursuit of her own personal ambitions? Would the suffrage movement lose more than it was gaining from Victoria Woodhull?

Elizabeth Stanton had no such doubts. She approved of Mrs. Woodhull and defended her against all detractors as "a grand, brave woman." But Susan Anthony's skepticism deepened at the next annual suffrage convention in Washington, in January 1872, when Mrs. Woodhull made a rousing appeal for the creation of a new political party, the Equal Rights Party, with herself as candidate for President. Miss Anthony was able to squelch this suggestion, but the idea lingered in the minds of some, including Mrs. Stanton.

After the convention, Susan Anthony resumed her lecture tour in the West. She wrote to Elizabeth Stanton expressing her opposition to the formation of a new political party. It would set men all the more against granting suffrage to women, if it meant giving power to a new and rival party. She made it clear that her name was not to be used in any plans to form such a party.

She was furious, therefore, when in April, while waiting for a train, she picked up a copy of *Woodhull & Claflin's Weekly* and read an announcement that the National Woman Suffrage Association would hold a convention in New York City the following month for the purpose of forming a new political party and nominating candidates for President and Vice President of the United States. The signatures to the announcement included not only Elizabeth Cady Stanton but Susan B. Anthony!

She sent off an angry telegram to Mrs. Stanton, demanding that her name be removed, and that the association avoid becoming involved in such a thoroughly unwise scheme. But when she returned to New York to attend the annual convention, she found that her instructions had been ignored. At the first session, Mrs. Woodhull announced, with the approval of Mrs. Stanton, that joint sessions of the new political organization and the National Association would be held.

Susan Anthony immediately countermanded the announcement. Mrs. Stanton called Miss Anthony "narrow, bigoted, and headstrong" and promptly resigned as president of the association. Susan Anthony was elected to replace her and, as president, was able to defeat a second attempt by Mrs. Woodhull to call a joint session with the embryo Equal Rights Party.

The next day, the Equal Rights Party was formally established. Mrs. Woodhull was nominated for President, Frederick Douglass for Vice President. This came as a surprise to Douglass, who had known nothing about it, and he refused the honor.

Susan Anthony and Elizabeth Stanton had disagreed before. In their relationship, each spoke her mind freely. Agreement was not automatic, nor was either one the stronger personality, dominating the opinions of the other. Often they arrived at a decision only after long and frank discussion of their opposing points of view. Mrs. Stanton was inclined to be the more impulsive: she had the greater imagination and was quick to take daring leaps into bold—and sometimes rash—action. Susan Anthony was essentially more earthbound; she would stop to look for the practical flaws in any proposed scheme, no matter how attractive it might seem at first. Mrs. Stanton had a high degree of respect for her collaborator's more sober judgments, gave them serious thought, and at times came around to her view.

This is what happened in the present case. She soon realized that Susan Anthony had been right in refusing to permit the National Association to support the unstable Victoria Woodhull and her Equal Rights Party. But others were slower to agree with Miss Anthony's judgment of Mrs. Woodhull, and the association was badly shaken by the whole episode.

Later that year, Victoria Woodhull caused another disturbance—it seemed cataclysmic at the time—by exposing the great Beecher-Tilton scandal. Two years earlier, Elizabeth Tilton had confessed to her husband, Theodore Tilton, the liberal editor and lecturer, that she had been carrying on an affair with the Reverend Henry Ward Beecher, the most popular and famous preacher of the day. Both men were active supporters of the woman's rights movement; Beecher had been the first president of the American Woman Suffrage Association. Mrs. Tilton begged her husband to take no action, particularly since the relationship was now over. Tilton agreed, but he brooded over the affair and spoke about it to some of his close friends, including Elizabeth Cady Stanton. The following year, Mrs. Stanton, in a moment of misplaced confidence, passed the story on to Vic-

toria Woodhull who, after months of dropping dark hints, revealed the details in the fall of 1872, first in a speech, then in
Woodhull & Claflin's Weekly.

The publication set off an explosion of sensational publicity
and controversy. Denials, charges, and countercharges were exchanged. All over the country, people took sides passionately.
Mrs. Tilton, after several times changing her version of what had
happened, left her husband. Tilton sued Beecher for alienation of
his wife's affections. The trial lasted almost six dramatic months,
but the jury was unable to come to a decision and the case was
finally dismissed.

During these events, Elizabeth Cady Stanton, in letters,
speeches, and articles, came out in support of Mrs. Tilton who,
as a woman, she asserted, was the principal victim of the scandal.
Victoria Woodhull lectured widely on the case, saying on
various occasions that she and Tilton had been lovers. Mrs. Stanton's defense of Mrs. Tilton and Mrs. Woodhull's pronounce-
ments on free love were seized upon by the enemies of the
woman's rights movement, who tried to use the whole incident
as further evidence of the connection between the movement
and immorality. How much actual damage was done to the
woman's cause was not clear. But what was clearer than ever, at
least to Susan Anthony, was that future entanglements with
irresponsible people like Victoria Woodhull, who for her own
private purposes had made the scandal public, must be avoided.

After Victoria Woodhull, there were other attempts by ec-
centrics or fanatics to divert the Suffrage Association into by-
paths of extremism. But Susan Anthony became adept at
detecting and heading off such proposed invasions. Never
again did she allow the association to become involved with
those who, in the end, would distort its character and goals.

Other women who challenged the Fourteenth Amendment
were less flamboyant than Victoria Woodhull. In 1871 and

1872, 150 women tried to vote under the amendment. In most cases they were not permitted to register; if they managed to register, they were not permitted to vote; if they actually voted, their votes were not counted. They would then bring suit against the election inspectors for denying them, as citizens, their right to vote.

There had been a few earlier attempts. In 1868, in Vineland, New Jersey, 172 women, including four black women, came to vote and were directed to drop their ballots into a separate box, and in 1870 the same separation of ballots took place in Hyde Park, Massachusetts, where forty-two women, led by the aging Grimké sisters, came to the polls. The separate boxes could then be conveniently put aside during the final count.

In 1871 seventy women came in a body to the polls in the District of Columbia, tried to vote, and were turned away. They brought suit against the Board of Election Inspectors. The court ruled that the Fourteenth Amendment did not affect the law of the District, which specifically limited suffrage to men over twenty-one. Four women in other states tried to vote that same year; three of them actually had their votes counted.

On November 1, 1872, Susan Anthony asked her sisters to go with her to register in Rochester, New York. The chief registration inspector refused to allow them to do so, saying it was against New York law. Susan Anthony had expected this and come prepared. She had brought along a copy of the Fourteenth Amendment and read aloud the section on which she was basing their right to vote. This, she contended, superseded the New York State constitution.

All the inspectors present listened to the discussion, and two of them agreed to take the responsibility of registering the Anthony sisters. As soon as Susan Anthony left the registration office, she went to ask other women to register. The newspapers carried the story, which persuaded still more women that perhaps they could vote. Altogether, fifty women registered in Rochester.

But when election day came, most of them had second thoughts. It was, after all, illegal for unqualified persons to vote. They could be fined up to $500 and be imprisoned up to three years. Susan Anthony knew this; before she herself tried to vote, she sought legal advice. Several lawyers refused to help her. Finally she found a retired judge, Henry R. Selden, who felt she had valid grounds for her action and agreed to defend her if she ran into trouble. Then she, her sisters, and eleven other women went to vote.

The voting inspectors were reluctant to let the women cast their ballots, since that might make the inspectors guilty of violating the law, but Susan Anthony promised to pay their expenses if they were charged with an illegality. The women then had the incredible experience of exercising the democratic right of all citizens to a voice in their government: they voted.

About two weeks later they were all arrested. Oddly enough, though she knew the law, Susan Anthony had never expected to be actually arrested. She had planned, by proving her own right to suffrage, to bring suit against those inspectors who had refused to register women or accept their vote. This would establish the precedent, once and for all, that inspectors all over the country must accept women as voters.

The pre-trial hearing was held on December 23 before a large audience of newspaper reporters, concerned women, and the curious public. When the militant lawbreakers appeared, they all proved to be, as one newspaper put it, "elderly, matronly-looking women with thoughtful faces, just the sort one would like to see in charge of one's sick-room, considerate, patient, kindly."

Bail was set at $500 each, pending trial. Everyone except Susan Anthony paid. She refused, applying instead for a writ of habeas corpus, planning to challenge the legality of her arrest. The writ was denied, and her bail raised to $1000. Again she refused to pay, saying she would go to jail first. But Judge Selden couldn't bear the thought of Susan Anthony in jail; in spite of her protests, he paid the bond himself. As they were leaving the courtroom, she learned that, by paying bail, she had lost the chance to put the case before the Supreme Court by writ of habeas corpus. She hurried back into the courtroom to get the bond canceled, but it was too late.

The trial took place on June 17, 1873. Before it began, she went through the county delivering a speech—"Is It a Crime for a United States Citizen to Vote?"—in which she discussed the constitutional issues involved. She had not committed any crime, she said, but had only exercised her voting right as a citizen as laid down in the Constitution, which had drawn no distinction between the sexes. In its very preamble, "It was we, the people, not we, the white male citizens, nor yet we, the male citizens, but we, the whole people, who formed this Union."

Some authorities interpreted the use of masculine pronouns —"he," "his," and "him"—as proof that only men were intended to have certain rights under the Constitution. "If you insist on this version of the letter of the law," she said, "we shall insist that you be consistent and . . . exempt women from taxation" and from obeying laws, since "there is no she, or her, or hers, in the tax laws" or in the criminal laws.

The legal papers served on her by the court were all printed forms containing only masculine pronouns. The clerk of the court had altered them to read "she" and "her." If government officials can manipulate pronouns for their purposes, she said, then women can do the same in order to exercise their citizen's right to vote.

The district attorney, fearing that her speech might prejudice a jury in her favor, transferred the trial to another county. She immediately gave her speech in as much of that county as she had time for. The rest of it was covered by another woman's rights leader, Matilda Joslyn Gage, who spoke on "The United States on Trial, not Susan B. Anthony."

The case attracted attention all over the United States. Much of it was sympathetic, especially in Rochester itself, where a local newspaper called her "our Susan B. Anthony" and described her as "a genuine lady—no pretense nor sham—but good Quaker metal . . . cheery, warm-hearted . . . utterly fearless . . . yet having a woman's delicate sensitiveness." The article quoted a woman who, after attending a suffrage convention, had said, "No, I am not converted to what these women advocate, I am too cowardly for that; but I am converted to Susan B. Anthony."

When the trial opened, every seat in the Canandaigua courthouse was filled. There were many lawyers and politicians present, including ex-President Millard Fillmore, all curious to hear how the constitutional question would be handled.

The judge was Ward Hunt, presiding over his first case. Throughout the trial he showed a strong bias against Susan Anthony. He refused to allow her to be called as a witness in her own behalf. Judge Selden, in his defense arguments, stressed the fact that she had acted in good faith, believing, upon his own advice, that she had a right to vote under the provisions of the Fourteenth Amendment. The only way to prove such a right was by trying to exercise it and then getting a court decision on the legality of such action. Her one motive was to test the constitutional question of woman suffrage.

The district attorney replied that her motives were irrelevant. She had violated the law and was guilty, an argument that he developed in a two-hour speech. Judge Hunt then pulled out of his pocket a written opinion, apparently prepared before the trial, and began reading it to the jury. The privilege of voting, he said, arises from "the Constitution of the State, and not of the United States." In New York the Legislature "has seen fit to say that . . . voting shall be limited to the male sex." Neither the Fourteenth nor the Fifteenth Amendment specifically contained the word "sex" or said that women could vote. Miss Anthony's arguments based on these amendments were therefore not "potent." She knew all this, said the judge, and such knowledge of the facts supplies criminal intent.

He concluded by saying there was nothing for the jury to consider since it was all a question of law "and I have decided as a question of law" that Miss Anthony did not have the right to vote. "I therefore direct that you find a verdict of guilty." He refused to let the jury be polled and, over Judge Selden's protests, cut off all further discussion and discharged the jurors. Several of them said, after they had been dismissed, that they would have voted not guilty.

The next day Judge Selden moved for a new trial, on the grounds that Miss Anthony had been denied her right to a trial by jury. Judge Hunt refused, and pronounced sentence. She was fined $100 and costs. Her response was, "I shall never pay a dollar of your unjust penalty." Ordinarily she would have been imprisoned until she paid, but Judge Hunt carefully refused to order her put in jail, thereby taking away her second chance of bringing the case before the Supreme Court.

After Susan Anthony's trial was over, the election inspectors were tried before Judge Hunt. They were found guilty and fined $25 apiece. Susan Anthony was ready to put up the money, as she had promised, but two of the men decided not to pay as a matter of principle and were jailed. The women who had voted kept them fed with superb meals, and hundreds of Rochester residents came to visit them. At the end of a week, President Grant pardoned them and remitted their fines. The cases against the other women who had voted were dropped. Susan Anthony's fine was never paid, but no further action was taken against her.

A great many lawyers, members of Congress, and newspapers, regardless of how they felt about woman suffrage, were outraged by the trial. They considered it a gross violation of the right to a trial by jury, a dangerous "over-reaching assumption of authority" by Judge Hunt. One newspaper said the judge "violated the Constitution of the United States more in convicting Miss Anthony of illegal voting, than she did in voting." She was urged to appeal the case, but the only way this was possible was for her to petition Congress. She did so, but her petition was rejected.

Another case, however, was appealed and did reach the Supreme Court. Virginia Minor of St. Louis, a friend of Susan Anthony's and president of the Missouri Woman Suffrage Association, had also tried to vote in 1872. The election inspector refused to register her, and she brought suit against him. As a married woman, in order to bring suit she had to be joined by her husband, Francis Minor. Mr. Minor was a lawyer; he had been among the first to suggest that the Fourteenth Amendment provided grounds for woman suffrage and had wanted to bring a test case before the courts.

He was able to carry it through the lower courts and all the way to the Supreme Court. But on March 29, 1875, the court ruled against him, saying that the Constitution does not confer suffrage upon anyone. The vote is regulated by each state, and all the Constitution could do, through the amendments, was to forbid discrimination on certain grounds. The Fourteenth and Fifteenth amendments had forbidden discrimination on the grounds of race, but not on those of sex.

Another path must now be followed to woman suffrage: an amendment to the Constitution specifically guaranteeing it. In view of all that had happened, this should have taken no time at all. Now that the Negro's hour had brought emancipation and the vote, surely the woman's hour was at hand.

There was a footnote, or rather a preamble, to the attempts to vote under the Fourteenth Amendment. In 1866, Elizabeth Stanton had decided to run for Congress, not because she thought she had the remotest chance of being elected, but to illustrate a constitutional point. Under the New York State constitution, women were denied the right to vote, but there was no stated restriction on their right to run for political office. To test this right, Mrs. Stanton offered herself as a candidate on a platform of *"free speech, free press, free men, and free trade,—the cardinal points of democracy."* If elected, she promised, she would work within Congress to secure universal suffrage so that women could vote.

She received a grand total of twenty-four votes, but also a vast amount of publicity and discussion, which had been her real purpose in running. Her only regret, she said, looking back upon her "successful defeat," was that she did not get photographs of her "two dozen unknown friends."

22

The "Antis"

The conclusive objection to the political enfranchisement of woman is, that it would weaken and finally break up and destroy the Christian family.

—Orestes A. Brownson, 1869

I would not . . . degrade woman by giving her the right of suffrage. . . . It would take her down from that pedestal where she is today, influencing by her gentle and kindly caress the action of her husband toward the good and pure.

—Senator George G. Vest, 1887

I called on Mrs. Frémont to see if she would head a petition. "Oh, no. I do not believe in suffrage for women. I think women in their present position manage men better." I expressed doubt as to whether it was our business in life to "manage men."

—Elizabeth Cady Stanton, 1866

*I*n January 1875, Martha Wright, one of the original ladies of Seneca Falls, died. She was thirteen years younger
than her famous sister, Lucretia Mott, and had been overshadowed by her. Since Martha Wright made few public speeches
and wrote even less than she spoke, her special contribution to
the woman's movement has often been overlooked.

She was one of its active leaders from the start. She had
presided over several conventions and at the time of her death
was president of the National Association. But she did more
than hold office and serve on committees: she provided a necessary element of calm judgment and perspective to check the
sometimes excessive enthusiasm or earnestness of more zealous
leaders like Elizabeth Stanton and Susan Anthony. "Martha
Wright," wrote Mrs. Stanton, "was uniformly in favor of toning
down our fiery pronunciamentos."

For this purpose she was perhaps even more effective than
Lucretia Mott, since Mrs. Wright had a touch of lightness lacking in her more serious sister. Susan Anthony called her "clear-
sighted, true and steadfast almost beyond all other women."

She was one of the first to support Mrs. Stanton in proposing
woman suffrage as a basic aim of the movement. And yet, in
many ways, she was more conservative than the other leaders.
Unlike Elizabeth Stanton and Susan Anthony, who feit that
marriage should be only one of many options open to women,
and who constantly urged that girls be trained for non-domes-
tic careers, Martha Wright believed that the greatest roles for a
woman were those of wife and mother.

But she wanted to change the demeaning view of those roles.
Being a wife and mother, she felt, should in no way diminish a
woman as a responsible, capable adult, entitled to full citizenship. She wanted women to help "make the laws, and administer justice," on an equal basis with men. She wanted women to
be respected and to have self-respect; she wanted them to de-

mand economic and political rights: "I for one have always gloried in the name of Woman's Rights, and pitied those of my sex who ignobly declared they had all the rights they wanted." Above all, she wanted women to be aware of their full value as human beings.

Susan Anthony was deeply distressed by the sudden death of Martha Wright. She had always looked to her for encouragement and support. And in 1875, Susan Anthony felt in special need of encouragement. The attempts to base woman suffrage on the Fourteenth Amendment had failed. This was a staggering defeat. From now on, there would be a long, heartbreaking struggle to get a special constitutional amendment passed, specifically giving votes to women. At the same time, campaigns would be carried on in every state and territory, hoping to win suffrage in at least some states, which in turn might make it easier to put through a Federal amendment. The territories of Wyoming and Utah had granted woman suffrage in 1869 and 1870. But the only states to follow between 1870 and 1910 would be Colorado in 1893 and Idaho in 1896.

Year after year, the women, led principally by Susan Anthony, worked on. They held national, state, and local conventions, appealed to Congress and legislatures, raised money, made speeches. Whenever a state or territory held a referendum on woman suffrage, or whenever a state adopted a new constitution, the suffrage associations sent speakers and campaign assistance. There were fifty-six referendum campaigns, forty-seven state-constitution campaigns. Susan Anthony, growing older but no less active, traveled all over the country, speaking, organizing, encouraging local suffragists.

And yet, in spite of all this work, in spite of the steadily increasing respectability of woman suffrage and its supporters, suffrage seemed further away than ever. All the antisuffrage arguments—the physical fragility of women, their mental inferiority or at least their inability to understand politics (woman suffrage would "double the ignorant vote"), the danger to feminine purity and modesty, the threat to the family and home, the horrors of exposing gently bred females to the coarseness of the voting booth, the Biblical injunctions to remain subservient to men—all these persisted to some degree, and new ones were added.

When the temperance movement, mushrooming after the Civil War, was linked to woman suffrage, another source of opposition arose. Americans had always been heavy drinkers, but after the war there was a marked increase in the amount of liquor consumed and produced. Saloons were everywhere. Much of this was due to the great influx of immigrants, who drank more often and even more heavily than the descendants of the original colonial settlers. The liquor industry became highly profitable and powerful, acquiring close connections with both criminal and political elements. The United States Brewers' Association was organized in the 1860s to defend the interests of the trade, and particularly to ensure its political protection.

As drinking increased, so did the outcry against it. It was denounced as a sin and a menace, a destroyer of the American family, a threat to the efficiency of the American worker, a seedbed of crime and political corruption.

On December 23, 1873, in the town of Hillsboro, Ohio, an appeal for temperance was made by Dio Lewis, a man who had been afflicted with an alcoholic father. The next morning a group of women held prayer meetings in front of the town's saloons. Almost immediately afterward a much larger group of women did the same in the nearby town of Washington Court House.

From then on, the "Washington Court House Movement" spread like a brush fire. Thousands of women in one town after another, with no organization or direction, acting almost spontaneously, gathered in front of saloons and wherever liquor was sold. They sang hymns, read from the Bible, knelt on the sidewalk and prayed against the "Demon Rum." Sometimes the saloonkeeper and his customers were so moved that they joined the women and even went so far as to pour their liquor out on the street. Some 3000 saloons closed their doors—though many reopened after the fever passed.

The crusade lasted only about six months before it faded out as quickly as it had begun. But it made people think about the effects of liquor, and out of it grew a number of temperance leagues. In November 1874 women from seventeen states met at Cleveland and organized the Woman's National Christian Temperance Union. It had an immediate appeal, not only in the United States but in other countries. Church and press gave it their blessing; the most devout and upright women approved of it. Churchwomen who had shunned the irreligious suffrage associations embraced the WCTU. Like the Washington Court House Movement, it was welcomed as a "blessed antidote to the radicalism, fanaticism, and . . . blunders of the woman-suffrage associations."

But there was a surprise in store for the conservative, anti-suffrage women. At the organization meeting of the WCTU, a formidable woman named Frances Willard had been elected corresponding secretary. Unlike the other officers, she was a thorough feminist, believing not only in woman suffrage but in taking women beyond the confines of their homes and increasing their self-awareness and self-confidence.

Though she spoke of the "sacredness and value" of the "vocation of motherhood," she spoke even more of training women for commercial vocations as well: "Every true woman should firmly grasp in her steady hand an honorable breadwinning weapon with which she may hold her own in this world of relentless competition." As president of the Evanston College for Ladies, she had encouraged the students to develop their talents and seek worldly as well as domestic accomplishments. She wanted to transform women from diffident, isolated, and politically naïve housewives into politically aware, self-reliant citizens.

In 1876, at the first international convention of the WCTU, Frances Willard came out openly for woman suffrage, and asked the organization to support it. She was opposed by a large majority, but a small liberal wing developed under her leadership. The politically adept Miss Willard continued to attract followers, especially from the more liberal western states. By 1879 she had gained enough support to be elected national president of the WCTU.

Under her aggressive direction, the WCTU burgeoned into the largest, most prominent association of women in the world. There were 200,000 women organized in 10,000 local units in every state and territory of the United States. Women who weren't especially interested in temperance joined the "White Ribbon Army" in order to take part in one of the many activities—from physical culture to social welfare—sponsored by Miss Willard's "Do-Everything Policy."

Frances Willard was a rousing orator, a magnificent showman. She changed WCTU gatherings from what had been hardly more than prayer meetings into great dramatic events, colorful and emotional, with bright banners and brilliant displays of flowers, stirring music, and even more stirring speeches.

Through it all, she managed to convert many conservative women to woman suffrage. Realizing that their chief concerns were the home and the church, she cleverly advocated suffrage on the ground that it was needed to protect the home. If women could vote, they could outlaw drinking, that archenemy of the happy, united family. She was careful not to outrage her listeners—in contrast to Elizabeth Stanton, who loved to jolt her audience into fresh and unconventional points of view. Instead, feeling that people reacted more to the words and manner of expressing ideas than to the ideas themselves, she achieved her aims through the use of carefully selected emotional appeals. She never talked about the need for woman suffrage as a basis for the equality and independence of women —in which she herself believed—but described how the sanctity of the home could be preserved and the moral purity of the nation uplifted if the spiritual influence of women could be exercised through the vote. Instead of bluntly urging women to become self-supporting, as Susan Anthony did, she led them gently in the same direction, calling it "useful womanhood." The slogan which she coined for the WCTU and also used for suffrage drives was "For God and Home and Native Land."

She joined Lucy Stone's American Woman Suffrage Association and became an associate editor of the *Woman's Journal*, but was always ready to help Susan Anthony and the National Association as well, especially in working for a Federal suffrage amendment. Susan Anthony welcomed whatever assistance she could get from Frances Willard and the WCTU, but Elizabeth Stanton was not happy about the intrusion of the "singing and praying" temperance women into the suffrage movement. She suspected that the WCTU might prove more of an embarrassment than a benefit to the cause of woman suffrage.

As time went on, Frances Willard committed the WCTU so solidly to suffrage that she was able to send thousands of women all over the country with petitions for both suffrage and temperance. To the existing suffrage organizations this was, as Mrs. Stanton had feared, an extremely mixed blessing. There is no doubt that the WCTU helped make suffrage respectable in the eyes of thousands of women who had once been repelled by the very idea of such unwomanly dabbling in the affairs of men. And there is no doubt that many thousands of workers were added to the suffrage effort through the enlistment of WCTU members in the routine work of getting out petitions and publicity. But the close association of temperance and suffrage proved to be disastrous.

To the makers and users of alcohol, votes for women began to mean votes against drinking. Soon the powerful liquor interests organized themselves to fight woman suffrage. They were a determined enemy, and threw all their resources into the campaign against it.

The beer and whiskey manufacturers set up influential lobbies and made large contributions to political campaigns. They put pressure on Congressmen and state legislators, threatening to work at election time against those who supported woman suffrage. They warned all the businessmen and farmers who depended on the liquor industry—the coopers who made the barrels, the farmers who grew the grain, the railroad men who transported the liquor, the local dealers and saloonkeepers who sold it—to work against suffrage and to keep their wives and daughters from joining suffrage associations.

In one Oregon suffrage campaign, everyone who sold liquor, from the saloonkeeper to the hotel owner, was required by the Brewers' and Wholesale Liquor Dealers' Association to get twenty-five men to vote against the state suffrage amendment. Intimidation, blackmail, bribery, boycotts—every ruthless device was used to keep men from voting for woman suffrage.

Among voters who couldn't be reached by such techniques, they hammered away at the idea that votes for women would mean the end of beer and whiskey for men. This was especially effective among the German and Irish immigrants, principally in cities like Boston and Chicago where they had settled in large numbers.

To carry on their work, the liquor interests raised vast sums of money. Special taxes of a few cents a barrel were levied, and with millions of barrels of beer and whiskey produced each year, this added up to a substantial war chest. Millions of dollars were raised to combat both prohibition and woman suffrage, regarded as twin movements leading to the same dire result of ruining the liquor trade. The woman suffrage associations, with their meager resources, could hardly stand up to that kind of money.

The immigrants had another reason for keeping votes from women. A great many of them, especially those from the south of Europe who arrived later in the century, had a strong Old World tradition of male dominance. They were dead set against woman suffrage and could be counted on to vote against it.

This was a source of great irritation to native American women. It was bad enough to see the vote given to the many foreign men who were ignorant of the democratic process and sometimes illiterate—many couldn't read or write in their own language, let alone English—while it was denied to even the most educated American women. It was galling for women property owners to have the obligation of paying taxes without the privilege of voting, while the landless foreigner had the vote without the tax. And then to have these same men use their voting power to prevent American women from voting was altogether too much.

An added irritant was the use that political parties made of the immigrant voters. Few immigrants had any experience with democratic processes or understood the men and issues for which they were voting. They often voted in return for favors from the local political boss, for jobs, food, assistance with family problems. They were easily manipulated by the local ward heeler from whom they took their voting instructions. Sometimes votes were openly bought and sold for varying amounts of cash, with the vote going to the highest bidder.

The political party leaders knew that American women as a whole could never be used in this way. And the suffragists' claim that once women got the vote they would reform politics and fight against political corruption didn't exactly stimulate the party leaders to promote woman suffrage.

Like the brewers and whiskey distillers, the major political parties felt they had much to lose if women ever got the vote. They did all they could, secretly as well as overtly, to prevent the calamity of woman suffrage, and in the meantime they encouraged the more pliant immigrants to vote as soon as possible. In fifteen states, foreign-born males didn't even have to wait until they were citizens; they could vote as soon as they had taken out their first papers, which required only a declaration of intent to become citizens. In a short time, with no effort at all on their part, foreign men were granted a privilege for which American women had fought and would continue to fight bitterly, against the most discouraging and humiliating odds, for years to come.

Perhaps the most painful opposition, in the eyes of the woman's rights leaders, came from women themselves. Some women were not against suffrage itself, but felt its time had not come. They wanted to wait until politics had been cleaned up, or until public opinion had ripened to the point where voting and other rights would be granted to women without requiring the use of unladylike tactics.

But there were some women who were flatly against suffrage at any time. They formed organizations like the Boston Committee of Remonstrants and the Association Opposed to Woman Suffrage. They insisted that most women didn't want to vote, weren't capable of voting, and would find voting altogether too much to handle along with their basic function of running a home. Suffrage would cause dissension between husband and wife; it might even destroy marriage.

Whenever the suffrage associations conducted a campaign for a woman's suffrage amendment or asked for a state suffrage referendum, the female antisuffragists would present arguments against them. They published magazines like *The True Woman* and *The Remonstrance*. They held meetings—mostly in their own homes, since they wouldn't do anything as unfeminine as hold public gatherings—in which they tried to work up opposition to suffrage. Ironically, these meetings often led conservative women to think more fully about suffrage, and some of them wound up in the pro-suffrage camp as a result.

There were also women whose careers were living examples of what the woman's rights movement was trying to achieve, but who were nevertheless as opposed to the movement as any housewife afraid to stir outside her domestic sphere. Catherine Beecher, the educator who had attacked the Grimké sisters for speaking in public, was one of these. Sarah Josepha Hale, editor of the influential *Godey's Lady's Book* and author, in 1830, of "Mary Had a Little Lamb," was another. She was a devoted supporter of higher education for women and even wanted them to become doctors, but rejected woman suffrage and the idea that women should invade the rougher world of men. She criticized Lucretia Mott for placing "the true dignity of woman in her ability to do man's work, and to become more and more like him. What a degrading idea; as though the worth of porcelain should be estimated by its resemblance to iron! Does she not perceive that, in estimating physical and mental ability above moral excellence, she sacrifices her own sex?"

One of the most famous female "antis" was Queen Victoria. In 1870 she said: "The Queen is most anxious to enlist everyone who can speak or write to join in checking this mad, wicked folly of 'Woman's Rights,' with all its attendant horrors, on which her poor feeble sex is bent, forgetting every sense of womanly feeling and propriety. . . . It is a subject which makes the Queen so furious that she cannot contain herself. God created men and women different—then let them remain each in their own position."

The Queen, obviously, was not very consistent. As Elizabeth

Stanton pointed out, "when the day dawned for Victoria to be crowned Queen of England," she had not gone before the House of Commons and declared "that she had not the moral stamina nor intellectual ability for the position; that her natural delicacy and refinement shrank from the encounter; that she was looking forward to the all-absorbing duties of domestic life. . . . Suppose with a tremulous voice and a few stray tears . . . she had said she knew nothing of the science of government; that a crown did not befit a woman's brow; that she had not the physical strength even to wave her nation's flag, much less to hold the scepter of power . . . that in case of war she could not fight and hence could not reign."

Victoria had done nothing of the kind. Without the slightest hesitation, she had accepted the crown and proceeded to exercise a great many woman's rights—and stubbornly insisted on those rights. And after chloroform was introduced to ease the pains of childbirth, she demanded that it be used on her. Religious and medical conservatives were shocked. They said God had decreed that women must suffer in childbirth as atonement for the sins of Eve. But Queen Victoria wouldn't accept this particular anti-woman's-rights dictum. She became one of the first women to use anesthesia during childbirth, and knighted Dr. James Simpson, the Scottish physician who developed this use of chloroform, though he was excommunicated by his church for doing so.

It was all very tantalizing. Votes for women always seemed just around the corner—yet as each corner was turned, suffrage moved skittishly away. The suffrage organizations became more accepted and more respectable. Elizabeth Stanton and Susan Anthony became loved and admired, "grand old ladies," in their later years. Other rights were granted: the right of married women to control their own property was extended to most states; more girls were able to get a better education; a few more professions and occupations opened their doors to a few more women. But the vote remained as elusive as ever.

Nevertheless, Susan Anthony patiently and hopefully continued to work for suffrage, against every kind of discouragement and setback, against the power of organized enemies like the liquor interests and the political parties. Nothing could deter her from spending her best energies on an all-out effort to win the vote for women.

Elizabeth Stanton, however, had other ideas.

23

Beyond Suffrage

We deny the right of any portion of the species to decide for another portion, or any individual for another individual, what is and what is not their "proper sphere." The proper sphere for all human beings is the largest and highest which they are able to attain to.

— Harriet Taylor, "Enfranchisement of Woman," 1851

Think what it is to a boy, to grow up . . . in the belief that without any merit or any exertion of his own, though he may be the most frivolous and empty or the most ignorant and stolid of mankind, by the mere fact of being born a male he is by right the superior of all and every one of an entire half of the human race.

— John Stuart Mill, *On the Subjection of Women*, 1869

So many of our followers think they do enough if they sing suffrage, which now calls down no ridicule or persecution. But the battle is not wholly fought until we stand equal in the church, the world of work, and have an equal code of morals for both sexes.

— Elizabeth Cady Stanton, 1899

*A*fter the days of Mary Wollstonecraft, the issue of woman's rights had subsided in England. A whole generation passed before Harriet Martineau, the British writer and feminist, took up the question, and some of her most widely read comments appeared in connection with American women. She had come to the United States in 1834 to spend two years traveling extensively throughout the country. In 1837 she published *Society in America*, a long, detailed report of her observations, which included several sections on women.

Though she found much to admire in the United States, she was sharply critical of the treatment accorded women. She pointed out the inconsistency of American democracy which had been founded on "the fundamental principle . . . that governments derive their just powers from the consent of the governed," yet, by denying women the right to vote, imposed its rule upon them without "the consent of the women thus governed." She asked, "Is it to be understood that the principles of the Declaration of Independence bear no relation to half of the human race?"

She discovered that in America, as in England, female education was deplorably inadequate. No technical or professional training was provided. Women were neither encouraged to earn their own living nor rewarded for doing so, receiving far less money than men for equivalent work. Girls were taught to consider marriage "as the sole object in life," though many were "unfit for that object." Intellectual activity or any show of independence on the part of women was "feared and repressed." Lack of physical exercise and their largely indoor, domestic existence added to the "vacuity" of women's lives and contributed, she believed, to the heavy drinking that she found even "among women of station and education in the most enlightened parts of the country." She concluded that they must have been led to excessive drinking by despair. If women went so far "as to plunge into the living hell of intemperance, there must be something fearfully wrong with their position."

Harriet Martineau's book had little direct influence upon her countrywomen. What finally stirred them was news of the woman's rights conventions in the United States, and in the early 1850s there began the organized action which had angered Queen Victoria.

British women learned about the American conventions from an article by Harriet Taylor, which appeared in the *Westminster Review* in 1851. That same year Harriet Taylor married the noted political economist and social philosopher John Stuart Mill. At their wedding, he protested against the current marriage laws, as Theodore Weld did when he married Angelina Grimké, and as Henry Blackwell would do a few years later when he married Lucy Stone. These laws, said Mill in his formal declaration, gave too much "odious" power to the husband and too little freedom to the wife.

As a member of Parliament, Mill introduced the first bill for woman suffrage in England in 1867. In 1869 unmarried women and widows were allowed, if they were taxpayers, to vote in municipal elections; in 1882 married women were granted property rights. But that was as far as British liberality would go.

In 1869, Mill published his famous essay *On the Subjection of Women*. Women, he wrote, are not only denied basic political and social rights, but have been brought up to accept their inferior status as right and natural. All of female education has been deliberately planned—by men—for that purpose. From earliest childhood, girls are taught that the ideal feminine character is the exact opposite of a man's. Where men are encouraged to control and direct their own lives, women are taught "submission and yielding to the control of others." Traditional morality and convention tell them that it is their duty and nature to live for others, "to make complete abnegation of themselves, and to have no life but in their affections."

Three things, said Mill, determine the character of women: first, the natural attraction between the sexes; second, "the wife's entire dependence on the husband, every privilege or pleasure she has being either his gift, or depending entirely on his will"; and third, that her social ambitions can be realized "only through him."

Put together these three things and "it would be a miracle if the object of being attractive to men had not become the polar star of feminine education and formation of character." The very foundation of a woman's life was made to depend upon her ability to attract a man. Men took advantage of this to hold women in subjection, "by representing to them meekness, submissiveness, and resignation of all individual will into the hands of a man, as an essential part of sexual attractiveness."

Mill rejected the argument that meekness and dependence are part of woman's true nature. No one really knows the true nature of men and women, or just what the real difference between them might be, since people have been taught to behave not according to their own natures, but in traditionally approved ways. "What is now called the nature of women is an eminently artificial thing—the result of forced repression in some directions, unnatural stimulation in others." The female character has been "entirely distorted from its natural proportions" by the nature of women's relationship with men.

Though men are quick to dogmatize about the nature of women, very few men ever get a chance to learn what women really are. Most men don't even understand their own wives, since wives deliberately or unconsciously hide part of themselves from their husbands. Their relationship makes it difficult for a wife to be completely frank and open with her husband. "The fear of losing ground in his opinion . . . is so strong, that . . . there is an unconscious tendency to show only the best side, or the side which, though not the best, is that which he most likes to see." Women have been taught to please their husbands, "to let him neither see nor feel anything . . . except what is agreeable to him."

If women were allowed "the free use of their faculties" and permitted the same choice of occupations as men, it would double "the mass of mental faculties available for the higher service of humanity." Everyone, including men, would benefit from this "widening of the sphere of action for women."

As for women themselves: "The mere getting rid of the idea that all the wider subjects of thought and action . . . are men's business, from which women are to be warned off—positively interdicted from most of it, coldly tolerated in the little which is allowed them—the mere consciousness a woman would then have of being a human being like any other, entitled to choose her pursuits . . . whether she attempted actual participation in them or not—this alone would effect an immense expansion of the faculties of women."

Women would be infinitely happier if they had "a life of rational freedom" instead of "a life of subjection to the will of others." Everyone would be better off, since if women were allowed to express their true feelings and use their own abilities, they would not be driven to devious and irritating attempts to control the actions of their husbands and children. "An active and energetic mind, if denied liberty, will seek for power: refused the command of itself, it will assert its personality by attempting to control others. . . . Those to whom others will not leave the undisturbed management of their own affairs, will compensate themselves, if they can, by meddling for their own purposes with the affairs of others."

It is true, he added, that women with families to care for have an outlet for their energies, but what happens when the children grow up and leave home? These women remain with undiminished energy, but with no use for it. And what of those who never have children, who "pine through life with the consciousness of thwarted vocations"? Society condemns them to a "dull and hopeless life" by forbidding them to exercise their practical abilities in a wider field.

It is "vitally important to the happiness of human beings" that they have a regular occupation which they enjoy. Yet for women, their sex brings "a peremptory exclusion from almost all honourable occupations," except those which men cannot perform or think unworthy of the male sex. Few men realize "the great amount of unhappiness . . . produced by the feeling of a wasted life."

If men learn nothing else, they must learn to avoid "the positive evil caused to the disqualified half of the human race by their disqualification. . . . Every restraint on the freedom of conduct . . . dries up . . . the principal fountain of human happiness, and leaves the species less rich . . . in all that makes life valuable to the individual human being."

John Stuart Mill's book was such a complete statement of everything Elizabeth Stanton felt about the position of women that she sent him a letter expressing her thanks. No one else, she wrote, "has so . . . logically revealed the causes and hidden depths of woman's degradation. . . . It is the first response from any man to show that he is capable of seeing and feeling all the nice shades and degrees of woman's wrongs, and the central point of her weakness and degradation. . . . Yours in deepest gratitude . . ."

Once suffrage had been accepted as a legitimate aim and the suffrage associations launched to carry on the campaign for the vote, Mrs. Stanton was ready for other projects. Although it was she who had first introduced the idea of woman suffrage, and had fought for its inclusion in the Seneca Falls Declaration against the advice of her closest associates, she had never thought that suffrage should be the only or even the chief goal of a woman's rights movement. She wanted to explore, as Mill had done, the reasons for women's inferior position, and then she wanted to attack and remove those reasons, operating on as broad a front as possible.

The original ladies of Seneca Falls had called their convention to protest against a whole range of injustices—against the legal, educational, and economic handicaps of women, and against "their social and religious degradation." In the years that followed, many of these grievances had been acknowledged, however grudgingly, and a beginning, however slight, had been made in eliminating them. In many states married women were given control of their own property and earnings; it was possible, if not easy, for girls to go to college and to get some kind of professional training. Women were permitted to speak in public, before mixed audiences.

To many women, the goal had narrowed down to getting the vote. Elizabeth Stanton considered this a great mistake. She wanted the younger suffragists to expand, not contract, their aims: "It requires no courage now to talk suffrage; they should demand equality everywhere." She told Susan Anthony: "It is . . . germane to our platform to discuss every invidious distinction of sex in the college, home, trades, and professions, in literature," as well as in religion and the civil law.

Susan Anthony did not agree and was distressed by what she regarded as Mrs. Stanton's digressions. Though Susan Anthony wanted women to consider every aspect of discrimination against them, she wanted suffrage to be the main goal, for the present at least, and the unifying force to bring women together. After suffrage was achieved, women could go on to other things more effectively, since they would have the power of the vote to help enforce their claims.

Elizabeth Stanton felt that "I get more radical as I grow older, while she seems to get more conservative." The more Susan Anthony wanted Mrs. Stanton to stick to the subject of suffrage, the more reluctant Mrs. Stanton became. When Susan Anthony wanted Mrs. Stanton to prepare resolutions and other material for a convention to be held in Des Moines, Mrs. Stanton wrote in her diary: "One would think I were a machine; that all I had to do was to turn a crank and thoughts on any theme would bubble up like water." She wrote to Susan Anthony: "Is it not time that some of our younger coadjutors do the bubbling? The fact is that I am tired of bubbling on one subject."

The fact was also that the two old friends who had worked so closely—"In thought and sympathy we were one"—had begun to pull apart. Though still the warmest of friends, they were no longer inseparable, and each began to go off in a different direction. Or rather Mrs. Stanton began going off. Suffrage had become too limited a field for her energies and interests. Susan Anthony, with her dogged single-mindedness of purpose, could pour her efforts into a few selected channels, but Mrs. Stanton, with her inquiring mind, her restless curiosity, and her extraordinary vitality, needed a larger scope.

For Susan Anthony, as for most of the woman's rights leaders, suffrage remained the principal aim. Though Mrs. Stanton was still the president of the Suffrage Association, Susan Anthony became the real force behind the movement. For years she had looked to Mrs. Stanton for advice and direction. One symbol of their relationship was that she always referred to the older woman as Mrs. Stanton, who, in turn, always called Miss Anthony Susan. But now Susan Anthony had full confidence in herself. She still discussed the work of the association with Mrs. Stanton, but she handled the practical details on her own. Her special genius continued to lie in organization, and she devoted her seemingly boundless energies to keeping the issue of suffrage constantly before the public.

Mrs. Stanton, on the other hand, was tired not only of suffrage but of attending the endless conventions and legislative hearings. She was tired of preparing and delivering lectures on suffrage, and suspected that the public was getting equally tired of the subject. The opportune moment had passed, and she wanted to try another tack. "Logically, our enfranchisement ought to have occurred in 1776, or at least in Reconstruction days. And that was what I urged in the sixties. Our movement is belated, and like all things too long postponed now gets on everybody's nerves."

More and more, Elizabeth Cady Stanton came to believe that the suffrage movement was too limited. What was the use of winning the vote if women kept thinking in the same old narrow ways? And if men kept thinking of women and treating them in the same old condescending ways? How would getting the vote affect those deeper conflicts which had nothing to do with political equality, important as that was?

The vote was fine as far as it went, but to concentrate only on suffrage at the expense of other aspects of a woman's life was unwise. Suffrage, she said, was only a "fragmentary" approach. Too many women thought of the vote as the ultimate key to personal fulfillment and equality. Mrs. Stanton knew that it was only a useful tool, only one token of a self-realization for women that must go far beyond practical tools and purely external symbols.

Mrs. Stanton may have thought suffrage was too limited, but she did not give up working for it. In 1880, to help the cause along, she tried to repeat Susan Anthony's attempt to vote. The Stantons had moved from New York City to Tenafly, New Jersey, and Susan Anthony was staying there while the two women worked on the monumental *History of Woman Suffrage*. They had decided that a record must be kept of this effort to broaden the democratic process. Since male historians would probably ignore a woman's movement as too trivial for anything more than passing mention, they would have to write it themselves.

Susan Anthony had saved every document, convention record, newspaper clipping about the movement, and she worked on the sorting and arrangement of the material, while Mrs. Stanton did the actual writing. On election day they were busy working. All the Stanton men were away, and Mrs. Stanton decided that since she owned the house and paid taxes on the property, she would try to vote.

The two women went to the polling booth. A leading citizen of Tenafly introduced Mrs. Stanton to the election inspectors and said he saw no reason "why she should not exercise this right of citizenship." The inspectors were shocked. One of them put his arms around the ballot box, holding one hand over the slot, and insisted that only men were allowed to vote. She informed him that women had voted under the New Jersey constitution until 1807 and furthermore, under the Fourteenth Amendment, all persons born in the United States—as she had been—were citizens and entitled to vote. The inspector replied that he knew nothing about either the state or Federal constitution, had never read either, but no woman had ever voted that he knew of and she couldn't vote either. Since he refused to remove his hand from the slot, she tossed the filled-out ballot in the direction of the box and left. She wrote to her children afterward: "The whole town is agape with my act. A friend says he never saw Tenafly in such excitement."

A few days after this episode, Mrs. Stanton and Susan Anthony were grieved to learn of Lucretia Mott's death. She was eighty-eight years old, and had been active in the movement almost to the end of her life. Her contribution to the cause of women and her influence upon her colleagues were immeasurable. Younger women entering the movement found her a potent source of inspiration. Two years before her death, while attending the thirtieth anniversary of the Seneca Falls convention, she expressed her pleasure with the "bright young women now ready to fill our soon-to-be vacant places. I want to shake hands with them all before I go, and give them a few words of encouragement." This was her last convention. She made a farewell address and, leaving the platform, walked slowly down the aisle, shaking hands as she went. Everyone stood up, and Frederick Douglass called out, "Good-by, dear Lucretia!"

24

"The Solitude of Self"

Some men tell us we must be patient and persuasive; that we must be womanly. My friends, what is man's idea of woman-liness? It is to have a manner which pleases him—quiet, deferential, submissive. . . . Patience and persuasiveness are beautiful virtues in dealing with children and feeble-minded adults.

—Elizabeth Cady Stanton, 1890

Weak and frivolous women have been made so by false education, customs and conventionalities. . . . Men drill all spontaneity out of women until the mass of them look and act as if they were not certain of anything.

—Elizabeth Cady Stanton,
letter to a young man about to wed, 1881

Call on God, my dear, She will help you.

—Mrs. O. H. P. Belmont
to a discouraged young suffragist

In the late 1880s, Elizabeth Stanton and Susan Anthony definitely parted on the importance of suffrage. "Miss Anthony," said Mrs. Stanton, "has one idea and she has no patience with anyone who has two. I cannot sit on the door just like Poe's raven, and sing suffrage evermore. I am deeply interested in all the live questions of the day." And again: "I cannot work in the old ruts any longer. I have said all I have to say on the subject of suffrage."

What Mrs. Stanton wanted to do now was to stir women up, to liberate their minds, to make them inwardly aware of themselves and their situation. She wanted them to stop thinking along purely traditional lines and explore the real nature of the relationship between the sexes; to examine with a fresh, uncluttered eye the institution of marriage, the controversial subjects of divorce and birth control. She wanted them to shake off the restrictive influence of religious thought.

She did not claim to have all the answers, but she did want women to think for themselves, without yielding to pressure from society or the church. Nor was she anti-male, as some people thought. She was against men's unjust treatment and prejudiced views of women; but she believed that once men accepted women as their equals, the two sexes could live together in a relationship that would be vastly happier and more fulfilling for both.

She had tried to get the woman's movement involved in these matters almost from the beginning. Lucy Stone and what would become the "Boston group" had rejected this broader approach. Now, in the late 1880s and '90s, Susan Anthony and the reunited National American Woman Suffrage Association were limiting their interests primarily to suffrage. So Mrs. Stanton acted alone, pursuing in print and on speaking platforms her personal campaigns to emancipate her sex.

She was in great demand as a writer and was kept busy

writing articles "for magazines and journals on every possible subject from Venezuela and Cuba to the bicycle." The bicycle had suddenly become popular, but it raised all kinds of questions: Should women ride? What should they wear? Should they ride on Sunday? If a girl rode a bicycle, would it not "destroy the sweet simplicity of her girlish nature"? What were "God's intentions" concerning woman and the bicycle?

Mrs. Stanton replied that if women were able to ride, it was evidently God's intention that they should; female riders should wear whatever was comfortable and convenient; and a woman had the right to choose "a spin of a few hours . . . in the open air to a close church and a dull sermon." Trees, flowers, and singing birds were as suited to worship as "that melancholy service that relegates us all . . . to the ranks of 'miserable sinners.' "

Among her favorite subjects were marriage and divorce. No matter how many civil and political rights women were able to win, their most serious problems must be solved, she said, within the framework of marriage. Equality, personal freedom and dignity, self-fulfillment could hardly be achieved if the traditional relationship between the sexes was accepted without question. "Woman's degradation is in man's idea of his sexual rights," she wrote to Susan Anthony. "Our religion, laws, customs, are all founded on the belief that woman was made for man. . . . How this marriage question grows on me. It lies at the very foundation of all progress."

She wanted full equality in marriage. "It is folly to talk of the sacredness of marriage and maternity, while the wife is practically regarded as an inferior, a subject, a slave." Marriage should be based on "loving companionship," which can exist only between equals. Property rights for married women were essential, but a wife must also have an equal voice in running the home and especially in raising the children. The right to control her own body, not only in the matter of bearing children but in sexual relations with her husband, was the most fundamental of all rights.

In 1873, Mrs. Stanton had startled a meeting of conservative women by saying it was not the duty of every man and woman to become a parent. She was openly in favor of contraception. In 1880 she wrote: "I did not see [when young] all that I now see with age and experience. . . . I then knew no better than to have seven children in quick succession." A few years later, visiting her daughter Harriot, now married and living in England, she talked to the cottagers' wives about the dangers of overpopulation: "So long as they filled their homes with infants their own conditions grew worse and worse with every generation." And when she heard of a woman doctor who was teaching women "how to avoid a too general perpetuation of the race," she considered it "a commendable kind of knowledge to hand down to our overburdened mothers."

She felt that marriage was made too easy, divorce too hard. She wanted to reverse this process. If there had to be marriage laws, one of them should raise the age at which people were permitted to marry. Most women married too young, before they had a chance to grow as individuals or to develop mature judgment.

If marriages turned out badly, they should be dissolved, without requiring "delinquencies," as under existing laws. She wanted divorce made respectable, without any "guilty" parties. "Incompatibility of temper . . . should be the primal cause for divorce. . . . The parties might simply declare that, after living together for several years, they found themselves unsuited to each other, and incapable of making a happy home." There should be no "public prying"; divorce, like marriage, was a private affair and neither the state nor the church should meddle in it.

The existing divorce laws were heavily in favor of the husband and father. The father retained guardianship, no matter what the cause of divorce, and could turn the children over to a complete stranger if he wanted to. Elizabeth Stanton wanted the children left with the mother if she was capable of bringing them up.

This last point was probably the only one which found general approval among women. To many women, as to men, the rest of Mrs. Stanton's views on marriage and divorce seemed dangerous. At a time when most people felt that easy divorce would lead to immorality and the destruction of the home, Mrs. Stanton was claiming that immorality was more likely to be the result not of divorce, but of unhappy marriages from which there seemed no escape. "No, no; the enemy of marriage, of the State, of society is not liberal divorce laws, but the unhealthy atmosphere that exists in the home itself. A legislative act cannot make a unit of a divided family."

If these views on marriage and divorce disturbed or irritated many of Mrs. Stanton's suffragist colleagues, her attacks on organized religion upset them profoundly. She had become increasingly convinced that a major cause of women's inferior status was the attitude of the church. Ministers kept telling women that their role in life must be one of self-effacing submission to God and husbands. Passages were quoted from the Bible to convince women that it was God's will for them to live in subservient obedience to their husbands, keep silent in public, and remain conscious of their guilt as the daughters of Eve. Since women were brought up to believe that the Bible was the direct Word of God, it was almost impossible for many of them to examine these ideas objectively, and even harder to reject them.

As the suffrage movement became more respectable, it attracted conservative and religious women who had refused to join earlier. When the WCTU took up suffrage, an even stronger religious element entered the movement. Elizabeth Stanton was troubled by this. How could women develop independence when their religion preached self-sacrificing devotion to the needs and wishes of others? How could they develop self-respect and dignity as long as they continued to believe that woman had brought sin into the world and was therefore condemned by God to remain in a state of remorseful atonement forevermore? Elizabeth Stanton kept raising these questions at conventions, to the annoyance of even Susan Anthony, who wanted to avoid all subjects that might cause division or create distractions from the main goal of suffrage.

Susan Anthony believed that women should get political rights first, then "religious bigotry will melt like dew before the morning sun." Elizabeth Stanton was not so sure that bigotry would disappear so readily. In any case, she felt that women must first get rid of their own religious superstitions, otherwise the right to vote would be of no benefit.

In the late 1880s, to counteract the influence of organized religion on women, Elizabeth Stanton began preparing *The Woman's Bible*. This was a two-volume work consisting largely of an analysis of the passages which were used to keep women in an inferior position. Assisted by seven other women, Mrs. Stanton, who had a thorough knowledge of Greek and Latin, studied the original texts of the Bible and all the commentaries.

She wanted to show that many of these were not translated or interpreted accurately. More than that, she wanted to convince women that the Bible was not the direct Word of God, but a series of writings by men, a compilation of Hebrew mythology and history. The position of women as laid down in the Bible was not divinely ordained; it was only the reflection of ancient patriarchal attitudes, which men had used ever since to reinforce their male authority. Women were under no obligation, moral or otherwise, to accept these dictates.

In connection with her work on *The Woman's Bible*, a group

of Jewish women came to see Mrs. Stanton to explain a phrase in the Hebrew prayer service. Mrs. Stanton had objected to the fact that in their daily prayer Jewish men said, "I thank thee, O Lord, that thou hast not created me a woman." The women claimed that their religion greatly revered women—"the wife and mother were considered to hold the most exalted position . . . their men thought it would be a desecration of the holy office of women to tax them with public affairs." Mrs. Stanton asked why, if this was so, did their men thank God for not creating them women? The reply was, "It is not meant in an unfriendly spirit, and is not intended to degrade or humiliate women." Mrs. Stanton rejoined: "But it does, nevertheless. . . . Oh no, ladies, the Jews accord us women no more honor than do the Gentiles."

The first volume of *The Woman's Bible* was published in 1895, the second in 1898. When the first appeared, it had a sensational, almost a scandalous impact. Newspapers in America, England, and Europe carried reviews and articles about it, often with long extracts from the book. Ministers denounced it as the work of Satan. But people bought it. Several editions sold out, and the revising committee was enlarged to thirty women working in America and Europe.

Mrs. Stanton had tried to make it clear that *The Woman's Bible* was entirely a private, individual production having nothing to do with the suffrage movement. But it was inevitably linked with that movement, just as Victoria Woodhull's views on free love had been linked with the earlier suffragists. In the minds of much of the press and public, it was another proof that the woman's rights movement was antireligious as well as antifeminine.

A great many women inside the suffrage organization were distressed by this linkage, and by the book itself. They felt that all women's causes would be harmed by this heretical, impious work. Resolutions opposing it were passed by suffrage and temperance societies. At the annual suffrage convention in January 1896, a resolution was introduced disclaiming any connection "with the so-called 'Woman's Bible.' " It was argued that since Mrs. Stanton was honorary president of the Suffrage Association, the public would assume that *The Woman's Bible* was officially sanctioned by that group.

Susan Anthony indignantly opposed the resolution, calling it an expression of religious intolerance. Mrs. Stanton, she said, had as much right to her views on the Bible as the most religious woman had to hers. The resolution would be "a vote of censure," passed by "narrow and illiberal" delegates. It would be a denial of the right of individual opinion which was a distinct feature of the association.

In spite of this argument, the resolution passed. And in spite of her argument, too, Susan Anthony really disapproved of *The Woman's Bible*. Several months later, in the summer of 1896, Miss Anthony went to California to help campaign for a woman suffrage amendment to the state constitution. Mrs. Stanton suggested that a speech of hers dealing with the Bible be distributed in pamphlet form. Susan Anthony replied: "I have been pleading with Miss Willard . . . to withdraw her threatened W.C.T.U. invasion of California this year . . . now, for heaven's sake, don't you propose a 'Bible' invasion."

Elizabeth Stanton had hoped for a more sympathetic response from her old friend. But she was used to criticism. By this time, after all the early years of ridicule and abuse, it bothered her very little. On the contrary, she felt that the heated discussion about *The Woman's Bible* meant that people were thinking about it. And to make women think, to make them look at things from new viewpoints, however hostile their reaction, was exactly what she had set out to do.

The National American convention of 1892 was held in Washington to coincide with the annual submission of a woman suffrage bill to Congress. On the morning of January 17 several women, including Elizabeth Stanton, addressed the House judiciary committee. Instead of repeating the familiar arguments in favor of woman suffrage, Mrs. Stanton made a remarkable speech in which she presented her ultimate reasons for the emancipation of women. The speech, which she called "The Solitude of Self," was repeated that afternoon at the opening session of the convention and was later issued as a separate pamphlet.

"The Solitude of Self" was generally considered, by herself as well as others, to be Elizabeth Stanton's best work. In it she emphasizes the essential isolation of each human being and the need to prepare for that isolation. "No matter how much women prefer to lean, to be protected and supported, nor how much men desire to have them do so, they must make the voyage of life alone, and for safety in an emergency they must know something of the laws of navigation. . . . The talk of sheltering woman from the fierce storms of life is the sheerest mockery, for they beat on her from every point of the compass, just as they do on man, and with more fatal results, for he has been trained to protect himself, to resist, to conquer.

"Whatever the theories may be of woman's dependence on man, in the supreme moments of her life he can not bear her burdens. . . . We may have many friends, love, kindness, sympathy and charity to smooth our pathway in everyday life, but in the tragedies and triumphs of human experience each mortal stands alone.

"But when all artificial trammels are removed, and women recognized as individuals . . . thoroughly educated for all positions in life they may be called to fill; with all the resources in themselves that liberal thought and broad culture can give . . . and stimulated to self-support by a knowledge of the business world and the pleasure that pecuniary independence must ever give; when women are trained in this way they will, in a measure, be fitted for those years of solitude that come to all, whether prepared or otherwise."

The convention at which this speech was given was the last attended by Elizabeth Stanton. It was also the last for Lucy Stone, who died the following year. Of all the original leaders, only Susan Anthony remained in office.

25

The Grand Old Ladies

I thought of the Seneca Falls days. Who would have believed then that in less than half a century, I, at that moment the laughing-stock of the press and public . . . would to-day receive such a tribute?

—Elizabeth Cady Stanton, diary, 1892

Once I was the most hated and reviled of women; now, it seems as if everybody loves me!

—Susan B. Anthony, farewell address, 1900

I never felt I could give up my life of freedom to become a man's housekeeper. When I was young, if a girl married poverty, she became a drudge; if she married wealth, she became a doll. Had I married at twenty-one, I would have been either a drudge or a doll for fifty-five years. Think of it!

—Susan B. Anthony, interview, 1896

In 1892, Elizabeth Cady Stanton retired as president of the Suffrage Association. She was replaced by Susan Anthony, then a mere seventy-two. The succession pleased a great many members. The more conservative ones preferred Susan Anthony as steadier, less given to radical excursions which might embarrass the movement. Younger members respected Mrs. Stanton's intellectual abilities, but they adored "Aunt Susan," who worked more closely with them and took a deep personal interest in their private troubles. Mrs. Stanton had become somewhat remote, spending a good deal of time on her non-suffrage writing or visiting her daughter Harriot in England.

Soon after her retirement, Mrs. Stanton was honored at a luncheon given by the New York Woman Suffrage League. By this time she was known as "the grand old woman of America," respected by the whole country, admired even by the press which had once denounced her ideas and ridiculed her presumption. The laudatory speeches went on until six o'clock, while Mrs. Stanton kept thinking of how differently she and her proposals for woman's rights had been received almost a half century before. "Courage!" she wrote in her diary that night. "What will not be the advance in another fifty years?"

This change in public opinion was emphasized again at the huge celebration held in November 1895, on Mrs. Stanton's eightieth birthday. It was arranged by Susan Anthony, though the official sponsor was the National Council of Women, which felt that Mrs. Stanton's birthday party would be a fitting symbol of a half century of progress made by women. Six thousand people attended; thousands more sent letters and telegrams. "Having been accustomed for half a century to blame rather than praise," wrote Mrs. Stanton, "I was surprised with such a manifestation of approval."

She thought of that first convention at Seneca Falls, when

her conservative friends had warned her: "You have made a great mistake, you will be laughed at from Maine to Texas and beyond the sea; God has set the bounds of woman's sphere and she should be satisfied with her position." They were right, continued Mrs. Stanton, "we were unsparingly ridiculed by the press and pulpit. . . . But now many conventions are held each year . . . social customs have changed; laws have been modified; municipal suffrage has been granted to women in England . . . school suffrage has been granted to women in half of our States, municipal suffrage in Kansas, and full suffrage in four States of the Union. Thus the principle scouted in 1848 . . . has slowly progressed. . . . That first convention, considered a 'grave mistake' in 1848, is now referred to as 'a grand step in progress.' "

In February 1900, Susan Anthony resigned from the presidency of the Suffrage Association. At the end of her farewell speech she, too, noted the immense change in public opinion. Fifty years ago, she said, "I [was] the most despised and hated woman in all the world." Now she was the object of universal love and respect.

The next day, after the convention ended, there was a mammoth celebration of her eightieth birthday. Supporters of suffrage and admirers of Susan Anthony came from all over the country to spend the afternoon listening to a program of speeches and music, followed by an evening reception at the Corcoran Gallery of Art. One of the speakers was Elizabeth Stanton's daughter Harriot Stanton Blatch, who read a greeting from her mother, now no longer able to attend such affairs. Another was a delegate from Wyoming, who presented Miss Anthony with a brooch consisting of an American flag made of gold and diamonds. Four of the stars were diamonds, representing the states that had already granted suffrage to women: Wyoming, Colorado, Utah, and Idaho. The presentation speech ended with: "We hope you may live to see all the common stars turn into diamonds."

Throughout the United States, newspapers carried sympathetic reports of the affair. These same papers had once printed grotesquely unflattering caricatures of Susan Anthony, and had referred to her as "this shrewish maiden." Now they warmly praised "The Napoleon of the Woman's Rights Movement," and competed with each other in listing her many virtues.

One editorial said there was "an element of tragedy in the fact that Miss Anthony," with all her worthy accomplishments, had nevertheless "missed wifehood and motherhood, the crowning honor and glory of a woman's life." The Cleveland *Leader* replied that yes indeed, "Miss Anthony has gained the love and reverence of millions of people . . . but then she has never known the unspeakable bliss of nursing children through the measles, whooping cough and mumps. She has lived a useful and perfectly unselfish life, but she doesn't know a thing in the world about the supreme happiness that lies in being housekeeper, cook, chambermaid, nurse, seamstress . . . every day in the year till nervous prostration puts an end to the complicated business.

"She has stood on a thousand platforms and listened to the applause of vast audiences, but she doesn't know the glory and honor there is in picking up a bucket of hot water and climbing a step ladder to wash the doors and windows. All the joy and rapture of housecleaning in the beautiful month of May are as a sealed book to her. She has made the life of womankind broader, deeper and higher . . . but she has no conception of the breadth, depth and height of satisfaction to be found in nursing a baby through three-months-colic. . . .

"She has been free and independent . . . but alas, she has never known the ecstasy of asking John for ten cents to pay street-car fare and she has never experienced the bliss of hearing him growl about the price of her Easter bonnet and groan over the monthly grocery bill. . . .

"It is said that on Miss Anthony's last birthday anniversary she received 3,000 letters congratulatory of the things she has gained in her eighty years of life. But there are wives and mothers who would cheerfully and heartily write her 300,000 more letters congratulatory of the things she has missed."

In her own way, however, Susan Anthony was both maternal and domestic. She loved children and young people, and managed to practice a great deal of mothering: she was a second mother to her own nieces and nephews and to the Stanton children, who were often sent to stay with "Aunt Susan" at the Anthony farm near Rochester. As she grew older and the age gap between herself and the new recruits to the suffrage movement widened, she assumed a maternal relationship to the young women entering the association. She took a deep interest in them as individuals with private lives, and in return they came to her with their personal problems. She could not have had a warmer or more satisfying relationship with some of them if they had in fact been her own daughters.

In 1891 Susan Anthony decided to "retire" to Rochester. Before this, when she wasn't traveling about the country, she had spent most of her time in Washington or on extended visits to Mrs. Stanton, with only brief stopovers in Rochester. But now she was ready to settle down permanently. The Anthony home in Rochester had been left to Mary, the youngest sister, born seven years after Susan. Mary and Susan renovated the house in 1891 and set up a thoroughly domestic establishment. The thirteen rooms were redecorated. Many of the furnishings were gifts from devoted friends, among them the mahogany table on which the resolutions for the Seneca Falls convention had been written. When Mrs. Stanton came to visit later that year, she found Susan "demurely seated in her mother's rocking-chair hemming table linen and towels for her new home."

The Rochester house became the headquarters from which Susan Anthony, incapable of any real retirement, directed the work of the Suffrage Association. She received and answered thousands of letters; many of these, from men as well as women, asked for advice on personal matters. New organizations wrote for assistance, young people wrote for information, wives wrote to ask for help or express their gratitude for her work. Her day began at six or seven in the morning and went on busily until ten at night, after which she took a long walk, stepping at a quick pace, before going to bed. In winter she finished off her day by sweeping the snow from the walks in front of the house.

Presiding over it all was Mary Anthony. It was she who really ran the whole establishment, including her sister Susan. She directed the renovation and redecoration of the house, and ran it smoothly once it was in shape. She did the shopping, even for Susan's clothes, took care of the housework and cooking, and nursed Susan through illness.

She had done a great deal of this long before Susan Anthony settled in Rochester. For years she had acted as a domestic backstop and manager for her sister. She had helped arrange the hundreds of trips taken by Susan; bought the tickets, prepared and mended the necessary clothes, packed the trunks. She had done the errands and cleared away hundreds of minor details, leaving Susan free for the major work of directing the suffrage movement. She had acted as secretary, agent, nurse, housekeeper.

But Mary Anthony was much more than a devoted sister helping a famous relative. She was a woman of sound achievement in her own right, whose substantial contribution to the woman's rights movement is overshadowed by the awesome accomplishment of Susan Anthony, just as Martha Wright's value is forgotten in the light of her older sister, Lucretia Mott. Susan Anthony said in an interview that it was not she but Mary who was the suffrage pioneer in their family. It was

Mary who had attended the woman's rights convention in Rochester in 1848 and signed the Declaration of Sentiments— "when I came home . . . I heard nothing but suffrage talk, and how lovely Lucretia Mott was, and how sweet Elizabeth Cady Stanton was." Susan had not thought much about woman's rights then and even made fun of it, "but sister Mary was a firm advocate." Even after Susan Anthony became active in the movement, one of her brothers-in-law said that she could preach woman's rights, but it took Mary to practice them.

Mary had spent most of her life teaching, becoming principal of a Rochester school. At the same time, she held leading positions in the city and state suffrage organizations. For eleven years she was president and moving spirit of the Rochester Political Equality Club. There were long periods when she carried on this work in addition to nursing her mother, who was an invalid for the last ten years of her life, and taking care of nieces and nephews whose own parents were ill or had died.

She wrote newspaper articles and did some public speaking. Her gently ironic style made her much sought after for the platforms of organizations in the Rochester area. In 1897 she began her famous Protests, which continued until 1907: whenever she paid her taxes, she sent along a note saying, "Paid under protest," with a paragraph or two of sharp comment. In one she discussed the "tyranny" of taxation without representation, which for women had remained unchanged since the rule of King George III. In another she objected to the extension of suffrage to Indian men who couldn't read or write English, thus making them politically superior to literate, educated women, and signed herself "Yours for the right to vote as well as for the privilege of being taxed." These Protests appeared in the newspapers and received wide publicity.

Disproving the current belief that women were helpless in financial matters, Mary Anthony had taken a small inheritance, added her own savings to it, invested it carefully, and managed to provide herself with an income. She had been able to give Susan Anthony a generous sum to help the sinking *Revolution*. When she died, she left her money to the woman's rights movement.

In the spring of 1888 the fortieth anniversary of the Seneca Falls convention was celebrated by the first convocation of the International Council of Women. The idea for an international association had originated with Mrs. Stanton while she was in England in 1882. The following year, when Susan Anthony made her first trip abroad, she and Mrs. Stanton discussed the possibility of such an organization and helped set up a committee of women to explore it. Public acceptance of woman suffrage and equal rights had grown not only in the United States and Great Britain, but in many foreign countries. When the International Council met in Washington in March 1888, there were delegates and speakers from nine countries, including India.

The second International Council meeting was held in Chicago, just after the opening of the Chicago World's Fair of 1893. It was held as part of the World's Congress of Representative Women, which met on the fair grounds and drew women from twenty-seven countries. Huge crowds gathered at the sessions to see the legendary Susan B. Anthony. She was warmly applauded whenever she spoke and wherever she appeared. Buffalo Bill, whose Wild West Show was one of the highlights of the fair, gave her a box for one of his performances and opened the show by riding up and saluting her. She stood up and waved to a wildly enthusiastic audience. Forty years earlier she had been jeered and denounced for talking about woman's rights in public. She found the change in attitude immensely encouraging, even though her goal of national suffrage had not yet been won.

Toward the end of that year, however, there were two victories to be recorded: Colorado granted women the right to vote, and so did New Zealand, whose Electoral Act of 1893 permitted anyone over twenty-one, regardless of sex, to vote.

The third meeting of the International Council was held in London in 1899. This time there were women from South America, Africa, the Middle East, China, Australia, New Zealand, and India. Susan Anthony, then seventy-nine, led the United States delegation. When she addressed the council, her voice was as strong and sure as it had ever been, and she was applauded and lionized in London as she had been in Chicago.

The next council meeting was held in Berlin in 1904. Again she was received with tremendous ovations. The Berlin newspapers said that she was not only the Americans' "Aunt Susan" —"She is our 'Aunt Susan' too." At the meeting, she was introduced as "Susan B. Anthony of the World." Though she was eighty-four by now, her voice carried clearly throughout the crowded hall. When the delegates were received at the royal palace, the Empress Victoria Augusta said, "Miss Anthony, you are the honored guest of this occasion." Susan Anthony suggested that Emperor William might do something about the position of German women. The Empress smiled and said, "The gentlemen are very slow to comprehend this great movement."

Elizabeth Stanton and Susan Anthony worked right up to the end of their lives. In 1900, at the age of eighty-five and with her vision seriously dimmed by cataracts in both eyes, Mrs. Stanton wrote in her diary: "I am writing articles, long and short, all the time. Last week I had something in seven different papers." Just two weeks before she died, a long article of hers on divorce was printed in a New York newspaper.

She spent the last week of her life preparing arguments to be sent to President Theodore Roosevelt in support of woman suffrage. The day before her death on October 26, 1902, she wrote a letter to Roosevelt in which she said: "Abraham Lincoln immortalized himself by the emancipation of four million Southern slaves. . . . We now desire that you, Mr. President . . . immortalize yourself by bringing about the complete emancipation of thirty-six million women."

During the last six years of her life, Susan Anthony suffered from a serious heart condition, but continued to work actively in spite of it. The year before her death she traveled to Portland, Oregon, to preside at the opening session of the annual suffrage convention. She was invited to address the congregation of the Portland Baptist Church, where so many flowers were sent up to the platform that she said: "This is rather different from the receptions I used to get fifty years ago. They threw things at me then—but they were not roses. . . . Now I get flowers instead of eggs, compliments instead of epithets."

That same year she took time out to respond tartly to ex-President Grover Cleveland's attacks on woman suffrage and women's clubs. Cleveland felt that God had assigned their rightful places to men and women: this "natural equilibrium, so nicely adjusted to the attributes and limitations of both . . . cannot be disturbed without social confusion and peril." A thoughtful lawmaker, he said, will have an "intelligent disapproval of female suffrage." Though "it is one of the chief charms of women that they are not especially amenable to argument," they should be reminded that suffrage is not an inherent or natural right. It is a responsibility best left to men, as intended by divine wisdom.

Besides, if women were enfranchised, "the votes of the thoughtful and conscientious would almost certainly be largely outweighed by those of the disreputable, the ignorant, the thoughtless, the purchased and the coerced." This was a common argument against woman suffrage—that, in general, only the worst would vote, since the finest women would shun the rude atmosphere of the public polls. "It would not be the best and most responsible" who would vote.

He admitted that the same might be said of male voters, but the results would be much worse among women. "We all know how much further women go than men in their social rivalries and jealousies. Woman suffrage would give to the wives and daughters of the poor a new opportunity to gratify their envy and mistrust of the rich."

When Susan Anthony was asked what she thought of Cleveland's statements, she replied that she had disposed of such antediluvian views half a century ago. "If he had said one new thing . . . there might have been a chance for argument, but no—just hash, hash, hash, of the same old kind!" The press took great delight in her condescending dismissal of Cleveland. A popular jingle ran:

> Susan B.
> Anthony, she
> Took quite a fall out of Grover C.

Fifty years earlier the target of ridicule would have been Susan B. Now, votes and at least some measure of equality for women had become so accepted—if not yet granted in actual fact—that Grover C., twice elected President of the United States, had changed places with her.

Susan Anthony died on March 13, 1906, at the age of eighty-six. Two months earlier she had attended her last convention, in Baltimore. At the end of her address, she said: "I am here for a little time only and then my place will be filled. . . . The fight must not cease; you must see that it does not stop." At her eighty-sixth birthday celebration, held in Washington a few weeks later, her final words in public were: "Failure is impossible."

26

"The Stone That Started the Ripple"

It is fifty-one years since we first met. . . . We little dreamed
. . . that half a century later we would be compelled to leave
the finish of the battle to another generation of women.
But . . . there is an army of them where we were but a
handful.

—Susan B. Anthony,
letter to Elizabeth Cady Stanton, 1902

If I had had the slightest premonition of all that was to follow that [first] convention, I fear I should not have had the
courage to risk it.

—Elizabeth Cady Stanton, *Eighty Years and More*

More than half a century had passed between the first Seneca Falls convention in 1848 and the death of Susan Anthony in 1906. It would take another fourteen years of unremitting effort under a new generation of leaders—one of whom was Elizabeth Stanton's daughter, the politically astute Harriot Stanton Blatch—before the Nineteenth Amendment granting votes to women was ratified in 1920. Seventy-two years after Seneca Falls, the women of America were finally admitted as participating citizens in their government—recognized as "persons" and entitled to the privileges of "all persons born or naturalized in the United States."

Getting the vote was a tremendous but limited victory. It was a highly useful weapon for improving the status of women and a great symbolic triumph. But it was not in itself, as Elizabeth Stanton had warned, an open sesame to full equality or to full recognition and respect.

In the later decades of the twentieth century, women were still regarded as a second sex, inferior, or "different" in a sense that implied inferiority. And this in spite of the visible advances—the vastly expanded educational and vocational opportunities, the larger social and sexual freedoms. Though the pressures were subtler, girls were still being steered into exclusively domestic lives and attitudes, or made to think that they were less than their brothers in everything from playing tennis to the capacity for abstract thought. And being less implied an automatic confinement to the kitchen or the typists' pool.

Even if they accepted marriage and motherhood as primary goals, with society's hearty approval and encouragement, they found that society then turned around and thought less of them for having done so. "Housewife" was still a term of opprobrium, and women were still apologizing for being "just a housewife."

On the other hand, to be a "career woman" was just as unsatisfactory. It implied that a woman was aggressive, bold, unfeminine, threatening to men, and probably incapable of attracting a husband or succeeding in marriage. Simone de Beauvoir said that while men are punished for being failures, women are punished for being successes. The most successful woman executive or professional was still pitied because she lacked a husband and children; or if she had them, the husband and children were pitied and she was made to feel guilty because they lacked her full-time devotion. And though she could enter a range of occupations undreamed of in the days of Seneca Falls, she was still getting—and accepting—lower pay and less advancement than an equally or less competent man.

For all the freedoms gained, a woman was still damned if she conformed to the accepted feminine image, and damned if she didn't. She was still being offered only half a loaf and finding herself left hungry, no matter which she chose. Nearly two centuries after Mary Wollstonecraft had asked that woman be regarded as "a human being, regardless of the distinction of sex," women were still being looked at through the distorting prism of their sex.

The myths concerning women, what they are and what they are capable of, were not dispelled by woman suffrage. Women were still arbitrarily prejudged according to a false image the world itself had created. What Carrie Chapman Catt, Susan Anthony's successor as president of the Woman Suffrage Association, had said in 1902 remained true: "This world taught woman nothing skillful and then said her work was valueless. It permitted her no opinions and said she did not know how to think. It forbade her to speak in public, and said the sex had no orators. It denied her the schools, and said the sex had no genius. It robbed her of every vestige of responsibility, and then called her weak. It taught her that every pleasure must come as a favor from men, and when to gain it she decked herself in paint and fine feathers, as she had been taught to do, it called her vain."

The ladies of Seneca Falls, especially Elizabeth Stanton and Lucretia Mott, wanted to do more than just dispel these feminine myths and images: they wanted women to get recognition and respect not only from society, not only from men, but from themselves. They wanted women to become conscious of their own worth and dignity, to stop being appendages to men, to develop their own minds, talents, lives. In this, they were carrying on the ideals and goals of Mary Wollstonecraft and Margaret Fuller.

After the long suffrage battle, these goals lapsed for a generation. They did not surface again until the upsurge of the women's liberation movement in the 1960s and '70s. In that movement the consciousness and spirit engendered by the ladies of Seneca Falls were revived.

Elizabeth Stanton wrote in her diary in 1892: "Our successors . . . have a big work before them—much bigger, in fact, than they imagine. We are only the stone that started the ripple, but they are the ripple that is spreading and will eventually cover the whole pond." After decades of stillness, the pond is stirring again.

Declaration of Sentiments and Resolutions

Adopted by the Seneca Falls Convention,
July 19–20, 1848

When, in the course of human events, it becomes necessary for one portion of the family of man to assume among the people of the earth a position different from that which they have hitherto occupied, but one to which the laws of nature and of nature's God entitle them, a decent respect to the opinions of mankind requires that they should declare the causes that impel them to such a course.

We hold these truths to be self-evident: that all men and women are created equal; that they are endowed by their Creator with certain inalienable rights; that among these are life, liberty, and the pursuit of happiness; that to secure these rights governments are instituted, deriving their just powers from the consent of the governed. Whenever any form of government becomes destructive of these ends, it is the right of those who suffer from it to refuse allegiance to it, and to insist upon the institution of a new government, laying its foundation on such principles, and organizing its powers in such form, as to them shall seem most likely to effect their safety and happiness. Prudence, indeed, will dictate that governments long established should not be changed for light and transient causes; and accordingly all experience hath shown that mankind are more disposed to suffer, while evils are sufferable, than to right themselves by abolishing the forms to which they were accustomed. But when

---

The Declaration of Sentiments and Resolutions was taken from the *History of Woman Suffrage*, Vol. I, pp. 70–73.

a long train of abuses and usurpations, pursuing invariably the same object, evinces a design to reduce them under absolute despotism, it is their duty to throw off such government, and to provide new guards for their future security. Such has been the patient sufferance of the women under this government, and such is now the necessity which constrains them to demand the equal station to which they are entitled.

The history of mankind is a history of repeated injuries and usurpations on the part of man toward woman, having in direct object the establishment of an absolute tyranny over her. To prove this, let facts be submitted to a candid world.

He has never permitted her to exercise her inalienable right to the elective franchise.

He has compelled her to submit to laws, in the formation of which she had no voice.

He has withheld from her rights which are given to the most ignorant and degraded men—both natives and foreigners.

Having deprived her of this first right of a citizen, the elective franchise, thereby leaving her without representation in the halls of legislation, he has oppressed her on all sides.

He has made her, if married, in the eye of the law, civilly dead.

He has taken from her all right in property, even to the wages she earns.

He has made her, morally, an irresponsible being, as she can commit many crimes with impunity, provided they be done in the presence of her husband. In the covenant of marriage, she is compelled to promise obedience to her husband, he becoming to all intents and purposes, her master—the law giving him power to deprive her of her liberty, and to administer chastisement.

He has so framed the laws of divorce, as to what shall be the proper causes, and in case of separation, to whom the guardianship of the children shall be given, as to be wholly regardless of the happiness of women—the law, in all cases, going upon a false supposition of the supremacy of man, and giving all power into his hands.

After depriving her of all rights as a married woman, if single, and the owner of property, he has taxed her to support a government which recognizes her only when her property can be made profitable to it.

He has monopolized nearly all the profitable employments, and from those she is permitted to follow, she receives but a scanty remuneration. He closes against her all the avenues to wealth and distinction which he considers most honorable to himself. As a teacher of theology, medicine, or law, she is not known.

He has denied her the facilities for obtaining a thorough education, all colleges being closed against her.

He allows her in Church, as well as State, but a subordinate position, claiming Apostolic authority for her exclusion from the ministry, and, with some exceptions, from any public participation in the affairs of the Church.

He has created a false public sentiment by giving to the world a different code of morals for men and women, by which moral delinquencies which exclude women from society, are not only tolerated, but deemed of little account in man.

He has usurped the prerogative of Jehovah himself, claiming it as his right to assign for her a sphere of action, when that belongs to her conscience and to her God.

He has endeavored, in every way that he could, to destroy her confidence in her own powers, to lessen her self-respect, and to make her willing to lead a dependent and abject life.

Now, in view of this entire disfranchisement of one-half the people of this country, their social and religious degradation—in view of the unjust laws above mentioned, and because women do feel themselves aggrieved, oppressed, and fraudulently deprived of their most sacred rights, we insist that they have immediate admission to all the rights and privileges which belong to them as citizens of the United States.

In entering upon the great work before us, we anticipate no small amount of misconception, misrepresentation, and ridicule; but we shall use every instrumentality within our power to effect our object. We shall employ agents, circulate tracts, petition the State and National legislatures, and endeavor to enlist the pulpit and the press in our behalf. We hope this Convention will be followed by a series of Conventions embracing every part of the country.

Resolutions

WHEREAS, The great precept of nature is conceded to be, that "man shall pursue his own true and substantial happiness." Blackstone in his Commentaries remarks, that this law of Nature being coeval with mankind, and dictated by God himself, is of course superior in obligation to any other. It is binding over all the globe, in all countries and at all times; no human laws are of any validity if contrary to this, and such of them as are valid, derive all their force, and all their validity, and all their authority, mediately and immediately, from this original; therefore,

Resolved, That such laws as conflict, in any way, with the true and substantial happiness of woman, are contrary to the great precept of nature and of no validity, for this is "superior in obligation to any other."

Resolved, That all laws which prevent woman from occupying such a station in society as her conscience shall dictate, or which place her in a position inferior to that of man, are contrary to the great precept of nature, and therefore of no force or authority.

Resolved, That woman is man's equal—was intended to be so by the Creator, and the highest good of the race demands that she should be recognized as such.

Resolved, That the women of this country ought to be enlightened in regard to the laws under which they live, that they may no longer publish their degradation by declaring themselves satisfied with their present position, nor their ignorance, by asserting that they have all the rights they want.

Resolved, That inasmuch as man, while claiming for himself intellectual superiority, does accord to woman moral superiority, it is pre-eminently his duty to encourage her to speak and teach, as she has an opportunity, in all religious assemblies.

Resolved, That the same amount of virtue, delicacy, and refinement of behavior that is required of woman in the social state, should also be required of man, and the same transgressions should be visited with equal severity on both man and woman.

Resolved, That the objection of indelicacy and impropriety, which is so often brought against woman when she addresses a public audience, comes with a very ill-grace from those who encourage, by their attendance, her appearance on the stage, in the concert, or in feats of the circus.

Resolved, That woman has too long rested satisfied in the circumscribed limits which corrupt customs and a perverted application of the Scriptures have marked out for her, and that it is time she should move in the enlarged sphere which her great Creator has assigned her.

Resolved, That it is the duty of the women of this country to secure to themselves their sacred right to the elective franchise.

Resolved, That the equality of human rights results necessarily from the fact of the identity of the race in capabilities and responsibilities.

Resolved, therefore, That, being invested by the Creator with the same capabilities, and the same consciousness of responsibility for their exercise, it is demonstrably the right and duty of woman, equally with man, to promote every righteous cause by every righteous means; and especially in regard to the great subjects of morals and religion, it is self-evidently her right to participate with her brother in teaching them, both in private and in public, by writing and by speaking, by any instrumentalities proper to be used, and in any assemblies proper to be held; and this being a self-evident truth growing out of the divinely implanted principles of human nature, any custom or authority adverse to it, whether modern or wearing the hoary sanction of antiquity, is to be regarded as a self-evident falsehood, and at war with mankind.

[At the last session Lucretia Mott offered the following resolution.]

Resolved, That the speedy success of our cause depends upon the zealous and untiring efforts of both men and women, for the overthrow of the monopoly of the pulpit, and for the securing to woman an equal participation with men in the various trades, professions, and commerce.

AUTHOR's NOTE: All the resolutions except the ninth, asking for the vote, were unanimously adopted. After a strong defense by Elizabeth Cady Stanton and Frederick Douglass, the ninth was passed by a small majority.

Chronology

1648   Margaret Brent (1600–1671) becomes first woman in America to demand the right to vote.

1792   *A Vindication of the Rights of Woman*, by Mary Wollstonecraft (1759–1797).

1828   Frances Wright (1795–1852) creates shock as first woman in the United States to speak in public before mixed audiences of men and women.

1833   American Anti-Slavery Society organized. Women not permitted to join, form Philadelphia Female Anti-Slavery Society, with Lucretia Mott (1793–1880) as a leader.

1836   First introduction to New York Legislature of Married Woman's Property Act. Ernestine Rose (1810–1892) circulates petition to support it, gets five signatures.

1837   Angelina (1805–1879) and Sarah (1792–1873) Grimké give antislavery lectures before mixed audiences; Massachusetts clergy attack Grimkés in Pastoral Letter.

          Society in America, by Harriet Martineau (1802–1876).

1838   Pennsylvania Hall burned down by mob protesting women's antislavery convention.

1840   Marriage of Elizabeth Cady (1815–1902) and Henry B. Stanton (1805–1887).

          American Anti-Slavery Society splits, partly over "woman question."

          World Anti-Slavery Convention held in London; female delegates denied seats. Elizabeth Cady Stanton meets Lucretia Mott.

          Ernestine Rose, Paulina Wright (1813–1876), and Elizabeth Cady Stanton join to work for Married Woman's Property Act.

1845   *Woman in the Nineteenth Century*, by Margaret Fuller (1810–1850).

1847   Stantons move to Seneca Falls, N.Y.
        Lucy Stone (1818–1893) makes her first public speech on plight of women.

1848   Married Woman's Property Act is passed in New York, giving married women the right to control their own property.
        July 13: Elizabeth Cady Stanton, Lucretia Mott, Martha Wright (1806–1875), Mary Ann McClintock, and Jane Hunt call first woman's rights convention.
        July 19 and 20: Seneca Falls convention.

1849   Elizabeth Blackwell (1821–1910) becomes first woman in United States to receive a medical degree.

1850   Margaret Fuller Ossoli drowns in shipwreck off Fire Island, N.Y.
        First National Woman's Rights Convention, Worcester, Mass.

1851   First public appearance of bloomer costume.
        First meeting of Susan B. Anthony (1820–1906) and Elizabeth Cady Stanton.

1854   Elizabeth Cady Stanton makes first address to New York Legislature; asks for expansion of Married Woman's Property Act and for woman suffrage.

1855   Marriage of Lucy Stone to Henry Blackwell (1825–1909).

1860   Elizabeth Cady Stanton again addresses New York Legislature, asking expansion of married women's rights and woman suffrage.
        New York Legislature passes act granting all rights requested except suffrage.
        Mrs. Stanton jolts tenth annual convention by recommending liberalized divorce laws.

1861   Civil War begins; United States Sanitary Commission established, with services performed largely by women.

1862   New York Legislature repeals those sections of Act of 1860 giving mothers equal guardianship of children and certain property rights to widows.

1863   National Woman's Loyal League established; under direction of Susan Anthony and Elizabeth Cady Stanton, League collects signatures on petition to Congress for Thirteenth Amendment, abolishing slavery.

1865   Women petition Congress asking to be included in Fourteenth Amendment, insuring the vote; are told they must wait because "This is the Negro's hour."

1866   First postwar National Woman's Rights Convention; woman's rights movement converts itself into American Equal Rights Association to work for both Negro and woman suffrage.

Elizabeth Cady Stanton runs for Congress to prove woman's constitutional right; gets twenty-four votes.

1867   New York constitutional convention; women ask that word "male," as well as "white," be removed from revised constitution. Request denied.

Kansas referendum on two propositions: one to remove word "male," the other to remove "white," from voting requirements. Both defeated.

George Francis Train joins Susan Anthony and Elizabeth Cady Stanton in Kansas campaign, offers to finance woman suffrage paper.

1868   *The Revolution* begins publication.

Woman Suffrage Amendment introduced into Congress for first time.

1869   *On the Subjection of Women*, by John Stuart Mill (1806–1873).

Suffrage movement splits: "New York" group, led by Susan Anthony and Elizabeth Cady Stanton, forms National Woman Suffrage Association; "Boston" group, led by Lucy Stone, forms American Woman Suffrage Association.

Territory of Wyoming grants woman suffrage.

1870   Territory of Utah grants woman suffrage.

American Woman Suffrage Association begins publication of *Woman's Journal*.

Susan Anthony gives up *The Revolution* because of financial difficulties.

1871   Victoria Woodhull (1838–1927) presents memorial to Congress on woman suffrage.

1872   Susan Anthony votes and is arrested.

1873   Trial of Susan Anthony; refuses to pay fine.

1875   Supreme Court rules against Francis and Virginia Minor in test case of women's right to vote under Fourteenth and Fifteenth amendments.

1878   "Susan B. Anthony Amendment" introduced into Congress, in exact wording used for Nineteenth Amendment, granting woman suffrage, ratified 1920.

1880   Elizabeth Cady Stanton tries to vote in Tenafly, N.J.
Death of Lucretia Mott.

1890   Suffrage groups reunite as National American Woman Suffrage Association, with Elizabeth Cady Stanton as president.

1892   Elizabeth Cady Stanton resigns as president of Suffrage Association; is succeeded by Susan Anthony.

1893   Colorado grants woman suffrage.
        New Zealand becomes first country to grant full woman suffrage.

1896   Idaho grants woman suffrage.

1900   Susan Anthony resigns as president of Suffrage Association; is succeeded by Carrie Chapman Catt.

1902   Death of Elizabeth Cady Stanton.

1906   Death of Susan Anthony.

1920   Nineteenth Amendment, granting woman suffrage, ratified.

Bibliography

In any listing of sources for a work on the woman's rights movement of the nineteenth century, special mention must be made of the indispensable and encyclopedic *History of Woman Suffrage*, from which many of the quotations in this book were taken. It was compiled largely because the leaders of the movement understood that if they didn't write their own history, the full story might never be known. Besides the chronological record of all events pertaining to the woman's cause, it contains important speeches, memoirs, essays, letters, and newspaper articles, including many written by the opponents of the movement. The completed *History* consists of six volumes, of which the first four cover the period under consideration.

Other important sources, from which quotations appear, are Elizabeth Cady Stanton's *Eighty Years and More*, and the compilation of her letters and diary edited by her son and daughter. I am indebted also to the invaluable biographies by Ida Husted Harper, Alma Lutz, Otelia Cromwell, Gerda Lerner, and Elinor Rice Hays, and to the collection of the Weld-Grimké letters by Barnes and Dumond. For information on the whole range of women's accomplishments during this period, Eleanor Flexner's *Century of Struggle* was particularly useful.

The best manuscript collections on the woman's rights movement are at Radcliffe and Smith colleges. There is also much valuable material in the Manuscripts Division of the Library of Congress as well as the New York Public Library.

Adams, Mildred. *The Right To Be People.* Philadelphia: Lippincott, 1967.

Anthony, Katharine. *Margaret Fuller.* New York: Harcourt, Brace, 1921.

———. *Susan B. Anthony: Her Personal History and Her Era.* Garden City, N.Y.: Doubleday, 1954.

Anthony, Susan B., and Ida Husted Harper, eds. *History of Woman Suffrage*, vol. IV. Rochester: Susan B. Anthony, 1902.

Barnes, Gilbert H., and Dwight L. Dumond, eds. *Letters of Theodore Dwight Weld, Angelina Grimké Weld, and Sarah Grimké, 1822–1844*. 2 vols. New York: Appleton-Century, 1934; rpr. Gloucester, Mass.: Peter Smith, 1965.

Benson, Mary Sumner. *Women in Eighteenth-Century America*. New York: Columbia University Press, 1935.

Bird, Caroline, with Sara Welles Briller. *Born Female*. New York: David McKay, 1968.

Birney, Catherine. *The Grimké Sisters*. Boston: Lee & Sheppard, 1885; rpr. New York: Haskell House, 1970.

Blackwell, Alice Stone. *Lucy Stone, Pioneer of Woman's Rights*. Boston: Little, Brown, 1930.

Blatch, Harriot Stanton, and Alma Lutz. *Challenging Years: The Memoirs of Harriot Stanton Blatch*. New York: Putnam, 1940.

Brown, Arthur W. *Margaret Fuller*. New York: Twayne, 1964.

Catt, Carrie Chapman, and Nettie Rogers Shuler. *Woman Suffrage and Politics*. New York: Scribner, 1926.

Cleveland, Grover. "Would Woman Suffrage Be Unwise?" *Ladies' Home Journal*, October 1905, pp. 7–8.

Cromwell, Otelia. *Lucretia Mott*. Cambridge, Mass.: Harvard University Press, 1958.

Cunnington, C. Willett. *Women*. London: Burke, 1950.

Dunbar, Janet. *The Early Victorian Woman*. London: George C. Harrap, 1953.

Earhart, Mary. *Frances Willard: From Prayers to Politics*. Chicago: University of Chicago Press, 1944.

Earle, Alice Morse. *Colonial Dames and Good Wives*. Boston, 1895; rpr. New York: Frederick Ungar, 1962.

Figes, Eva. *Patriarchal Attitudes*. New York: Stein and Day, 1970.

Filler, Louis. *The Crusade Against Slavery, 1830–1860*. New York: Harper & Row, 1960.

Fletcher, Robert Samuel. *History of Oberlin College from Its Foundation Through the Civil War*. 2 vols. Oberlin, Ohio: Oberlin College, 1943; rpr. New York: Arno, 1971.

Flexner, Eleanor. *Century of Struggle*. Cambridge, Mass.: Harvard University Press, 1959; rpr. New York: Atheneum, 1968.

———. *Mary Wollstonecraft*. New York: Coward, McCann & Geoghegan, 1972.

Fuller, Margaret. *Woman in the Nineteenth Century*. New York: Tribune Press, 1845; rpr. New York: Norton, 1971.

Furnas, J. C. *The Life and Times of the Late Demon Rum*. New York: Putnam, 1965.

Gattey, Charles Neilson. *The Bloomer Girls.* New York: Coward-McCann, 1968.

Greeley, Horace. *Recollections of a Busy Life.* New York: J. B. Ford, 1868; rpr. New York: Arno, 1970.

Grimké, Sarah M. *Letters on the Equality of the Sexes and the Condition of Woman.* Boston: Isaac Knapp, 1838; rpr. New York: Source Book Press, 1970.

Hallowell, Anna Davis. *James and Lucretia Mott: Life and Letters.* Boston: Houghton Mifflin, 1884.

Harper, Ida Husted, ed. *History of Woman Suffrage*, vols. V and VI. New York: National American Woman Suffrage Association, 1922.

———. *The Life and Work of Susan B. Anthony.* 3 vols. Indianapolis: vols. I and II, Bowen-Merrill, 1899; vol. III, The Hollenbeck Press, 1908.

Hays, Elinor Rice. *Morning Star: A Biography of Lucy Stone, 1818–1893.* New York: Harcourt, Brace & World, 1961.

Hecker, Eugene A. *A Short History of Women's Rights.* Rev. ed. New York: Putnam, 1914; rpr. Westport, Conn.: Greenwood Press, 1971.

Irwin, Inez Haynes. *Angels and Amazons: A Hundred Years of American Women.* Garden City, N.Y.: Doubleday, Doran, 1934.

———. *The Story of the Woman's Party.* New York: Harcourt, Brace, 1921.

Jensen, Oliver. *The Revolt of American Women: A Pictorial History of the Century of Change from Bloomers to Bikinis, from Feminism to Freud.* New York: Harcourt, Brace, 1952.

Johnston, Johanna. *Mrs. Satan: The Incredible Saga of Victoria C. Woodhull.* New York: Putnam, 1967.

Kraditor, Aileen S. *The Ideas of the Woman Suffrage Movement, 1890–1920.* New York: Columbia University Press, 1965.

———, ed. *Up from the Pedestal: Selected Writings in the History of American Feminism.* Chicago: Quadrangle, 1968.

Langdon-Davies, John. *A Short History of Women.* New York: Viking, 1927.

Lerner, Gerda. *The Grimké Sisters from South Carolina.* Boston: Houghton Mifflin, 1967; rpr. New York: Schocken Books, 1971.

Lifton, Robert Jay, ed. *The Woman in America.* Boston: Houghton Mifflin, 1965.

Lutz, Alma. *Created Equal: A Biography of Elizabeth Cady Stanton, 1815–1902.* New York: John Day, 1940.

———. *Susan B. Anthony.* Boston: Beacon Press, 1959.

Martineau, Harriet. *Society in America.* 3 vols. London: Saunders and Otley, 1837; rpr. New York: AMS Press, 1966.

Massey, Mary Elizabeth. *Bonnet Brigades: American Women and the Civil War.* New York: Knopf, 1966.

Mill, John Stuart. *On the Subjection of Women.* London: Longmans, Green, 1869; rpr. Greenwich, Conn.: Fawcett, 1971.

O'Neill, William L., ed. *The Woman Movement.* Chicago: Quadrangle, 1971.

Parrington, Vernon Louis. *Main Currents in American Thought.* Vol. II. New York: Harcourt, Brace, 1930.

Peck, Mary Gray. *Carrie Chapman Catt.* New York: Wilson, 1944.

Postgate, Raymond. *Story of a Year: 1848.* New York: Oxford University Press, 1956.

Reische, Diana, ed. *Women and Society.* New York: Wilson, 1972.

Riegel, Robert E. *American Feminists.* Lawrence: University Press of Kansas, 1963.

————. *American Women: A Story of Social Change.* Rutherford, N.J.: Fairleigh Dickinson University Press, 1970.

Sachs, Emanie. *The Terrible Siren: Victoria Woodhull (1838–1927).* New York: Harper, 1928.

Schneir, Miriam, ed. *Feminism: The Essential Historical Writings.* New York: Random House, 1972.

Shaplen, Robert. *Free Love and Heavenly Sinners.* New York: Knopf, 1954.

Shaw, Anna Howard, with Elizabeth Jordan. *The Story of a Pioneer.* New York: Harper, 1915.

Shaw, Bernard. "Woman—Man in Petticoats," in Elsie Adams and Mary Louise Briscoe, eds., *Up Against the Wall, Mother . . . ,* pp. 197–200. Beverly Hills, Calif.: Glencoe Press, 1971.

Sinclair, Andrew. *The Better Half: The Emancipation of the American Woman.* New York: Harper, 1965.

Smith, Page. *Daughters of the Promised Land: Women in American History.* Boston: Little, Brown, 1970.

Stanton, Elizabeth Cady. *Eighty Years and More: Reminiscences, 1815–1897.* London: T. Fisher Unwin, 1898; rpr. New York: Schocken Books, 1971.

————, Susan B. Anthony, and Matilda Joslyn Gage, eds. *History of Woman Suffrage.* 3 vols. Rochester, N.Y.: Susan B. Anthony, 1887.

————, et al. *The Woman's Bible.* 2 vols. New York: European Publishing Company, vol. I, 1895; vol. II, 1898.

Stanton, Theodore, and Harriot Stanton Blatch, eds. *Elizabeth Cady*

Stanton: As Revealed in Her Letters, Diary and Reminiscences. 2 vols. New York: Harper, 1922.

Suhl, Yuri. *Ernestine L. Rose and the Battle for Human Rights.* New York: Reynal, 1959.

Tanner, Leslie B., ed. *Voices from Women's Liberation.* New York: New American Library, 1971.

Taylor, Harriet. "Enfranchisement of Woman," *The Westminster and Foreign Quarterly Review,* July 1851, pp. 289–311.

Wade,·Mason. *Margaret Fuller: Whetstone of Genius.* New York: Viking, 1940.

Wardle, Ralph M. *Mary Wollstonecraft.* Lawrence: University of Kansas Press, 1951.

Whitridge, Arnold. *Men in Crisis: The Revolutions of 1848.* New York: Scribner, 1949.

Willard, Frances E. *Occupations for Women.* New York: The Success Company, 1897.

Wollstonecraft, Mary. *A Vindication of the Rights of Woman.* London: Joseph Johnson, 1792; rpr. New York: Norton, 1967.

Woolf, Virginia. *A Room of One's Own.* New York: Harcourt, Brace, 1929.

Wormeley, Katharine Prescott. *The Sanitary Commission of the United States Army.* New York: Published for the Benefit of the United States Sanitary Commission, 1864.

Index

A

abolition, *see* antislavery

Adams, Abigail and John, 21, 25

Amendments to Constitution: Thirteenth, 210–212; Fourteenth, 212–213, 242–244, 249–250, 253, 255, 259, 279; Fifteenth, 226–227, 231–232, 235, 244, 253, 255; Sixteenth (proposed woman suffrage), 227, 232, 233; Nineteenth, 259, 288–289, 303

American Anti-Slavery Society, 34, 37–38, 48–49, 54, 67, 116–117, 197, 199; split in, 48, 117, 232

American Equal Rights Association, 214, 215, 223–224, 231–233

American Revolution, 24–25, 31, 94–95, 160–161, 215, 278

American Woman Suffrage Association, 233–237, 248, 263

anesthesia in childbirth, 95, 268

Anthony, Daniel, 109–112, 115, 174, 201

Anthony, Lucy Read, 109–111

Anthony, Mary Stafford, 109, 250, 295–298

Anthony, Merritt, 197–198

Anthony, Susan Brownell: and antislavery, 117, 197–200; background and early career, 109–115 ff., 123; and bloomer costume, 142, 150, 152–154, 158; and Civil War, 208, 210–212; described, 113, 166–167, 241, 248; epigraphs from, 108, 155, 184, 194, 230, 238, 291, 302; later years and death, 293–296, 298–301, 303; and Lucy Stone, 120, 191–193, 225, 228, 234; as Lyceum lecturer, 240–242; and Married Woman's Property Act, 174–175, 178–181, 196; and *The Revolution*, 221–224, 231, 235–236, 240, 242, 298; as speaker, 160, 166–171 *passim*, 180, 196–197, 228, 240–242; and suffrage, vi, 212–232 *passim*, 238, 240, 242–255 *passim*, 259, 268–269, 276–278, 282, 293, 300–301; and Suffrage Association, 167–168, 232–234, 237, 239, 246–248, 277, 282, 290–295 *passim*; and temperance, 113, 119, 156–158, 162–165, 263; tests voting rights, 250–255, 278; trial of, 251–254; and woman's rights, v, 120–121, 155, 156, 159–171 *passim*, 196–205 *passim*, 258, 286, 290, 292, 293; and workingwomen, 228–229

Anthony-Stanton relationship, 109, 115, 119–120, 155–156, 164, 166–171, 197, 217, 224–225, 248, 276–277, 282, 295

Anti-Slavery Convention of American Women, 35

Mott, Lucretia Coffin (*cont.*)
55, 85, 101, 106, 171, 185–186;
and suffrage movement, 215,
225, 234, 245; and Mary Wollstonecraft, 18, 53; and woman's
rights, 2–3, 13, 85, 95–107 *passim*, 109, 115, 138–139, 155–162
passim, 171, 185, 267, 279, 305,
311; at World Anti-Slavery
Convention, 2, 49–51, 55, 83–
85, 158; mentioned, 92, 149,
204, 205, 296, 297
Mott, Lydia and Abigail, 114, 139
Mount Holyoke College, 126

N

National American Woman Suffrage Association, 167, 237,
277, 282, 288–289, 292–293,
296, 304
National Woman's Loyal League,
211–212
National Woman Suffrage Association, 232–237, 239, 245, 247,
248, 249, 258
New York constitutional convention, 215–216
"New York" group, 225–226,
228, 234
New York Herald, 104, 139, 162,
165
New York State Teachers' Association, 171, 196–197
New York Tribune, 80, 104, 116,
120, 140, 165, 198–199, 203, 216

O

Oberlin College, 126–134, 190
On the Subjection of Women,
272–275
Owen, Robert, 88
Owen, Robert Dale, 203

P

Paine, Tom, 20, 31
Pastoral Letter, 9, 38–41, 129
Philadelphia Female Anti-Slavery
Society, 34, 37, 49, 54, 100
Phillips, Wendell, 115, 137, 138,
153, 201, 204, 212, 214, 215, 224
Pillsbury, Parker, 222
Pinckney, Eliza Lucas, 23
press: on bloomer costume, 148,
150–151; on conventions, 93,
103–105, 107, 116, 139–140,
147–148, 162, 165, 293; on
woman's rights leaders, 137,
205, 251, 253, 287, 291, 292,
294–295; on women, 8, 10, 56
public speaking by women, 10,
32–35 *passim*, 38–48 *passim*,
54–55, 98, 129–130, 132, 135,
163, 165, 171, 206, 241, 276,
304, 310–311
property acts (*see also* Married
Woman's Property Act of
New York): England, 272;
Maine, 89; Massachusetts, 185;
Tennessee, 146; Wyoming,
228; other states, 268, 276
Punch, 150

Q

Quakers, 2, 10, 37, 51–54, 85, 105,
109–111, 112, 116, 145

R

Reform, Age of, 31–33, 94–95
religion (*see also* Bible, Quakers),
58, 84; attitude of church
toward women, 8, 9–10, 38–41,
42, 49, 51, 85, 88, 95, 97, 107,
129, 157, 158, 161–162, 222,
260, 268, 282, 285–287, 309, 311;

W